CROSS CURRENTS

CROSS CURRENTS

Exploring the Implications of
Christianity for Our Times

An Anthology of Forty Years of
Cross Currents

Edited by William Birmingham

Foreword by Joseph Cunneen

CROSSROAD · NEW YORK

1989

The Crossroad Publishing Company
370 Lexington Avenue, New York, N.Y. 10017

Printed in the United States of America

Library of Congress Cataloging-in-Publication Data

Cross currents : exploring the implications of Christianity for our
  times : an anthology of forty years of Cross currents / edited by
  William Birmingham.
    p.   cm.
  ISBN 0-8245-0956-0
  1. Theology. I. Birmingham, William. II. Cross currents.
BR53.C76 1989
270.8'25—dc20   89-37964
                                          CIP

To Joseph L. Caulfield and Erwin W. Geissman,
founding editors and friends,
who live in our grateful memory

Contents

Foreword 9
  Joseph Cunneen

Introduction 13
  William Birmingham

Christian Faith and Civilization 29
  Emmanuel Mounier

The Church of Sinners 46
  Karl Rahner

Guilt and Guilt Feeling 63
  Martin Buber

The Meaning and Value of Atheism Today 93
  Jean Lacroix

Hoping and Planning 109
  Jürgen Moltmann

Are Some Things Valued by All Men? 125
  Everett E. Hagen

Feminism, Socialism, and Christianity 138
  Mary B. Mahowald

The Need for Political Saints 163
  Leonardo Boff

Classical Western Spirituality and the American   176
    Experience
    Thomas Berry

Global Spirituality and the Integration of East and West   193
    Beatrice Bruteau

The American Economy, Religious Values, and a New   216
    Moral Imperative
    Madonna Kolbenschlag

Violence and the Gospel   241
    Georges Khodr

Toward a Darkly Radiant Vision of America's Truth   258
    Vincent Harding

Faith and Metaphysics Revisited   281
    Eugene Fontinell

Chosenness and Universality: 305
    Can Christians Claim Both?
    Raimundo Panikkar

Foreword

We were just a bunch of post–World War II graduate students drinking too much coffee, or arguing late at night over beer instead of preparing for exams. We were mostly Roman Catholics, many of us using veterans' benefits to get an advanced education previously unavailable to our families. We wanted to break out of the religious/ethnic ghettos of an earlier generation, we knew that religion had been the weakest course in the Catholic schools we had attended, we found the anticommunism of Communion breakfast speakers ridiculous if not insulting—and yet we were still drawing more strength from our parents' faith than we yet realized.

We had encountered a few brilliant individual teachers, mavericks yet believers, sometimes refugees or converts, most of whom would not write major books because they were overworked and underpaid, or the publishers wanted only Thomist textbooks. We had no illusions about Catholic education but were not convinced that Fordham should simply try harder to be like Yale, while still getting a cardinal to hand out degrees. It was more than a larger endowment that Notre Dame needed to be as good as Chicago, but we did not see that faith had anything to fear from reason and suspected that even the highest products of reason needed a scrupulous appraisal nourished by familiarity with the Hebrew prophets and the Christian gospels.

One of our group talked about a Mass she had attended, celebrated by a worker-priest in a suburban Paris apartment, and how moved she had been by the informal but intense participation of the workers. Another had been a friend of Dom Luigi Sturzo during his Brooklyn exile, and told us how much he had learned from this courageous priest who had founded the Popular (later Christian Democratic) party in Italy as an antifascist movement responsive to the hopes of peasants and workers. A third had attended an international student conference and brought back mimeographed notes by a Jesuit paleontologist, Teilhard de Chardin, that made the religion-evolution debate seem hopelessly outmoded. A fourth spoke of an article by Walter Dirks, founder (with Eugen Kogon) of the important German monthly *Frankfurter Hefte,* which rejected the argument that Marxism was necessarily materialistic and atheistic as sheer ignorance. A fifth called our attention to the careful historical scholarship of a U.S. Jesuit, John Courtney Murray, on the problem of church and state, which he believed could help define the freedom of both.

The more often we met, the more obvious it became that the questions that kept recurring were not special to Catholics, that if you took the trouble to master slightly different vocabularies you would find them addressed, often with greater penetration, by men and women of varying spiritual traditions, indeed by those who professed themselves unbelievers. We were not totally unprepared for such discoveries since none of us believed that Christianity possessed some constantly updated answer-book to contemporary dilemmas. And those of us who, as unprepared G.I.'s in the last stage of our advance into Germany, had in horror discovered the Nazi death camps, knew, without fully realizing all its implications, that the Holocaust meant the failure of organized Christendom.

Cross Currents became the place where our conversations could continue and widen. In practice, the journal has proved to be an ongoing exchange on faith and intelligence, a discussion perhaps even more necessary today. We could make no sense of a notion of faith that meant postponing the task of human liberation to a posthistorical reckoning, and were sure that believers had an extra obligation to use the brains God had given them in the service of their brothers and sisters. Faith, we knew, could often turn into fanaticism, but reason, we had been shocked to learn, could also organize mass extermination. There still seemed a need for an international and ecumenical journal that, because it was unembarrassedly Christian in orientation, would ask others with different heritages to remove the motes from our understanding. The nuclear murder unleashed on Japan was only a further warning that an all-inclusive dialogue must be inaugurated on ways of dealing with differences that did not create new out-groups. Happily, the old imperialisms were crumbling, but the lust for power was not to be wished away; if new masters were not to reimpose even greater burdens on the oppressed, we would have to study issues in nothing less than planetary terms. Survival could depend on using our heads, and true piety would require not only a constant growth beyond denominational and tribal boundaries but an effort to learn—in many instances re-learn—the inner laws of the earth's energy, a reverence for our common mother.

The task of *Cross Currents,* therefore, has been to puncture the easy rapture of the self-inflated dogmatist, whether religious or secular. Since we had a special obligation to transcend the pretensions of U.S. nationalism, there was extra reason to be suspicious of those offering "democracy" as an excuse for invasion of small countries that wanted to experiment, however imperfectly, with non-capitalist economic and social arrangements, or who assume that a world dominated by Western-style media would automatically be more "free."

As we invite a new generation to join our conversation, it is perhaps with fewer illusions than in 1950. But there are also new seeds of hope. More and more women have insisted on being part of the dialogue; Latin Americans, Asians, and Africans are increasingly calling for a Christianity that would express their own cultural presuppositions, all the while complaining about Western modes of "reason" in much the same terms North American women use to protest male domination of academe; a broadening familiarity with traditional non-European religions is fostering a deeper communion with our threatened earth. No basic issues have been resolved, old and new injustices cry out to heaven, faith continues in search of intelligence.

In the summer of 1950 we asked our printer, Alexander Donat, a Polish-Jewish survivor, along with his wife and son, of the Nazi will for Jewish extermination, to print, on credit, 50,000 folders announcing the launching of *Cross Currents*. A few weeks later Pope Pius XII released an encyclical, *Humani Generis,* which cast a dark shadow over many of the contributors we had listed for early publication. There wasn't a minute to lose. We had to work hard if we were to get out our first issue before Christmas.

WILLIAM BIRMINGHAM

Introduction

C onvergence and the response to it have marked Christian faith since the Second World War. It has run like a thread through *Cross Currents* from the time that, some forty years ago, Joseph and Sally Cunneen together with a disparate group of friends set out to publish a quarterly that would explore the implications of Christianity for our times.[1]

That thread of convergence is the editorial principle on which the selections in this anthology have been based. It is important to note that the editors were not, early or late, attempting to publish some sort of convergence quarterly. There was, to say the least, no master plan, unless selecting articles meaningful to a particular set of editors at a particular time in their own and their world's history may be termed a master plan. Retrospect, however, makes the theme of convergence visible. In my judgment, it enables readers to find fresh meanings in essays that remain valuable in themselves.

By convergence I mean the process of drawing together in conscious relationship—"always the knit of identity, always distinction," Whitman says, "always a breed of life." Convergence begins with the rejection of dichotomy, of a world described as me/not-me, us/not-us, light/dark. It must be distinguished from merging, dissolution of me into us, of us into amorphous commonality, of concrete human ways into a pseudospirituality of disembodied humankind. To converge is to let the other in; to appropriate from the other and to let the other appropriate in

13

turn; to experience identity and to remain distinct. Convergence demands "the art of intimacy and distance, the capacity of beings to be totally present to each other while further affirming and enhancing the differences and identities of each."[2] Such convergence breeds life, a life that may find one of its paradigms in the doctrine of the Trinity.

Our times thrust the option of convergence on Christianity. Belated and partial awareness of Hitler's Holocaust kingdom forced Christians to confront their own history of social and theological hate and to seek vitality and forgiveness by tapping their Jewish roots. Their realization that no single mode of confronting Jesus in whom they professed faith as Christ could exhaust the possibilities of Word made flesh turned individual churches toward one another in a search for deepened wisdom. The Christian encounter with other, equally live spiritual traditions—in Africa and the Americas, the Middle East, India and the rest of Asia—developed and deepened; and as those varieties of religious experience entered Christian awareness, they drew forth new meanings within Christianity itself.

Simultaneously, Christians have had to face the dominant faiths of our century, secularism and communism. In much of the West secular faith defines through economics our standard of living and through the social sciences our very selves. Those moved by Christian faith to question Western secularism have had to consider the theoretical solutions offered by Marx and their incarnations in the Soviet Union and China. From dialectic with both these faiths have emerged the theological work of, say, Reinhold Niebuhr and John Courtney Murray, on the one hand, and Gustavo Gutierrez, Jon Sobrino and Leonardo Boff, on the other.

The fact of convergence has changed the beliefs of some who call themselves Christian but left untouched the beliefs of others. In both cases, however, the experience of Christian faith has changed. Neither the pope nor Billy Graham can believe as if the other did not exist, and both must acknowledge that somewhere in an African village there lives at least one animist gifted with a saving faith, which only the callous would dub anonymous Christianity. Convergence has turned Christian anthropology upside down.[3]

1

The first issue of *Cross Currents* appeared in Fall 1950. Its introductory editorial suggests that "despite the confusion of a world in upheaval—of which the current fighting in Korea is only a symptom—a new City is in the making, in which mankind is seeking, with perhaps more fervor than ever before, its lost unity" (1), and concludes, "we must try to find out—Christians and non-Christians alike—what it might mean to be a Christian today" (2).

Emmanuel Mounier, in "Christian Faith and Civilization"— the lead article in that issue as well as this collection—centered on the interpenetration of the sacred and the secular: to be a Christian, he says, is to be "a citizen of the earth. . . . to recognize that the supernatural has its place in our lives and in history . . . that it is everywhere, even though it may not be everything" (41). He speaks of the "sacramental reality of civilizations," and adds: "Perhaps we . . . Occidentals, nurtured in a civilization of the word, are too exclusively sensitive to the word which reduces to a formula, and not enough to the word which dances in the imagination" (45).

The clash between formula and dancing image has resonated through more than 150 issues of *Cross Currents*. All the founding editors were Roman Catholics, as are most of the present editorial board. The organizational church to which they belonged—and enjoyed belonging—was and largely remains addicted to formulas, especially those produced through analytic deduction from abstract principle. An unstated editorial guideline from the beginning dictated a preference for the existential, the phenomenological, the experiential, and the social, for conversation rather than competition between religious ideas and reality, for the dance of word and Word.

Over the years, the dance has remained the same, and been

transformed. The first issue brought Emil Brunner, Nicolas Berdyaev, Gabriel Marcel, and Henri de Lubac to the attention of readers. In later issues many readers met for the first time the work of such thinkers as Jean Daniélou, M.-D. Chenu, Karl Jaspers, Yves Congar, Paul Ricoeur, Henri Marrou, and Friedrich Heer. Karl Rahner's essay "The Church of Sinners" was his first appearance in English. The culmination of *Cross Currents'* European phase came in the Fall 1959 issue, which included Teilhard de Chardin's "Building the Earth." (The first of Teilhard's works to appear in the United States was "The Psychological Conditions of Human Unification," Fall 1952.) Teilhard's vision of an emerging common human consciousness and common human soul remains startling:

> *We have reached a crossroads in human evolution* where the only road which leads forward is towards a common passion.
> To continue to place our hopes in a social order achieved by external violence would simply amount to our giving up all hope of carrying the Spirit of Earth to its limits.
> But Human Energy, like the Universe itself the expression of an irresistible but infallible movement, could not be prevented by any obstacle from attaining freely the natural term of its evolution. . . .
> We must believe without reservation in the possibility and the necessary consequences of universal Love.
> The theory and practice of total Love have never ceased, since Christ, to become more precise, to transmit and propagate themselves; so that with two thousand years of mystic experience behind us, the contact which we can make with the personal Focus of the Universe has gained just as much explicit richness as the contact we can make, after two thousand years of Science, with the natural spheres of the World. Regarded as a "phylum" of love, Christianity is so living that, at this very moment, we can see it undergoing an extraordinary mutation by elevating itself to a firmer consciousness of human value. (330)

The same issue contained two articles on that seemingly most secular and most American of philosophers, John Dewey.[4] The moment at which Teilhard's planetary consciousness began to be articulated was also, in *Cross Currents* at least, the moment at which a peculiarly American love for the concrete became a dominant theme. The 1960s saw greater emphasis on the American way of seeing, experience-oriented and metaphysically pragmatic.

In more and more articles, extraordinary changes became evident. At times they were explicit, more often they were implicit. Certainty ceased to be taken for granted as a value; faith yielded meaning rather than knowledge; organizational Christianity emerged as a necessity for preserving the original charism, rather than a triumphant creation of the Divine will; orthopraxy replaced orthodoxy as the primary sign of commitment; the religious included the secular, and the secular included the religious. To speak of the Church was to speak of the mystical body formed by those gathered, physically or spiritually, in Christ's name and according to his word. The problems of the organizational churches continued to be taken seriously, but were not equated with the central question of what Christianity might and might not mean for our times.

In brief, in an increasing percentage of articles the way of seeing had changed. John McDermott's "The American Angle of Vision," contrasted the criteria of truth and experience in their application to faith, both organizational and lived (Spring and Fall, 1965). His brother Robert ("Religion as an Academic Discipline," Winter 1968) explored the necessity of a provisional commitment to any religious or spiritual way that the individual Christian might wish to study; to know another way as an object, he suggests, is to know it not at all. One effect of these articles was to illuminate meanings in material that had been published earlier, Karl Rahner's "Church of Sinners" and Jean LaCroix's "The Meaning and Value of Atheism," for example. Another effect was to stimulate meditation on the nature of Christian faith and reflection when described not theoretically but in terms of a philosophy of religion at once pragmatic, experiential, and confessional. Eugene Fontinell's reflections on faith and metaphysics in this book illuminate the content of controversial essays he wrote during the 1960s and indicate their further implications for the communities of faith.[5]

If it means anything, American thought means openness to the breadth of experience. When it closes itself off either from the new or the seemingly foreign, it distorts its peculiar genius. Recent decades have brought forth new ways of seeing that demand an ecumenism hitherto unparalleled. The old ecumenism, with its goals of organizational unity among Christians and minimized differences with Islam and Judaism, had completed its creative work by establishing the practice of interconfessional and interreligious respect. It became increasingly evident that the merger of Christian churches might best be left to Providence and that, granted those things held in common by the religions of the Book, their differences, far from being a source of scandal, were worthy of celebration. The newer ecumenism is challenged to heal deep wounds in human self-understanding: assumptions concerning separateness and superiority, concerning the social structures that incarnate good and evil, concerning the righteousness of violence in the service of good.

The 1960s and 1970s saw publication of special issues on Africa and colonialism ("For White America," edited by James J. Lamb, Fall 1968), the life and thought of Sri Aurobindo (edited by Robert McDermott, Winter 1972), the emerging revolution of thought and action in Latin America ("Latin America in Search of Liberation," Summer 1971), and Native American spiritual ways ("The Good Red Road," edited by Mary Louise Birmingham, Summer 1976). Each in a different way challenges such conventions as the inherent superiority of Christian to non-Christian and non-Western wisdom, the freedom of Christian faith from contempt for women, the unquestioning equation of economic prosperity with a high standard of living, and the individualist presupposition that the reform of society and the salvation of its members begins in the solitary heart and not in the existential structures of communal being.[6] In the 1980s two special issues—one devoted to Jacques Ellul (edited by Carl Mitcham, Spring 1985) and the other to Thomas Berry (Summer/Fall 1987)—center on the imperial will to dominate nature that arises from an image of humankind as separate from and above all else in creation and offer alternative spiritual ways through which the human might take its place within nature, redeemed by meanings made conscious and redeeming because it makes present to consciousness the incarnation of the holy. Mounier's dance of civilizations becomes the dance of all creation, and creation the dance of the divine.[7]

The process of convergence hurts. When countercurrents meet, turbulence ensues, the stream swells, much that is good is carried away. But other goods rise up; not only dross remains. Take liberation theology. The Latin American theologians, whose view of the political realm is less Marxist than Iberian, nevertheless bring to consciousness a fact which, once recognized, strips Christians of the ability to describe their communities as Body of Christ or people of God unless they recognize that as body and people, as community, they are divided by class. And unless empirical reality in no way describes it, its class structures inhere in the Christian churches not as a result of a sin of the world outside but as a sin of their own heedlessness or choice. This freedom to sin tarnishes one venerable image of the church, to be sure, but simultaneously suggests that the church and the churches possess the freedom to make and remake themselves, the freedom to speak an incarnated Word that they have not yet uttered.[8]

Perhaps more painful is the changed Christian self-definition that convergence implies. As Christians undertook surrender of anti-Semitism and sought instead to acknowledge Judaism as a saving religion, one part of their self-definition changed. Another part changed when the Christian churches began to acknowledge one another as valid social ways of embodying Christ in body and spirit. Many Christians have found these limited changes intolerable, as the growth of fundamentalism in its various forms indicates. The process of worldwide religious convergence demands much more. However differently, for example, a Presbyterian and a Roman Catholic may approach liturgical practice, both advert to a common Book and seek their justification in it. Christians who attempt to enter, without imposing Christianity on it, the nothingness at the heart of Zen—or to discover the divine embodied in Krishna without dissolving him into Christ—have taken a perilous first step. They hope that the second will lead up the mountain's path; it may plunge them into the abyss. Or, as happens often enough among comparative religionists, they may become aesthetes of faith, living through moment after spiritual moment, each of them precious but none integrated through choice of a coherent self and commitment to a living community of believers.

The process of convergence undermines the idea of the absolute (or the Absolute) as a reality that exists in itself, both unchanging and unconstituted by its relationships. The God of Christian belief, the Christ of faith, the wondrous Trinity as later defined—none becomes untrue, but none continues to be taken as absolute, as unconditioned by time and place. Each remains a radiant teaching that expresses teleologically the divine project, spiritually the divine meaning, and cosmically the divine presence not only in all that humankind sees and does but in all that the universe itself accomplishes in its movement from its explosive beginning to its mystery-filled end, the Omega point that Teilhard de Chardin dimly discerned and eloquently expressed. The world remains "charged with the grandeur of God," as Gerard Manley Hopkins proclaimed; but God is so present that, if the world chooses well, its grandeur will permeate the divine. And part of the world's grandeur will be the other ways that open the human to the holy. More, Christians may more fully experience their own way precisely when it has ceased to be an absolute but thrives instead through its relationship to other ways. The truth of the great creation myth of the seven days (Gen. 1:1–2:4) may find reawakened meaning in the Rig Veda's "Hymn of Creation" and its wondering whether the One does indeed know whence creation flows.

The question posed to Christian awareness is not, do I believe in absolutes? but, do I believe absolutely?[9] Are the central Christian myths—the myth of the divine made flesh, of the healing preacher of good news to the oppressed, of his perseverance through suffering and unto death, of his resurrected life of presence to his people, the myth of the one God whose oneness is found in interrelationship of persons—are those myths, at the same time that they are related to other myths paradigmatic of other ways, truly mine? Are they, in brief, the myths that energize me as Christian person and, in some way, my community as Christian community?[10] And am I as person and my immediate religious community as community so present to those other ways that they and their myths enlighten my—our—way?

The process of convergence includes the secular as well as the religious. A Christian task is to discern the holy within the explicitly profane, the sacred within the rigorously secular, while allowing them to remain themselves—unbaptized. Just as Buddhism must remain Buddhism, so must, say, poetry remain poetry, science remain science, and politics remain politics. Some Christians may be too facile in incorporating Emily Dickinson into communal prayer, Carl Sagan into creation mystery, and Fidel Castro into images of the Kingdom. And some may be too ready to announce their kingdom of Apollonian values while dispensing themselves from the grubby imperfections (and sin) of the everyday world.[11] The desire to rule and the desire to merge are as tempting today as it once was to find implicit in the Bible—or in the Fathers, or whatever source had been given a place of privilege—the truths disclosed by modern thought. Believers let the secular in at great risk, for the secular subverts traditional images of ultimate reality, just as belief in the incarnation subverts the transcendence of God. Without that convergence, however, hope in the world shrivels.

2

The selections that make up this anthology were neither written nor originally published to conform to the theme of convergence. Among the authors represented, some—Karl Rahner, for example—would find problematic my unqualified contention that the Christian, the Church, and the churches will profit from meeting one another, meeting other religious ways, and meeting the "world" on an equal footing with no privilege of place being given to or claimed by Christianity. It has little basis in either the scriptures or tradition. Most theological definitions exclude it. The historic efforts of missionaries contradict it. The claims of secularist humanism deny it. Few varieties of atheist experience would wish to admit it.[12] None of this is surprising: even an imagination as bounteous as Dante's could not redeem Virgil.

The initial issues of *Cross Currents* were at ease with language that editors now modify or eliminate in the rare instances that authors use it. God is He. Catholics and Protestants invariably speak of their particular capitalized Church, whose Roman Catholic pronoun is feminine since she is Holy Mother. In article after article, the authors refer to the relationship between God and man, with women left to fend for themselves. And so on. Indeed, the evolution of the language used to express religious ideas might serve as a subtext through which to trace lines of convergence other than those that are our central concern. The insights of feminist theology, for example, have subverted all simple reflection on God as Father, for the metaphor now seems impoverished unless one simultaneously holds in mind its equally valid polar opposite, the Divine motherhood.

Following Mounier's incarnational vision of the Christian faith and civilization are two essays that consider different aspects of sin and guilt. Karl Rahner examines existential Christianity, the blemished church. One might today wish to stress as well the sinful organizational structures of the various Christian churches—as well as those of other religions. Martin Buber then deals with guilt—guilt based on the fact of participation in evil— and stresses that the fact of past guilt remains, and must remain conscious, even as the reborn conscience seeks to bind the wounds that its evil has inflicted on the world. This attention to sin and guilt has much to do with the process of convergence. No Christians, even those who have been individually exempt from feelings of anti-Semitism, dare approach Judaism without acknowledging the sins of their communion against the Jews. At some future point, it is to be hoped, Judaism and Islam will approach one another in the same spirit.

The personal and social function of guilt feelings is this: to convince both individual and community of their limits—neither is God—and to inculcate the disposition to change, which is the foundation of experienced hope. Jürgen Moltmann's essay lays bare the anatomy of hope, which does not project the future through analysis of the past but through openness to the new signs that the future brings. Moltmann's message seems especially important as the 1980s draw to a close: Mikhail Gorbachev has thrown open the windows of the Kremlin, and fresh winds blow through the Communist citadel; yet, in Washington, most Sovietologists continue to center on the past, resisting the possibility that it can reveal little unless the unexpected present—*glasnost* and *perestroika*—is taken into account. Jean Lacroix's "The Meaning and Value of Atheism" might well serve as a starting point for fresh reflection on the shift from cold war to convergence. Creative disbelief—a creature far different from secularistic dismissal—contributes to the health of belief; as atheism plays a diminishing role as the state religion of the USSR and assumes its place as one fundamental commitment possible to the citizen, Soviet communism may achieve some of the humanism to which it has pretended.

Everett Hagen poses the question "Are Some Things Valued by All Men?" and answers that, from what the anthropologist's eye can see, humans agree on one value, respect. The implications are great. In the United States, the Emancipation Proclamation brought freedom from white owners, but it was freedom without respect from the former slaves' white fellow citizens. And for that continuing sin, American society pays a great price. The industrial nations have built material prosperity through the spirit of conquest over a nature that they see as other, an enemy for whose inner dynamism they lack respect. And now, in the oceans and the atmosphere, humankind pays the price. At the spectrum's other end, the practice of respect for the saving way that is not ours makes possible fuller understanding of and delight in the varieties of human spiritual experience.

The many reasons that the women's movement awakened resistance from so many men, and not a few women, need not burden us here. One of the least discussed may, however, be among the most important: the women's movement strikes at the foundations of the hierarchical imagination that, despite the efforts of Jesus, has been the organizing principle of Western culture and at the spirit of individualism that has been an energizing force in Western civilization since the Renaissance. Mary

Mahowald's weaving together of feminism, communitarianism, and Christianity implies that a new way—or, better, a new human self—is coming into being, a way that leads to the convergence of the masculine and the feminine incarnated in persons and in their communities. The new self that she envisions is profoundly relational. The relationships admit of no hierarchy—equality in Mahowald's world is ontological—and work for the common good takes precedence over self-interest, however enlightened or creative.

The great religious traditions have done too little to map out paths of holiness for those whose work is the world. The Middle Ages at their occasional best did see holiness as communitarian, the contribution of men and women monastics to society at large. (The dangers of religious specialization are apparent enough; they are surely one cause of the Reformation). Leonardo Boff's call for a spirituality of action, especially political action, stems logically from the premise of liberation theology. If Christian mission arises from a call to side with the oppressed and work with them for justice, Christians need to articulate a way of "being contemplative while working for liberation." Gandhi and Martin Luther King, whose contributions to spirituality Boff does not mention here, offer possible, though incomplete, models from outside his Latin American Roman Catholic tradition. So do some of those who have resisted one or another of our century's totalitarianisms of the right and the left. Boff has admirably laid out meaningful traits of liberationist contemplation. It would be useful to bring together insights from other traditions facing the same question—the Tibetan Buddhist and the African-American Christian, for example.

Of the four articles that follow Boff's, two explicitly consider spirituality. Those by Georges Khodr and Vincent Harding do so implicitly. Thomas Berry draws attention to the demonic element in Western spirituality: its divorce of the human and the Holy from nature. The person and the Persons, he is saying, are neither above nor apart but are within nature. "The human is that being," he says elsewhere, "in whom the universe activates, reflects upon and celebrates itself in conscious self-awareness" (*Cross Currents,* Summer/Fall 1987, 216). His ecological hope rests on thought and work that emanate from a spirituality founded on that awareness, an awareness that could find its social realization through the American experience. Beatrice Bruteau's integrating perceptions complement Berry's, for his hope demands not only a new way of seeing but a deepened understanding of love. Without rejecting Buber's metaphor of I-thou, she derives from the spiritualities of East and West a meeting of subjectivities, of the beloved experienced not as penetrating other—thou—but, as *I,* as oneself. Hers is an Emmaus vision, a eucharist of persons.

Georges Khodr is rigorous in his theological analysis of violence. He courageously faces the fact that one manifestation of God presented by the Hebrew Scriptures is that of a God of violence, the Lord of armies, the Power that enables his people to conquer. Nor does he hesitate to separate himself from that manifestation of God. The implications for spirituality are plain: even the holiest of writings must face the critical scrutiny of the informed conscience if a new Jerusalem is to be built. It is not a matter of picking and choosing; it is a matter of purifying the foundations on which religious faith—any religious faith—is built. If violence is, in fact, evil—at best a possibly moral way but as likely an anti-Christian option—traditions that celebrate it must be called into question.

Vincent Harding gives us a darkly radiant vision of the American self. He suggests that a nation engaged in the pursuit of loneliness seek instead its ancestors, the forebears not of individual families but of whatever hope society offers. The ancestors of American hope are some of them white, some of them Native American, some African-American, some Latino, some Asian. But they are all of them the common ancestors from whose spirits is inherited the best of what we are; and if we ignore them, or acknowledge only those who belonged to our tribe, we debase our heritage. The task of convergence might be described as the spiritual reconciliation of opposites; Harding would begin that work where he is, where Americans are, and the idea makes sense.

Convergence brings pain. The burden that Georges Khodr places on persons of biblical faith should not be minimized:

rejecting one scriptural perception of God awakens fear that all the Bible's religious insights may at some point begin to dissolve. Eugene Fontinell faces the same fear from a Roman Catholic perspective: "As one belief or knowledge claim after another succumbs, Christians are tempted to retreat to an ever-dwindling storehouse of allegedly unchanging beliefs. . . . Indeed, I would argue that without some mode of belief in the reality of God and resurrection, the Christian community forfeits its reason for being. . . . the point I would insist upon, however, is that no claim can be defended in isolation from the developing thought and experience of *both* the religious *and* the wider human community."

Raimundo Panikkar was born to a Portuguese Roman Catholic mother and an Indian Hindu father. He holds doctorates in science, philosophy, and theology. He can call three continents home. In conversation, he once described himself as a Christian in faith and a Hindu in practice. His person, in other words, might be taken as a symbol of convergence. To read his essay on the contradiction between the claim that Christian faith is both chosen and universal as an exercise in negative criticism would be mistaken. Panikkar has written instead a prolegomenon to a reborn Christian self-understanding. To be chosen is to see the unchosen as other; to maintain that one's faith supercedes all others is to reject the religious experience of millions of human beings over thousands of years. Vincent Harding might call it a denial of our ancestors, so many of whose names we do not know. We must at least reverence their variegated ways by honoring the faiths of their children.

Notes

1. Convergence is not the only thread, of course. Joseph Cunneen and I gathered psychologically oriented articles in *Cross Currents of Psychiatry and Catholic Morality* (New York: Pantheon, 1964; Meridian paperback, 1966). Intra-ecclesial articles have proved useful, especially to Roman Catholics. War, peace, and nonviolence have been

consistent themes in articles that have often enough broken new ground. As the soil out of which liberation and contextual theology grew, Latin America and South Africa have been a frequent concern. Feminists have contributed notable articles, surprisingly often on subjects not directly related to the oppression of women.

2. Thomas Berry, "Twelve Principles for Reflecting on the Universe," *Cross Currents,* Summer/Fall 1987, 217.

3. Rejection of convergence changes the experience of faith quite as much as does embracing it. Contemporary fundamentalism—whether Islamic, Christian, or Jewish—largely derives from the fact of convergence experienced as a threat to values that have worked in the past.

4. "Process and Experience: Dewey and American Philosophy" by Robert C. Pollock, and "Dewey and Christian Experience" by Ralph C. Sleeper. Pollock, one of the great teachers, influenced profoundly several of the more active *Cross Currents* editors.

5. The articles were expanded into *Toward a Reconstruction of Religion* (Garden City, NY: Doubleday, 1970; Cross Currents paperback, 1979).

6. Rosemary Radford Ruether's "The Becoming of Women in Church and Society" (*Cross Currents,* Fall 1967) deserves special mention; it catalyzed the process of spiritual reconstruction for many men and women.

7. A traditional carol portrays a courtly and cosmic Christ who opens his recital of gospel events:
To-morrow shall be my dancing day,
I would my true love did so chance
To see the legend of my play,
To call my true love to my dance.
Sing, oh! my love, oh! my love, my love, my love,
This have I done for my true love.
"They scourged me and set me at nought," this Christ says, and
"Judged me to die to lead the dance."

8. Within this context, I use the term *church* to designate the social reality of the Christian phenomenon. The *churches* are each of them more and less adequate embodiments of that phenomenon both through their Christian ways of life and through their organizational forms.

9. William F. Lynch makes the distinction in *Images of Hope* (Baltimore: Helicon, 1965). Though Lynch is applying it to questions of psychology, it makes sense in this context as well.

10. *Myth* taken as sacred story seems an apposite designation for the doctrine of the Trinity. It might be interesting to see the controversy

over the *filioque* clause as a dispute over ways of effectively telling the same story.

11. Denis Goulet's "Tasks and Methods in Development Ethics" (*Cross Currents,* Summer 1988, 146–163, 172) has special value for those who wish to meditate on the irrelevance of any ethics, religious or secular, that avoids engagement with the practicalities of implementation.

12. Walter Kaufman's introduction to his translation of Martin Buber's *I and Thou* is notable for its praise of religious language. In the 1950s the Jesuit thinker William F. Lynch baptized a child one of whose godparents was Jean Paul Sartre. Having made his commitment, Lynch told me, Sartre was assiduous in his attention to his godchild's religious welfare.

EMMANUEL MOUNIER

Christian Faith and Civilization

Emmanuel Mounier sought less to give definitive answers than to explore possible solutions, aware that what he said might not survive in the marketplace of ideas. Founder in 1932 of the political-cultural review Esprit, *he became a pivotal figure in the French noncommunist Left following World War II. As this essay indicates, his personalism goes far beyond a philosophy of individuation and embraces the breadth of social reality. His concern in this excerpt might be summarized in the word* incarnation: *Christian faith believes that the Incarnation happened; the Christian task is to make that isolated faith event a planetary reality.*

L et us begin by questioning history: if it is the book of God, read in the light of faith, it carries a sort of natural revelation which may enlighten us.

Let us pose this initial problem: has the life of faith, gradually incorporated into the Church and into the Christian world, had a notable influence on the destiny of our civilization, and if so in what way?

We have all heard of Christianity as a revolutionary leaven. The Gospels at first glance contain enough explosive material to blow up the family, the state, class harmony, the institutions of property, frontiers, the framework of race, propriety—in fact the entire social pattern. It was precisely this that the Roman Emperors feared. They did not persecute visionaries; they persecuted subversives. Now what did these subversives do? Within three centuries they made themselves masters of the Empire, but without an armed struggle. And what of the society which bred them? Did they withdraw from it like ascetics into the desert? Did they everywhere conscientiously object, refusing to obey? Did they try to imagine new forms of life? No. They were in the army and the court, the forum and the senate, the baths and the market-place; they refused to worship false gods, even at the cost of their lives—but that was their only rebellion. The strongest voices against pagan corruption, such as Tertullian, took the greatest pains to advise conformity in everyday life, to underline the regularity of their citizenship.

"There are now neither free men nor slaves," they proclaimed. And in fact the condition of the slave under a Christian master was profoundly altered. The most scandalous dispositions of slaves were abandoned. But slavery itself remained. Twelve and thirteen centuries after the revolutionary doctrine, all medieval theology, from St. Bonaventure to St. Thomas and Duns Scotus, still justified it. Slavery finally disappeared only because of economic pressure.

"Thou shalt not kill," they preached. But until the end of the second century, this was not a question of conscientious objection among the disciples. Even in the tenth century war was considered a normal state of affairs. It required the approach of the first millennium to produce the great reactions of the Assemblies of Peace and the Truce of God. The theology of the just war, broached in the thirteenth century, reached its full development only in the sixteenth.

Some would perhaps explain reluctance on the part of the first generations of Christians to build a Christian civilization, by the hypnotic fascination of the Gospels and their teaching, or by the common belief of the time that the Empire and the world would soon come to an end at the Second Coming. But when this illusion passed? Constantine brought Christianity to the throne of the Empire. Did one see Christian legislation as a result? Not even for the exclusive use of Christians. A little later when the clergy obtained jurisdictional privileges, they remained as an ecclesiastical nucleus in the general law without any influence over secular society. It has been said that in the later Empire the bishops became almost everywhere *defensores civitatis,* the principal municipal authorities. Today, we know they were not invested with any functions of the kind. When the ancient authorities succumbed to the attacks of the barbarians in the fifth and sixth centuries, the bishops assumed their functions in the absence of other authorities. The Church alone could preserve the organization, the resources, the traditions of the State. To what else could one turn?

It was only at the beginning of the seventh century that the Church began to grow directly enmeshed in temporal society. The bonds between the Church and the secular government were tied with increasing tightness by the unexpected and undesired inheritance of the Empire. It was only as an aftermath that theologians formed a theory to fit this new situation. That is what Maritain has called the Theocratic Utopia. Contrary to the popular opinion this was neither the doctrine nor the official practice of the Middle Ages, but only a thesis of the schoolmen. The dominant temptation of medieval Christianity was to struggle against the distinction, maintained by the Church, of two powers and two societies. It was not content to think that the faith was directly established in the organization of the world. By a sort of holy impatience, a return to the old temptation of the Jewish law, it wished to realize immediately and constitutionally the Kingdom of God in the stuff of this world under the temporal jurisdiction of the Pope.

Modern historians, both Christian and secular, have shown us that this perfect domination of the state by the Christian organism has never existed—unless in the nostalgic imaginations of some contemporary Christians ill adapted to the struggle in this our world.

I have taken my examples from the world of public life; I could have selected them as well from philosophy or art. No more than they have sought to build a state materially different from the pre-Christian state, have the Christian ages striven to found a new art or a new thought. It is well known how the Middle Ages lived on the foundation of ancient thought. Most of the first flowerings of Christian thought were concerned with theology and morality. Ideas were shaped and reshaped only insofar as they were useful to refine the dogma and teaching of the Church.

When Plato seemed to St. Thomas to deviate dangerously from Christian truth, it is another pagan, Aristotle, whom he hurls in the service of the Word into the attack on Plato. It was the same in art. The first churches were converted basilicas. Christ was at first represented by Bacchus. You know the famous letter of St. Gregory to Mellitus on the construction of churches: "Do not destroy the idolatrous temples in England. It is sufficient to destroy the idols they contain. Purify the buildings with holy water, construct altars; throw out the relics. . . . Whoever wishes to reach a summit ought to ascend gradually, step by step, and not by leaps." It is faith and morals which absorb the Pope's attention, with a superior indifference to means as long as the spirit of the means be good. This is far from the creative, formative dogma, from the Gothic arch subduing heavy stone to Christian prayer.

Let us linger for a moment on this point; it is of sufficient historical importance to raise a problem. What are we to conclude?

If it were a question of only the first Christian centuries, an interpretation would come immediately to mind. The material of history is rebellious. Just as in the case of culture, where moral habits implant themselves in us slowly, so it required many years for Christianity to rebuild a world settled in its foundations, a world which opposed to any change the enormous power of inertia. This is certainly a part of the answer. But two objections limit this explanation. If it were simply a matter of material resistance to a clear intention, there would be no problem. The more troubling fact is the absence of the intention—an intention of realizing a civilization clearly bearing a Christian trademark, wished and sought after as a new and unique civilization, instead of aspiring to a Kingdom not of this world, although beginning in this world and using its materials.

1

Fifty years ago, no one would have dared to predict a place for the Christian message in the history of civilization. He would have been afraid of being left behind the times. Today a powerful current has formed to support the basic indifference of the faith to the things of the world. It was born in a Protestant atmosphere in reaction against a religion confined within the limits of reason and of the success which religious liberalism had won there. The paradox of faith for Kierkegaard is that of an absolute isolation, so absolute that it imitates supreme egoism. It can in no way enter into the ranks of the general—into ideas, institutions, customs. The servant of faith can absolutely not be understood by anyone, nor can he be of aid to any other servant of the faith. If he is powerless to communicate faith to anyone even in the order of faith, how much less will he be able to communicate it at the level of organization? Christendom is a "horrible illusion." So far is Christendom from being a realization of Christianity that the whole problem today is to reintroduce Christianity into Christendom. It is not the dullness of our time which separates the Christian from Christ. It is the dullness of Christendom which has "abandoned Christ". Today a man becomes a Christian "much as he puts on his socks." He no longer sees the infinite opposition between the Christian order and the way of the world. This is absurdity and heresy. Mankind has wished to anticipate eternity and pretends to have installed a Church triumphant. It succeeds only in instituting a Christianity set up in trade and fingering the scales—in other words, the very contrary of Christianity. Christianity is a choice in the depth of the heart which is offered to each person and not to an organization. "The many" is meaningless, and time, for Kierkegaard, has no other meaning than as a part of the "continued rarefaction" of Christianity. In such a perspective, Christianity has nothing to look for from history. The idea of expansion is radically foreign to it. Its pretended progress resembles what the doctor says in one of Holberg's plays: "The fever has completely disappeared, but the patient is dead."

The rejection of history, such as one finds in the early Barth, is properly speaking a Protestant idea. It would be difficult for Catholic thought to maintain it so strictly. It finds favor, however, with certain temperaments—how this happens, we would have to investigate not only by an examination of ideas, but also by a psychological and sociological analysis. The myth of automatic progress is simply inverted by such people into the counter-myth of the systematic regression of civilizations—our own in particular. Of particular interest is the way such affirmations tend to erect a sort of closed theology and religious myth—neither exempt from socio-political infiltrations—as a true anti-history, by a resentment against history which serves as a counterpart of its naive idealization in the opposing camp.

This tendency to ignore phenomena is Greek; it is not Christian. It is strongly encouraged by the vague and confused relationship of the spiritual to the temporal. For the Christian the spiritual is, in the strict meaning of the words, the presence in our life of the eternal life, in opposition to our natural activities. But this eternal life is itself bred in the flesh and ordinarily presents itself to us only through the agency of natural activities. Instead of maintaining at all cost the central point of view of a religion which has the Incarnation as its axis, we have little by little allowed our concept of the spiritual to be contaminated by the eclectic and rootless idealism in which *spiritual* and *moral* signify the soul without the body, the breath of life without life, good will without the will, culture without earth. We do not have to carry the spiritual to the temporal; it is there already. Our task is to discover it there and to give it life, indeed to sacramentalize it. The temporal in its entirety is the sacrament of the Kingdom of God.

Here we are then—torn between the absolute demands of the Incarnation and the patent detachment of the first Christian period from the work of civilization. How are we to reconcile them?

Undoubtedly it would be better not to decide the question in the abstract, but rather to consider how the situation came about. If we consider more closely how Christianity has seized on civilization whenever it has spread itself, we will discover a very singular type of influence. This influence has been massive, and it is so deep-seated and profound that it conditions even those who remain detached from it.

First of all the faith disturbs human institutions as such as little as possible, at least as long as they do no violence to the justice of

God. Neither in the word of Christ nor in apostolic or patristic teaching do we hear the anathemas which were later hurled against human institutions by Luther and Jansenius. Christ was the point overturning the Jewish order, the Jewish nation and the exclusive rule of the Law which in the Jewish theocracy composed a single entity. But He has only praise for the profound permanence of this Law, and He fled the sovereignty which would have permitted Him, in His *human* capacity, to overthrow it immediately. "Render to Caesar" dominated the preaching of the Apostles. When he described the two cities, St. Augustine took every precaution lest he make the city of God an imaginary and separate city and he underlined its incorporation into the earthly city. "It is indifferent to the city of God what attire the citizens wear, or what rules they observe, as long as they contradict not God's holy precepts, but each one keeps the faith, the true path to salvation." (*City of God*, 19:29). Let us take up the word of Augustine: we can truthfully speak of a sort of Christian *indifference* to the matter of civilizations, not an indifference of abstention but of relation. Standing on the ground in a dense forest, one path alone seems to lead to the goal. Flying overhead many paths appear equally satisfactory. This relative indifference is inevitably scandalous to one who places his entire stake in direct action. He can see this partial unconcern, which he believes purely negative, only as an abandonment of the post. "If all imitate you," said Celsus to the Christian, "the King will remain alone and abandoned, all the things of the world will fall to the power of the barbarians, and your sect itself and the true wisdom will disappear from the midst of men." Did not Origen justify him when he said that the Christian ought to "deny himself to the public magistrates because he has higher ministers?"

In fact, this sacred indifference is very difficult to maintain in its spiritual exactness. There is a constant temptation for the *interior* Christian to withdraw from the affairs of the world. Is this what the transcendence of his faith asks? By no means. Notice that the Fathers did not say, "Avoid the affairs of the world, they are insignificant," but on the contrary, "Because they are insignificant do not withdraw from them. Take them as they come." And when they added "Penetrate the works of others with the Christian spirit," they started the Christian on an end-less road of supplementary tests and travails. The Christian was thus bound to the world with ever stronger ties until he had to seek with difficulty the secret ways to answer the call of grace.

Refusing to throw into confusion the world it has entered, the Christian idea turned instead to the task of introducing itself by indirect means. Like Christ in the upper room, it insinuated itself imperceptibly into the whole intact, without breaking through the gates, and at first it dropped out of sight. Where is it? How does it operate? What is it doing? No one knew. It did not wish to be handled, administered, rationalized. At first there was no change to be seen. He who like Thomas had not the living faith did not wish to believe it was there—was acting—but soon the catalyst was at work and the reaction was produced.

A man is pointed out—he has freed his slaves, without any sensation. He keeps them in his home and exacts obedience from them. But instead of machines, they are now men. They are treated with kindness; they are free to marry at their own choice. A second man follows suit—five, ten, a hundred. An institution from time immemorial, one which seemed eternal, has been broken as the surface of a stone after the silent frosts.

Recollect the attitude of the apostles toward the Jewish ob-servance. The first Christian community, the depositary of a universally explosive doctrine, was composed entirely of Jews committed to Mosaic practice. It even seems that the first Chris-tians to preach outside Jerusalem addressed themselves only to Jews. The presence of Hellenic Jews who long since had aban-doned part of the Mosaic ritual posed a problem. The problem reached an acute stage with the stoning of Stephen, who had emphasized the Hellenist point of view in his preaching. But after this dramatic climax, the fever dropped. James preached concil-iation, and limited the obligations of Gentiles to a respect for the Law, without as yet attempting to suppress it. Paul heightened the scandal by vigorously asserting the universalist message. Many within the Church wished to submit all Christians of whatever origin to circumcision and to the strict observations of the Old Law. James was again the peacemaker and obtained concessions from Paul.

The same movement applied toward the Empire. Christianity in insinuating itself within the Empire allowed her not only to survive but to grow more and more monstrous. The capricious omnipotence of the State soon passed even beyond the frontiers of madness. Who resisted it? Men who obeyed all her laws, followed all her customs, but who on one solitary point refused to submit, obstinately refused. One point and only one, a seeming trifle—the cult of the God-Emperor. But this was a vital point. As a hundred light blows delivered against a selected area can by vibration after vibration dislocate a powerful bulwark, so the Empire began to break under this chorus of *no, no, no.* Henceforth, wherever the Moloch-state reappears, Christianity will tirelessly undermine it with her power of disassociation.

In these examples, Christian inspiration has played the same role: it has not *constructed,* it has *disassociated.*

When, instead of this negative action, the Christian spirit has directly influenced a process of civilization, it seems as if it always has produced its temporal effects as by-products, at times almost without being aware of them. Theologians leaped into the depths of the Trinity, and two centuries raged for or against *procession* and *succession.* From a turmoil of councils and heresies there passed into history, by the definition of the divine Persons and their relationships, the double principle of the individual and the community which thereafter ruled over the fluctuation of societies. Generations of spiritual energy were expended to maintain in the Incarnate Word the integrity of the human nature and the fullness of the Incarnation: thanks to which European civilization alone will never withdraw from this world but will unite human activity with the spirit of contemplation. God alone was preached and no subordinate *latria* tolerated; at the same time, science was freed from the spirit of magic and thus became possible, by the unity of God, the unity of the world. Christianity contributes more to the most material works of mankind when it increases in spiritual intensity than when it loses itself in problems of tactics and management. Kierkegaard thought that it experiences only indirect communication. One might say that it experiences only indirect fertility. We are touching here on a master structure of divine and human history: *Seek ye the Kingdom of God and its justice and the rest shall be added unto you.*

Another figure from the Gospels enables us to picture, in a similar way, the operation of supernatural action in the temporal order. It is the figure of the leaven—of yeast or of salt. Some men even today follow with nostalgic eyes or despair the last remnants of medieval Christendom. One might ask himself if this earthly Kingdom, the temptation to which the Christian era had to submit even as the Jewish people before them, was not formed on a perverted representation of the presence of the Spirit in history. The theorists of Caesaro-Papist Christendom believed that the faith commanded them to organize the world under God. The problem is to know when it is not at least as important, and more in conformity with the teaching of the Gospels, to disorganize the world under God—I mean to render it transparent before God when the inevitable weight of *management* has succeeded in erecting a screen between the world and God. We must have administration and yet preserve the inspiration behind the administration. Christ did not prepare a systematic outline of new Christian ideas: the idea of creation, of a supernaturally ordained nature, of sin, of redemption—ideas to overturn the world.

Discreet and concealed, Christian inspiration reveals its strangeness even more by the ambivalence which it assumes in presenting itself to our mind or to our will. It transmits the Word of God to sovereign liberties. Therefore it cannot translate it into a language perfectly clear to men, for that would be no longer the Word of God, and it would impose necessity on our liberty. It offers itself always in such a way as to give light to those who seek the light, and, to follow the powerful aphorism of St. Paul, to give darkness to those who reject the light. The condemnation of atheistic communism directs our attention to the danger of a system of human relationships which grows perverted by closing its eyes to the total nature of man, but it serves also, against its own intention, to consolidate the social blindness and egotism of class.

Another aspect of this same ambivalence is the way in which Christianity operates through the very currents which set themselves in opposition to her. Here we are still in the dialectic of indirect communication. God does not communicate Himself clearly under any human name, through any human act. Some find Him by analogic affirmations. These are the faithful. Certain mystics find Him through negatives wrapped in an infinite love. Some find Him by an apparent negation accompanied by an apparent hostility, which is often only the negation of idolatrous representations of God. These last are those atheists who, though declaredly atheists, yet live in good will in the theological sense of the word, and under other names actually give themselves to God as the end of their lives. On the Day of Judgment many men, as we know from the words of Christ, will be astonished to learn that they have performed in Christ works which in their conscience never seemed directed toward Him.

2

The Church is not charged with maintaining order in the state, nor with the equable distribution of goods, nor with the greatest happiness of the greatest number. It is a community of life in Christ. The Church is not in herself a professor of philosophy, nor a custodian of morals, nor a guardian of society—neither is she a dispenser of riches, a foyer of culture, a center of works. Less still is she a power or an academy. This is what the first Christians saw. For the first two centuries the Church was devoted to the process of evangelization. The bishops were the great artisans of this first conquest. They multiplied into a considerable number, creating an indefinite (and dangerous) parceling out of churches. Only gradually was the mission consolidated and the parish constituted. Without a set plan she made her way empirically by diverse paths which took a long time to find a common end. Little occupied in organizing herself, the Church was far less occupied in organizing the world. Not that she scorned the task. It was simply not her affair and she left it to those whose care it was.

But since the Church, in imitation of her Master, is fully incarnate, her mission, which is not of this world, must be accomplished in this world. Properly speaking there are not two histories alien to one another, sacred history and profane history. There is but one history, that of humanity on the march toward

the Kingdom of God. "Sanctified history" *par excellence,* but
extended between two poles, a supernatural pole and a temporal
pole, with marked boundaries about each of them and an infinitely graduated composition between them. Even as the Church
refuses the separation of the two worlds, so she affirms their
vigorous distinction.

"The supernatural is not given its due," wrote Bernanos. A
single dimension of history, abstracted for the occasion of a
limited and necessarily incomplete act, may reveal an historic
pattern. But the totality of history in each of its moments assumes its significance for the Christian only in an historic super-
naturalism which classifies all events in terms of collective salvation and the attainment of the Kingdom of God. For the Christian
the Kingdom has already begun amongst us and through us. That
is why history is neither farce nor melodrama, but a divine
comedy coupled with a divine tragedy. In many religions sacred
history is mythical. It is not a comedy in which man plays a part
but a magical scenario which man undergoes as a fantasy of the
gods, and which ends badly for him. For Christianity God is so
intimately bound up with the history of man that at the last man
is drawn into the glory of God. And that begins here and now,
under our eyes. It is then entirely impossible for a Christian to
speak as if he were separating his occupations—to the Church or
to the life of faith, the supernatural domain; to this doctrine or
that action, the organization of the earth. The earth cannot be
organized outside the faith, even as the faith cannot develop
without the forces of the earth. We are penetrated and determined, both individually and collectively, by their influence.

Nevertheless the life of the Church and (in us) the life of faith
engrafted upon her, are transcendent in their effects or historic
expressions. We know the realities sought by faith only in a
mirror or through an enigma. Bound to the ordinary resources of
our spiritual life and of the teachings of the Church, we cannot
see clearly the relationship between these obscure truths and
civilization. It is presumptuous to dogmatize at random and to no
purpose. In our lifetime what have we not heard of "monarchists
because Christians", "democrats because Christians," "progressives because Christians"?

Each individual member of the faithful should keep in mind

that he is a citizen of the earth, and that if he attempts a complete imitation of Christ, he must completely assume, like Christ, the duties and charges of that citizenship. He must not conceive the grandeur of God in terms of the stupidity of the world. But this anxiety for free play with the things of this world ought not allow him to forget that as a Christian he cannot enclose his earthly citizenship in self-sufficiency. "You are," St. Thomas says, "fellow-citizens of the saints, you are members of the household of God." The panoply of virtues which is theoretically adapted to the natural order of the earthly citizen is no longer sufficient for a fallen nature in the true works of this earth. Still less can it satisfy the demands of our supernatural citizenship. Therefore it is not enough, in order that we may live organically as Christians, to recognize that the supernatural has its place in our lives and in history, but we must recognize that it is everywhere, even though it may not be everything. A Christian today must cease to be an idealist, or a spiritualist. This implies at the same time and with the same force that he will bury himself in the tradition and the life of the Church in order that he may no more be half a Christian than half a man. It implies that he be as deeply sensitive to the devitalization of our supernatural plan of natural truths, as he is sensitive to the devitalization of our supernatural message by the weakness of our *présence* in the world. Arduous work was needed to dissociate modern scientific achievements from their dramatization by scientism, while the Church was freeing her teaching from its decrepit representatives—before science and the faith could be enticed into pacific coexistence. The truths which the modern world has disentangled in the matter of civilization cannot, as they are and without *digestion,* become Christian truths. First there is necessary the alliance of two virtues rarely united: boldness and patience, wonder and fidelity. The adventure is well worth the doing.

3

There emerges from our analysis one consequence which especially preoccupies the man of action. If the passion for the Kingdom of God is the dominant passion for the Christian, is there not some risk in turning it away from the organization of the earth? It is necessary here to fasten more securely the bond between the spiritual and the temporal, and to do this we will consider now the question we have so far described only indirectly. We might phrase it so: *Is the development of civilization a help or a hindrance; is it superfluous or necessary for the life of faith?*

We can now descend one step and ask: is a well-ordered and happy civilization a Christian civilization? It is always possible to give to order and happiness meanings which will comprehend both heaven and earth. But in the plan to which we have assigned the name civilization, order is the rational management of relationships, happiness is a convenient satisfaction of needs. Even if we suppose they could establish themselves in a durable equilibrium and even decorate themselves with such moral virtues as are bound to the balance of health and strength, they would not constitute a Christian order, for that consists in faith, hope, and charity and their reverberations on the whole of life. There would even be a risk of their closing themselves in a confined whole so well adjusted that the true destiny of man would then find no place in which to take root.

But these conditions are not contemptible for the true destiny of faith. To say that they are necessary to it would be to steal from faith the profound gratuity it affirms from time to time by flowering against all the rules of logic. But although sovereignly free, the grace of God has sovereignly chosen to submit within ourselves to the conditions of the Incarnation. Christ has played fair. His activity within history has been free of deceit. In this sense we can say that He wishes it to undergo the conditioning of matter and of the body. The bond between the spiritual and the physical is tied more strongly than by necessity. It is tied by a will founded on love.

The more one considers the multitude, the greater part these conditionings play. The social encyclicals, following the doctors, endlessly recall that as a general rule and for the great number, a minimum of physical development, of health, security and material ease is essential to the exercise of a Christian life. Cro-Magnon man could not receive the Christian message. That is why Christ did not come until 200,000 or 300,000 years after the creation. The true proletarian can with difficulty see the spiritual life project itself amid the privileges of culture to which he has no access.

But it is not only a question of minimal conditions. The discussion lies on the frontiers of the *vital* minimum, and the influence of the structures of the spiritual life goes far beyond that. One always speaks of the spiritual as if the material universe did not fill History with its presence, and of the Church as if it were fully realized and radically separated from the world and from time. Altogether different is our condition: "We are not the sons of God, and it hath not yet appeared what we shall be." In step with humanity the Church is between the *already known* and the *yet awaited* joined to the *still to come,* and only this dialectic defines its true position in history. This *still to come* notably allows for the progressive expression in matter and in the history of civilizations of truths attained by the act of faith. Since in this world we do not see them face to face, but in a mirror and across the enigma of these expressions, how could the most intimate destiny of the life of faith not be bound to them?

There are in history "historic accidents of grace." Perhaps history has also known through our fault or through bad guesses some true historic mischances. It is an historic commonplace that the march of the legions prepared the path for St. Paul. The map of penetration of the great religions covers again that of the diffusion of epidemics. The roads are the same for microbes and for the word of God, the carrier is the same. The lassitude of an agitated and wandering population at the end of the Empire inspired the Benedictine vow of stability and favored the impetus of that order. The rapid growth of the feudal organism, into which the Church might easily have inserted herself, failed to stifle the Church under the laic power of the ninth century, and Gregory the Great detached her from the established order to return her spiritual liberty to her. It was the birth of the new communal society, the displacement toward the cities, the agitation of populations by a commerce threatening the old feudal stability, which provoked the rise of the great mendicant orders in the thirteenth century. The attraction of the riches of the Orient and the eco-

nomic crisis of feudalism were not strangers to the impulse of the
Crusades. At the beginning of the fifteenth century, in the re-
forms of the Canons Regular toward interior piety, simplicity of
life, open-hearted humanism, one may read the weariness of a
society overwhelmed by the weight of scholastic cavilling and of
a monastic order corroded with formalism. We could pile up
examples indefinitely showing the way of bourgeois austerity in
the Jansenist sect, or of commercial comfort in religious liberalism. Even today where the last remnants of feudal and peasant
civilization still predominate, is the sociological basis of the
Church without influence on the behavior of Christians? And
what of the massive absence of the world of the workers? Can we
think that certain reconquests of the religious life are possible
unless some aberrations are removed? "In History there is more
than History," one commentator has said. There is an invisible
regency of the Incarnate Word, perhaps a secret legality which
forms a sort of natural revelation. It seems that profane history
pays even less attention to Christianity than Christianity to her,
and that like Christ it consents to undergo violence but not to
exercise it. Therefore we must safeguard the discretion of Him
whom we imitate, in our manner of proposing Him to the institutions of this world. But on the other hand we must watch closely
this tight bond between the facts of civilization and the condition
of the spiritual in which the witness of the faith can blockade
himself and worse still be altered by all sorts of faithless aberrations.

History and civilization viewed in this perspective appear to
us no longer as realities foreign to the Kingdom of God. To cut
one off from the other is to cause the Kingdom to pass into the
pure irrational and to renounce the interior unity of the Christian
vision. And so certain Christians, unwilling to accept their in-
ability to assimilate history, prefer to give it a catastrophic essence and to be pleased by this. It is a little as if they found it
unworthy of the transcendence of Christ that He had a body
wholesome in itself and pleasant to view, and thought that it
could affirm itself only in deformed limbs. History and civilizations are as a collective sacrament of the Kingdom of God. That
means that they are in our dispensation necessary mediators.

And sometimes, when Christian society has not fully communicated to them the wholeness of its message, they effect a true substitution for it, just as bread without salt or leaven replaces the living God. Or rather, the unleavened bread, without manifesting His full significance, becomes the living God received in His silence and His humility. It is only at the summit of that sacramental reality of civilizations that our subject finds its full significance. Perhaps we other Occidentals, nurtured in a civilization of the word, are too exclusively sensitive to the word which reduces to a formula, and not enough to the word which dances in the imagination. *Verbum Dei* but also *Gesta Dei* and *Corpus Dei*. Civilizations too, unconsecrated, are only a fragile crust. Even then a sort of reverential fear prevents us from taking them too lightly, for they have the form of that which was made to be consecrated.

Translated by Erwin W. Geissman

KARL RAHNER

The Church of Sinners

Karl Rahner, S.J., widely considered the foremost Roman Catholic theologian of this century, grappled throughout his most creative years with human solidarity, "the grammar of a possible expression of God's own life", and saw the Christian church as a sacrament of that solidarity. "At the heart of his thought," his fellow Jesuit Leo J. O'Donovan says, "was the conviction that by our very creation and still more by God's redemptive grace we belong together"; ("Karl Rahner, S.J. [1904–1984]: in Memoriam." Cross Currents, Summer 1984, 206). In this essay, Rahner rejects the idea of an idealized church. "The Church is a sinful Church: it is part of her creed and no mere conclusion of experience. And it is terrifying." Human solidarity, the event of belonging together, may well begin with the indeed terrifying insight that we humans tinge what we touch with the darkness of evil as well as the radiance of hope.

In Catholic dogma the concept of the "Church of sinners" is for the most part very briefly treated. There is really so much that is more important and magnificent to be said of the Church. The fact that the Church is a "Church of sinners" does not occupy a very prominent place in theological interest, perhaps also because it is only too clearly an every-day experience. Nonetheless the subject is essentially of great significance in the teaching of the Church, not merely because one is concerned here with one of the most troublesome questions of theology in all dogmatic history, but because it is of such importance for the faith of the individual. The question is paramount because in the final analysis the problem as understood here is not so much that of the obvious, everyday experience, but of its dogmatic implications, whose answer therefore must be sought in Revelation and not in any confused, sin-distorted experience of men.

We say we are confronted with a thorny problem which is ever recurring in the history of the teaching Church. Christianity has always professed belief in the "holy" Catholic Church. And again and again historically the question has arisen, where then is this Church which so confidently declares that she is holy, the very Church on which the splendor of God's own holiness rests? And repeatedly with appeal to this article of faith the Church in the concrete has been rejected as a sinful one. Repeatedly some new Church has been established as the true, holy one and proclaimed to be the real Church of God and of His Christ. Tertullian declared that the great Church of his day was not the true Church of the spirit and of spiritual men but a brothel, because she did not cast out adulterers once and for all from her community. Montanism and Novatianism gave a similar teaching in the third century. Donatism in the time of Augustine, Messalianism and other heretical currents in monasticism, as well as movements such as that of the Cathari, the Spiritualism of a Joachim of Flora, the Spiritualists among the Franciscans, the Hussites in the Middle Ages. And even the Reformers of the sixteenth century, who taught so impressively the sinfulness and corruption of man, fought a large part of their struggle against the Catholic Church with accusations against a corrupted Papacy and the unholiness of the Church generally.

No less in the life of the individual, the experience of an unholy Church in inner conflict with his faith almost always plays a significant role. When anti-clericalism breaks out somewhere, what charge is more often hurled against the clergy than that their lives are in contradiction to their preaching? What more frequently said than that Church-going Christians are no better than others and that therefore the Church has failed? Such reproaches and the attacks on faith which grow out of them are, humanly speaking, not wholly unjust. Here after all is a Church proclaiming herself necessary for salvation, preaching in the name of the one holy God, declaring herself to be in possession of all truth and grace, insisting on being the only ark of salvation in the deluge of sin and corruption, believing that she must convert and save everyone. And it is precisely this Church, making such claims, that often seems to measure with a double standard. She preaches to poor tormented men the Sermon on the Mount with its "impossible" demands, but her official representatives seem personally to have let themselves off from these demands quite cheaply. Do they not seem to live in comfort? Are they not often greedy, arrogant, haughty? Are there not repeatedly scandals reaching into the ranks of their Religious orders, whose very purpose is to strive after sanctity and perfection? Are the "bad" popes a hostile epithet only or are they not historical fact? Have not even the sacred institutions of Catholicism been misused repeatedly throughout the world for sinful purposes: the confessional and the sacraments, the exploitation of the papacy for transparently political ends, etc.? That we are all men (so go the complaints) is not to be wondered at; and that even churchmen, ecclesiastical leaders, are men and sinners, in itself also is not astonishing. If it were only a question of this, it would be naturally unjust to probe the dark spots of Church history for her sins; but it is the Church herself who makes the claim to be essentially more than a human institution in which inevitably very human ways prevail. She insists that she is the representative of God in the world, the "holy" Church. She even declares that in herself she is through her "conspicuous holiness and inexhaustible fruitfulness of all good, a great and stable motive of credibility and an irrefutable witness of her divine mission" (Vat. Council, Denz. 1794). Precisely here is the crux: were the Church more modest (so runs the eternal objection of unbelief) we could be indulgent to her and forgive her everything we forgive ourselves. But because she sets herself up as the holy one, she must endure scrutiny of her life and history by norms and standards of judgment that exceed the human. But even then, is not the claim to holiness which she makes a unique presumption which proves rather precisely the opposite?

From yet a third angle the subject has relevance. It is not, that is, a question of how we as Christians who believe in the holiness of the Church meet our experience of unholiness there. More important is the dogmatic aspect, what, namely, Revelation itself says on the subject. In other words we do not wish at the moment to advert to the human indignation (we know perhaps better than earlier ages that "public opinion" even with considerable unanimity is a very problematic thing indeed, and that not uncommonly men will discover what they wish to discover), but to regard the Church's own testimony on this point of her unholiness. For the fact of the "Church of Sinners" is part of what the Church believes about herself. If someone, for example, with superficial optimism should pronounce the Church to be altogether perfect, she would not reply: Thank God here is someone finally who judges me with justice. Rather would she have to declare very bluntly: That is heresy and the truth concerning me is not in you; your indulgent spirit is wrong in that you have not taken into consideration the estimate of God Himself, either of that sanctity which He has bestowed on me His holy Church, or of the sanctity which I, the unholy Church of Sinners, surely lack; you yourself do not have the holiness you ought to have, otherwise you would not believe that you had found perfection in me—any more than he who in his disillusionment berates me because I actually do not have it.

1

The Church of God and of His Christ is a Church of Sinners. What this means can be considered under two headings: the sinners in the Church and the sinful Church.

1. It is a teaching of faith that sinners belong to the Church. Literally sinners, the eternally lost, can really and truly belong to the Church. This is a truth of faith which the Church has continuously taught from patristic times against Montanism, Novatianism, Donatism, through the Middle Ages against the Albigensians, the Fraticelli, against Wyclif and Hus, down to modern times against the Reformers, Jansenism and the Synod of Pistoia. The reverse proposition that sinners, deprived of grace

and seen by God in His foreknowledge to be lost, do not belong
to the Church, is a heresy definitely and conclusively condemned
by the Church herself. Still it would be rash to say that this is an
obvious fact which it is fantastic to question. It is actually far
from obvious. There is merely this much obvious: there exists a
civil, religious society called the Catholic Church and to it belong
others besides the superficially respectable bourgeoisie, the good
citizens, the paragons of virtue, and the genuine saints. So much
is clear enough. But this is not what is normally meant in Catholic dogma by the terms "Church" and "sinner." For "Church" in
the dogmatic concept is the visibility, the sacramental sym-
bolism, the abiding presence of God and His grace in the world;
it means the historical presence of Christ in the world until the
dawn of His second coming and his manifestation in His God-
head. "Church" is the human thing which is bound up with the
Divine, distinct from it certainly, but united. And the "sinner" in
the church is here not the man who on occasion falls short of the
code of penal law, which can happen to the best of us. Rather
the sinner in the proposition of faith is the man who really
lacks the grace of God, who strays far from Him, whose destiny
works itself out with fearful consequences to perdition. And it is
this kind of sinner that belongs to *this* kind of Church. He is not
merely registered as it were in her parish files; he is a part of her,
he is a small bit of the concrete embodiment of God's grace in the
world, a member of the Body of Christ. Is this a belaboring of the
obvious? Or is it not rather a truth so inconceivable that it far
outdistances everything which the protests of unbelief against
the unholiness of the Church can marshal?

This specific truth of Revelation is notwithstanding in both
Scripture and Tradition clearly indicated. The Kingdom of
Heaven is likened to a net which draws in from the seas of the
world both good fish and bad. Only on the shores of eternity will
the angels of judgment sort out the bad catch from the good and
cast it into the furnace (Mt. 13, 47–50). At the very wedding-
banquet of Heaven some will sit down who have not on a wed-
ding garment and these will shortly be tied hand and foot and
cast out (Mt. 22, 11 ff). There are some who, like the virgins
awaiting the bridegroom's arrival, have not enough oil for their

lamps (Mt. 25, 1–13). There are "brethren" who through continued disobedience to the Church become finally like pagans and abandoned sinners (Mt. 18, 17). Even the steward of the Lord's household can be cast out (Mt. 24, 45–51). Of the truths that the Lord teaches in these parables, the Apostles also give witness: there are sinners in the Church, men to whom the Spirit speaks: "I know your works; you are called living, but you are dead." Here is the terrifying aspect: one has actually the appearance of life, but is dead.

It was hard enough for the Church of the earliest centuries to accept this truth of faith without dismay, and even in St. Augustine, who enjoys, by virtue of his struggle with the Donatists, no little authority on this point in the history of dogma, it is not always quite clear whether, with his theories of wheat and chaff and of the free mingling of Jerusalem and Babylon, he always clearly and decisively regarded dead members as true members of the Mystical Body of Christ, or meant merely that the dividing line between these states is already drawn but reveals itself only at the end of time. In this respect the doctrinal consciousness of the Church has clarified itself in the course of time on our particular proposition that there are sinners and that they belong to the Church. In the Church are sin and rebellion. And these sins and shortcomings are a distinct part of the embodiment and manifestation of that divine salvation and grace which we call "Church."

This belonging of the sinner to the Church must necessarily be viewed from another angle, i.e., as negatively limited: the sinner does not belong in the same full sense as the non-sinner. For it is in the first place very obvious that one can and must speak of a belonging to the Church in whatever directions and dimensions the Church herself exists, and that whoever therefore does not belong in a single given dimension can not be regarded as her member in the fullest sense. Both Leo XIII in his encyclical "Satis cognitum" (1896) and Pius XII in "Mystici Corporis Christi" (to point only to more recent official teaching utterances) emphasize that it would be a kind of Nestorianism with regard to the Church and a rationalistic Naturalism to see in her no more than an external, legal organization, a mere visible

society, a "confession" in the sociological sense of the word. She
is rather the living Body of Christ, vitalized by the Holy Spirit of
God, to Whose reality belong the divine life, the grace and the
power of future aeons. But the sinner himself does not possess
the Holy Spirit, it is clear; nor unfortunately does he belong to
the Church in this full sense of the word. Now such a statement
implies no contradiction to previously cited propositions from
dogma in which the sinner is without qualification called a member of the Church. For in those propositions the concept
"Church" is taken in the sense of the visible society, as only on
that supposition could the absence of interior contrition in the
sinner be inconsequential for his membership.

    That this sense of "Church" is not in contradiction to the
teachings just cited of Leo XIII and Pius XII will be clear from
the following thoughts. The Church has so to say a sacramental
structure. But in the concept of sacrament one must distinguish
between sacramental sign as such (and the condition of its validity) and the sacramental sign insofar as it *de facto* produces the
sacramental grace and is filled with it. Both aspects are perhaps
best kept distinct, for in certain circumstances there can be a
"valid" sacrament which does not produce grace in the recipient.
Now the Church is, so to speak, the prime sacrament. Therefore
here as well one must distinguish between the body of the
Church insofar as it is visible as a symbol of grace, and the
Church as a body insofar as it is reality filled with grace, and, in
consequence, also between a merely valid and a fruitful belonging to the Church. In the first category of membership is the
sinner, but not in the second. Nor is it to be feared that by this
distinction the abiding presence of sinners in the Church is
diluted into a negligible business of some external, quasi-can-
onical sort. The point is the sinner belongs to the visible Church
still, but that visible membership has ceased to be the effective
sign of any invisible membership in a spiritually fruitful, holy
community. The sinner has as it were given the lie to this sign
(somewhat as when one receives a sacrament validly but illicitly),
for he has defrauded the status which he enjoys of the significance and effectiveness to which it is ordained by its whole

nature as the inner living bond of men with God and with each other in the Holy Spirit.

2. With that we come to the explicit affirmation of what this teaching of faith in all its austerity expresses: the Church is sinful. After what has so far been said, one can no longer in any context of faith maintain that there are sinners "in" the Church as in an external confessional organization, but that this carries no implication about the Church herself. For we have already seen that these sinners are, literally, according to traditional teaching, members, intimates, therefore a portion of the very visibility of the Church itself. This must now be further clarified. To see it more clearly we have to consider two things. If one should freely admit that there are sinners in the Church, but then maintain that this fact has nothing to do with the real Church, one would be implying an idealistic conception of the Church which is theologically very questionable. "Church" becomes an idea, an ideal, something which should be, a thing to which one can appeal from the concrete realities, something which can be approached merely but never quite realized. This kind of ideal one can naturally always cherish, one can acknowledge it, it is an intangible thing beyond contamination by the wretchedness of the every-day. But it will not be found in theology. There the Church is something very real: she is the one Church that is and is to be believed, in all circumstances and at all times the visible and validly organized sum total of the baptized and in her external profession of belief, in submission to the Roman pontiff, one. Of such a Church one can hardly say that she has nothing to do with the sins of her members. To be sure she does not sanction sin. Obviously there are in her ranks men (perhaps even many) who in some true sense must be reckoned saints. But if she is something real, and if her members are sinners and as sinners remain members, then she is herself necessarily sinful. Thus the sin of her children is spot and stain even on the Mystical Body of Christ. The Church is a sinful Church: it is part of her creed and no mere conclusion of experience. And it is terrifying.

If what we have said is true, then it is also obvious that the official leaders of the Church, those men whom the theologically untrained, portions of the Catholic laity included, regard as being in themselves in effect "the" Church (as if the layman were not also the Church and the leaders alone were her faithful image), can also be sinners and that such was and is actually the case in a very conspicuous way. Then it is once again so much the more clearly brought home, the concrete Church—again, only as 'concrete' is she a church—is a sinful Church. For it is obvious that the sin exists not only in the private life of the churchman but can enter very essentially into the concrete context of his activities as a representative of the Church as well. When the Church acts, guides, decides (or omits to decide when a decision should be made), when she preaches—and she should of course always preach in a way corresponding to the demands of the times and of this historical situation—these activities do not occur by abstract principle nor through the Holy Spirit alone. Rather is this entire activity of the Church the activity of concrete men. And if these men are sinful, if they are shamefully narrow, sinfully self-centered, insolent, self-willed, materialistic, sluggish, their sinful shortcomings will inevitably affect those actions which they perform in their capacity as churchmen and transact in the Church's name as concrete Church affairs. There is no teaching according to which the inspiration of the Holy Spirit, which is always with the Church, would restrict this influence of sin in Church leaders to their private lives and not permit it to invade the area of their work in the Church. To maintain otherwise would be to hold an unrealistic, abstract ideal of an invisible Church. Of course the individual Christian can brood over such influences.

He can also, if sin should be enjoined upon him—indeed at such times he must—refuse obedience, but where nothing sinful is enjoined he may not refuse even though he be certain that a command is at least partly inspired by a sinfully narrow, legalistic or willful spirit. In any case he can never object that such doings of churchmen are not the deeds of the Church. But this is to admit that the Church in her activity can be sinful. And that this happens contrary to the interior inspiration of the Spirit and against her own traditionally preached norms and laws is obvious. But it is surely the significant point in this phenomenon of the sinful Church that she herself can really so suffer and notwithstanding (in contrast to all human organizations fallen away from their primitive ideals) remains herself, the Spouse of Christ and the vessel of the Holy Spirit. She remains despite her sin the uniquely saving Church, from whose ranks one can never desert by having recourse to her own ideal, i.e., because she ostensibly is no longer what she "once" was (she never was!), what she should be and claims to be.

Let us add at once that we are not saying the Church is a mere paradoxical union of visible sin and hidden grace. She is holy because she stands always in vital union with Christ, the fountain of all holiness. She is holy because her whole history with all its glories and its scandals is pressing constantly in the energy of her vital principle, the Holy Spirit, towards that last day in which all her truth, her law and her sacraments are orientated, when God Himself unveiled will appear in the world. She is and remains infallible when she proposes in certain circumstances a solemn decision affecting faith or morals. Her sacraments, independently of the worthiness of their ministers, are of objective validity and effectiveness: in themselves holy and sanctifying their recipients. She had never succumbed to the temptation to accommodate the truth and the norms which her very human leaders preach, to the weakness and lukewarmness of men (how little obvious is this wonder of the power and grace of the Holy Spirit: yet the marvel recurs ever anew through the centuries!). She has at all times in a sinful world stood for the holiness of God and of His Christ, and if we should consider for a moment how readily men incline to order their principles by their acts, we would acknowledge the eternal "contradiction" between the preaching of the Church's Gospel and the human practice of her preachers, not so much as scandal but as very proof of the effectiveness of the Spirit of God working in a holy Church. Indeed the Church is possessed in so many of her members, of an empirically recognizable sanctity, that even in her external appearance, for men of good will who are illumined by the grace of faith, she is a steady motive of belief and an incontrovertible evidence of her own divine mission. Through the centuries, in ways which have not always been obvious, she has been miraculously the ever-fruitful mother of saints, the holy Church, the

Spouse of Christ whose aspect even now is assurance for the faithful that she will one day be the Bride who can enter without flaw into the wedding-feast of the Lamb. Naturally none of this gives the Church or us as her children the right to keep aloof, proudly and pharisaically from sin which, we must not forget, is not in the world merely, but in herself as well. The Church literally remains sinful, even in those respects in which she is much better than those outside her, although in a uniquely distinct way for she alone through her sins can disfigure Christ's "manifestation" in the world which she is, and conceal Him from men who must seek Him in death and life. If, however, there is both sanctity and sinfulness in the total manifestation of the Church, one is not thereby saying that they have the same relation to her hidden essence and belong to her in the same way. Her historically tangible sanctity is the real expression of what she is, of what she remains indestructibly until the end of time: the presence on earth of God and of His grace. The Church is immeasurably more than a club or a canonical body or a confessional organization because the Holy Spirit of God has united Himself with her inseparably. The Holy Spirit, hidden in Himself, provides ever anew reminders of His abiding presence in the tangible sanctity of the Church. It is in the holiness—not in the sin— that the inner glory is reflected "image-wise", which is the imperishable heritage from which her form derives. And in contrast to all other historical creations, including the "church" of the Old Testament, the visibility of the Church can never become so disfigured by sin that the vitalizing Spirit would depart from her, or, remaining, no longer be able to be seen historically. For the power of death shall never overwhelm her (Mt. 16, 18). The sin perceptible in the appearance of the Church is of course really inflicted upon the Church herself, in that she is essentially "body" and historically "form", and insofar as sin can exist in these dimensions. For the existential source of sin, i.e., the "heart", lies deep and obscure beneath the historical and the social, into which it always necessarily penetrates, when as a matter of fact it becomes the sin of the Church. But sin in the Church is never the expression of what the Church is in her own deepest living roots, but is rather the disguising contradiction of it; it is, so to speak, an external sickness in her body, not internal hereditary defect in her spirit. For guilt as such is always a contradiction of God and Christ; Who being Himself without sin suffered and conquered it; a contradiction of the Spirit of Christ, through which He sanctified His Bride by baptism in the word of life. The guilt is therefore also in contradiction to what the Church is. One cannot sin in order that the grace of God may be seen more abundantly (Rom. 3,5: 6,1) a truth threatened by a "sin-mysticism" or cult of a dialectic, gnostic kind today furtively spreading even among Catholics. Hence the Church is never sinful in order that the grace of God may overflow more freely. Sin in her remains a reality which contradicts her essence; whereas her sanctity is a manifestation of that essence.

Now from this proposition follows closely another two-fold one. First: In the concrete order of salvation, at whose center is always the cross of Christ, sorrow for past sins, remorse, anxiety, even despair, can all serve to manifest and to cooperate in the fulfillment, as it were, of Calvary in the world.

When the Church suffers from sin, she achieves redemption from her guilt, for she suffers her guilt in Christ Crucified, because sin, since it is not in the secret recesses of the heart but in the world and thus also in the Church, remains sin (since the "heart" has necessarily to project its acts into the world). But at the same time sin is also the consequence of sin (because it is the embodiment of the secret malice of the heart), and being absorbed as such by the Church, gives her the possibility of atoning for it and conquering it. When we encounter sin in the Church we should not forget this. As a matter of fact, we do not normally take scandal so much at the sin of the Church as at its consequences. We are scandalized by the hardhearted cleric, for example, not so much because he is without charity before God, as because he is niggardly with us, or because his refusal hurts our pride in the Church whose members we are in the eyes of the world. It embarrasses us before unbelievers. Why do we not so love the Church that we humbly and silently put up with the disgrace of her sins? That would sooner make her holy than our protests against her scandals however right and just protesting may be, and however little the protesters themselves deserve to be blamed by the man who had not beforehand examined his conscience, recognized his own guilt and tried to improve. Second: If the sin in the Church is merely contradiction to her spirit, is distortion and sickness in her external form alone, sin is not therefore negligible. For the Church should be the manifestation of the grace and holiness of God in the world, the temple of the Holy Spirit. But sinners in the Church make this outer form of hers an expression rather of the evil of their hearts, a "den of thieves." Thus the frightful truth remains, however much one is obliged to stress that sin and sanctity in the Church's form do not bear an identical relation to her inner essence.

2

We come to our second heading: the man of sin confronted by the Church of sinners. We do not ask how and in what sense this Church of Sinners is simultaneously the holy Church. This question was at least implicitly contained in what has been said. Another question seems to us here more important, namely how we ourselves, the children and members of this Church, shall deal with the fact of her sinfulness. Or more precisely, what must be our own position, that this eternal scandal of the Church may not be to us a scandal only, but an impetus to the renewal of our own Christianity and through us of that of the Church? In the first place, this Church in her concreteness is *the* Church, the unique Church, the Church of God and of His Christ, the homeland of our souls, the place where alone we find the living God of grace and of eternal salvation. For this Church is one with Christ and God's Holy Spirit, distinct but inseparable. From this Church there is no escape which could be toward salvation. One can seek freedom in an undisciplined private life. One can flee into a sect or something similar. There one may hear less about sin, punishment, scandal and with these things be less burdened. Such a man may then protest that he has nothing to do with "this" Church; he is perhaps closer to his ideals—he is certainly not closer to God. Nor can one appeal from the concrete Church to another theoretical one. There is only that ideal which has united itself forever with this Church and forever abides in her alone. And from this ideal one has fallen away if one seeks to cut oneself off from the unity of this Church, from her love, her belief, her obedience for the sake of self-made ideals. Thus one can never in an "aequivoca generatio" seek to found the Church anew; she is for all times till the end of days founded by one Lord. One may be complaining, weeping, entreating, raging, accuse and flee from her—but only to her; one can never justly leave her. One cannot abandon her without in some measure losing that which one pretends to wish to preserve.

All spirituality however austere which no longer endures the "figure of the handmaid" and the "mark of the sinner" on the Church—in humility and love and with the forebearance and patience of God—is soon found to be romantic delusion. Similarly one must sacrifice the madness of remaining in the Church and asking to preserve the prerogative of choosing between the "divine" and the "all too human." Wherever and insofar as the Church herself does this, then we really have the same right, whether in theology, or church art, in prayers and approaches to God, to assume the freedom of the children of God, and no one may demand more of us—as Pius XI says, speaking of dogma—than what the Church, the one mother of us all, demands. The more fully we know this Church, her life and teaching, the more objectively and the more freely we listen to her, the more we are impressed with her breadth and her generosity in rescuing us from ourselves into the greatness of God even where she seems to be forever setting down limits and speaking harsh words. But if, on the other hand, we begin to distinguish in opposition to this distinction between divine and human which she herself proposes, then where do we have a guaranteed norm for our distinction? Where is the guarantee that we are not indulging our own narrow taste, that we are not rejecting the Holy Spirit, when we attempt to curtail and to purify the human in the Church, when we think we are obliged to note abuses and to do away with them?

Nevertheless, even holding the orthodox position, the sincere believer will see sins and stains, scandal and rebellion in his mother. And if he is really a Christian (if his heart and eye are fixed on the uncompromise of the Gospel, perhaps more than in the case of most he can discern abuse) shall he conceal or minimize them? No. Naturally if he be a mature man he will not place himself on the side of those who would show their objectivity and liberalism by assembling from all corners of the past and present the scandals of the Church and at every opportunity displaying them before all who will or will not see. Also he will understand that the darker pages of a great history (and the Church's history is really great even if viewed from a purely human angle) need not necessarily constitute the chief content of a history primer for the immature. He will not say it is a falsification or blurring of history if the story of the Church is not made into a "chronique scandaleuse"; the history of the Spirit of God operating in the Church is always more attractive than the recital of human wretchedness. Despite all this for the sincere Christian there will remain in the total story a conspicuous dark residue, and this darkness will confront him not merely when he examines church history; he shall have to meet it in his life, especially when he lives with the Church. How this grim residue reacts on the individual will depend naturally in good part on his psychic temperament.

But when in fact we perceive sin unmistakably in the countenance of our Holy Mother, when we encounter within the precincts of God's house the sad realities of pride, vanity, commercialism, imperiousness, gossiping, double-bookkeeping, narrowness—what actually should our attitude be? We shall see these things as men who intimately know from experience that they themselves are also sinners. When we see the sins of others we forget so easily that we are only too inclined to pray: "Lord, I thank Thee that I am not as one of these sinners here, these self-righteous Pharisees in the house of the Lord,"—in a word, that we ourselves can be Pharisees in the guise of humble publicans. When sin in the church calls up our own sin into consciousness, when it brings us clearly face to face with our personal connivance—whether we be priests or laymen, great or small in God's kingdom—and the realization that it is our sins which are the sins of the Church, that we have contributed our part of the Church's poverty and plight (no less true because our own petty sins have not been recorded in the scandal chronicle of the Church) then we are in the healthy, Christian position to see the sins of the Church in the right light. We may then, perhaps, insofar as it lies within our power and line of duty, protest, complain, struggle and try to better: but we shall first and last weep for our own sins with which we too crucify the Son of God in His Church and darken the light of His Gospel for the world. And we shall carry and endure the disgrace of the Church as our own; she is in reality ours because whether we will or no, we belong to her and we have sinned in her. So shall we rejoice in the comfort of God, inconceivable and to the world forever incomprehensible, which He gives to us, each singly: a Mother whose sin is encompassed in His own mercy, whom He blesses and sanctifies, in and despite her daily sin, who never puts her trust in her own strength but in God's mercy alone which is grace and not merit.

When we can see the sin of the Church in this light, our eyes will increasingly turn to the hidden and the manifest glory and holiness of our Mother. If often we see little of it, it is not because we look into the world and on the Church with admirable exactitude and critical realism, but because our eye is the eye of the self-satisfied sinner, limited and ensnared. But happily when once we have wept honestly over the sin of the Church and for our own sins, when once we have begun to admit our personal guilt and see that all true holiness is a wonder of God and of grace and not a human vanity, then this eye of ours, washed with the tears of repentance, does become clear-sighted to the holy wonder of God working in His Church. The every-day is seen as new: her hands, despite all, overflow today as always with graces; she now and always administers the sacraments of Christ; from her heart rise unceasingly the imploring of the Spirit and its inexpressible groaning; the angels of God ever and again waft up like incense to the throne of the Most High the prayers of the just of this Church; her lips continue to preach the Word of God, faithfully and inexorably in the clear constancy and steadfastness of love; in her motherly womb she continues to conceive life for her children; the Spirit of God raises up for her endlessly holy sons—children and wise men, prophets and hidden men of prayer, heroes and humble bearers of crosses—and in her, till the end of time the redemption of the Lord recurs. And we shall always be able to pray, even if in tears—be they tears of repentance or of joy—I believe in the holy Church.

The Scribes and the Pharisees—they are not in the Church alone but everywhere and in all disguises—will always drag "the sinful woman" before the Lord and accuse her (with secret satisfaction that she is, thank God, no better than themselves)— "Lord, this woman has been taken again in adultery. What sayest Thou?" And this woman will not be able to deny it. No, it is scandal enough. And there is nothing to extenuate it. She thinks only of her sins, because she has rarely committed them, and she forgets (how could the humble maid do otherwise?) the hidden and shining nobility of her holiness. And so she does not attempt a denial. She is the poor Church of Sinners. Her humility, without which she would not be holy, knows only her guilt. She stands before Him to Whom she is espoused, Who has loved her and given Himself up for her to sanctify her, she knows her sins better than all her accusers. But He is silent. He writes down her sins in the sand of world history which—with her guilt—will soon be effaced. He is silent a little while, which to us seems thousands of years. And He judges this woman only through the silence of His love which gives grace and absolves. In every century new accusers confronted this "woman", and stole away, one after another, beginning with the eldest, for there was not one who found her who was himself without sin. And in the end the Lord will be alone with the sinner. He will turn and gaze at His fallen Spouse, and ask: Woman, where are they who accuse thee? Has no man condemned thee? And she will reply with unspeakable remorse and humility: No man, Lord. The Lord will go to her and say: Then neither will I condemn thee. He will kiss her brow and say: My Spouse, my holy Church.

Translated by William F. Gleason

Guilt and Guilt Feeling

Martin Buber was more than anyone else in the twentieth century responsible for making Jewish religious sensibility penetrate Christian and humanist consciousness. His Ich und Du *and Freud's* Das Ich und Es—*the parallel between their titles has been widely noted— were both published in 1923. What Freud's* The Ego and the Id *accomplished in describing the mechanisms of psychic determinism, Buber's* I and Thou *matched in delineating the possibilities of human relatedness. This essay, first delivered as one of Buber's 1957 William Alanson White Lectures, centers on those who, having confronted existential guilt, ascend to the heights of conscience. They do not closet their guilt, Buber says, but allow it to remain illuminated; they affirm their continuity with themselves, selves that did in fact embody sin; finally, they strive to heal the wounds that they have inflicted on the world—"for the wounds of the order-of-being can be healed in infinitely many other places than those at which they were inflicted." Buber's cosmic sense is especially evident here, and welcome for the realistic hope it offers.*

A t the London International Conference for Medical Psychotherapy of 1948,[1] "The Genesis of Guilt" was fixed as the theme of the first plenary session. The first speaker, a Hollander, began with the announcement that in his special group the question had been discussed as to whether the genesis of guilt or the genesis of guilt feelings was meant. The question remained unclarified. But in the course of the discussion it was left to the theologians to speak of guilt itself (by which, indeed, they did not actually mean personal guilt, but the original sin of the human race). The psychologists concerned themselves merely with guilt feelings.

This distribution of themes, through which the factual occurrences of guilt in the lives of "patients," of suffering men, hardly enters into view, is characteristic of most of what one calls the psychotherapeutic discipline. Only in the most recent period have some begun to complain that both in the theory and in the practice of this science only the psychic "projection" of guilt, but not the real events of guilt, is afforded room. But this omission has not been presented, and methodologically grounded as such. It has been treated as a limitation that follows as a matter of course from the nature of psychology.

Nothing of the kind is self-evident, however; indeed, nothing of the kind by right exists. Certainly, in the course of the history of the spirit each science that has detached itself from a comprehensive context and insured for itself the independence of its realm has just thereby severely and ever more severely limited its subject and the manner of its working. But the investigator cannot truthfully maintain his relationship with reality—a relationship without which all his work becomes a well-regulated game—if he does not again and again, whenever it is necessary, gaze beyond the limits into a sphere which is not his sphere of work, yet which he must contemplate with all his power of research in order to do justice to his own task. For the psychotherapist this sphere is formed from the factual course of the so-called external life of his patient and especially the actions and attitudes therein, and again especially the patient's active share in the manifold relations between him and the human world. And not only his decisions are included in this share, but also his failures to come to a decision when, in a manner perceptible to him, they operate as decisions.

To the valid scientific realm of psychotherapy belong the "inner" reactions of the individual to his passive and active life experience, the psychic elaboration of the biographical events, whether it takes place in conscious or in unconscious processes.

The relationship of the patient to a man with whom he stands in a contact that strongly affects his own life is for the psychologist only important as such in so far as its effects on the psyche of the patient can serve the understanding of his illness. The relationship itself in its reciprocal reality, the significant actuality of what is happening and has happened between the two men, transcends his task as it transcends his method. He limits himself to those of its inner connections that his work of exploring the mind of the patient makes accessible to him. And yet, if he wishes to satisfy not merely what he owes to the laws of his discipline and their application, but also what he owes to the existence and the need of man, he may—in fact, he must—go beyond that realm where an existing person merely relates to himself. He must cast his glance again and again to where existing person relates to existing person—this person here, the "patient," to another living being who is not "given," to the doctor, who may be completely unknown to him. The psychotherapist cannot include this other person, these other persons in his work. It is not for him to concern himself with them. And yet he may not neglect them in their reality; he must succeed in grasping their reality as adequately as possible in so far as it enters into the relationship between them and his patient.

This state of affairs manifests itself with the greatest intensity in the problem that occupies us here. Within his methods the psychotherapist has to do only with guilt feelings, conscious and unconscious (Freud was already aware of the contradiction that lies in the concept of unconscious feelings). But within comprehensive service to knowledge and help, he must himself encounter guilt as something of an ontic character whose place is not the soul but being. He will do this, to be sure, with the danger that through his new knowledge the help which he is obliged to give might also be modified so that something uncustomary will be demanded of his method; indeed, he must be ready even to step out of the established rules of his school. But a "doctor of souls" who really is one—that is, who does not merely carry on the work of healing but enters into it at times as a partner—is precisely one who dares.

1

The boundaries set by the psychotherapists' method do not, in any case, suffice to explain the negative or indifferent attitude that psychotherapy has so long taken toward the ontic character of guilt. The history of modern psychology shows us that here deeper motives are at work that have also contributed to the genesis and development of the methods. The two clearest examples of it are provided us by the two most noteworthy representatives of this intellectual tendency, Freud and Jung.

Freud, a great, late-born apostle of the enlightenment, presented the naturalism[2] of the enlightenment with a scientific system and thereby with a second flowering. As Freud himself recognizes with all clarity,[3] the struggle against all metaphysical and religious teachings of the existence of an absolute and of the possibility of a relation of the human person to it had a great share in the development of psychoanalytic theory. As a result of this basic attitude, guilt was simply not allowed to acquire an ontic character; it had to be derived from the transgression against ancient and modern taboos, against parental and social tribunals. The feeling of guilt was now to be understood as essentially only the consequence of dread of punishment and censure by this tribunal, as the consequence of the child's fear of "loss of love" or, at times when it was a question of imaginary guilt, as a "need for punishment" of a libidinal nature, as "moral masochism"[4] which is complemented by the sadism of the "superego." "The first renunciation of instinctual gratification," Freud stated in 1924, "is enforced by external powers, and it is this that creates morality which expresses itself in conscience and exacts a further renunciation of instinct."[5]

Of an entirely different, indeed diametrically opposed, nature is the teaching of Carl Jung, whom one can describe as a mystic of a modern, psychological type of solipsism. The mystical and religio-mystical conceptions that Freud despised are for Jung the most important subject of his study; but they are such merely as "projections" of the psyche, not as indications of something extra-psychic that the psyche meets. For Freud the structure of the psyche culminates in the "superego," which represents, with its censory function, only the authoritative tribunals of family and society; for Jung it culminates, or rather is grounded in, the "self" which is "individuality in its highest meaning"[6] and forms "the most immediate experience of the divine which can be grasped at all psychologically."[7] Jung does not recognize at all any relationship between the individual soul and another existing being which oversteps the limits of the psychic. But to this must be added the fact that the integration of evil as the unification of the opposites in the psyche is put forward as a central motif in the process of "individuation," of the "realization of self."[8] Seen from this vantage point, there is in Jung's panpsychism, as in Freud's materialism, no place for guilt in the ontological sense, unless it be in the relationship of man to himself—that is, as failure in the process of individuation. In fact, in the whole great work of Jung's we learn nothing of guilt as a reality in the relation between the human person and the world entrusted to him in his life.

With the other psychoanalytic doctrines it stands, in general, much the same. Almost everyone who seriously concerns himself with the problem of guilt proceeds to derive the guilt feelings that are met with in analysis from hidden elements, to trace them back to such elements, to unmask them as such. One seeks the powerful repressions in the unconscious as those that hide behind the phenomena of illness, but not also the live connection the image of which has remained in the living memory, time and again admonishing, attacking, tormenting, and, after each submersion in the river of no-longer-thinking-about-that, returning and taking up its work anew.

A man stands before us who, through acting or failing to act, has burdened himself with a guilt or has taken part in a community guilt, and now, after years or decades, is again and again visited by the memory of his guilt. Nothing of the genesis of his illness is concealed from him if he is only willing no longer to conceal from himself the guilt character of that active or passive occurrence. What takes possession of him ever again has nothing to do with any parental or social reprimand, and if he does not have to fear an earthly retribution and does not believe in a heavenly one, no court, no punishing power exists that can make him anxious. Here there rules the one penetrating insight—the one insight capable of penetrating into the impossibility of recovering the original point of departure and the irreparability of what has been done, and that means the real insight into the irreversibility of lived time, a fact that shows itself unmistakably in the starkest of all human perspectives, that concerning one's own death. From no standpoint is time so perceived as a torrent as from the vision of the self in guilt. Swept along in this torrent, the bearer of guilt is visited by the shudder of identity with himself. I, he comes to know, I, who have become another, am the same.

I have seen three important and, to me, dear men fall into long illnesses from their failing to stand the test in the days of an acute community guilt. The share of the psychogenic element in the illness could hardly be estimated, but its action was unmistakable. One of them refused to acknowledge his self-contradiction. The second resisted recognizing as serious a slight error he remembered that was attached to a very serious chain of circumstances. The third, however, would not let himself be forgiven by God for the blunder of a moment because he did not forgive himself. It now seems to me that all three needed and lacked competent helpers.

The psychotherapist into whose field of vision such manifestations of guilt enter in all their forcefulness can no longer imagine that he is able to do justice to his task as doctor of guilt-ridden men merely through the removal of guilt feelings. Here a limit is set to the tendency to derive guilt from the taboos of primeval society. The psychologist who sees what is here to be seen must be struck by the idea that guilt does not exist because a taboo exists to which one fails to give obedience, but rather that taboo and the placing of taboo have been made possible only through the fact that the leaders of early communities knew and made use of a primal fact of man as man—the fact that man can become guilty and know it.

Existential guilt—that is, guilt that a person has taken on himself as a person and in a personal situation—cannot be comprehended through such categories of analytical science as "repression" and "becoming-conscious." The bearer of guilt of whom I speak remembers it again and again by himself and in sufficient measure. Not seldom, certainly, he attempts to evade it—not the remembered fact, however, but its depths as existential guilt—until the truth of this depth overwhelms him and time is now perceived by him as a torrent.

Can the doctor of souls function here as helper, beyond professional custom and correct methods? May he do so? Is he shown at times another and higher therapeutic goal than the familiar one? Can and may he try his strength, not with conscious or unconscious, founded or unfounded guilt feelings, but with the self-manifesting existential guilt itself? Can he allow himself to recognize, from this standpoint, that healing in this case means something other than the customary, and what it means in this case?

The doctor who confronts the effects on the guilty man of an existential guilt must proceed in all seriousness from the situation in which the act of guilt has taken place. Existential guilt occurs when someone injures an order of the human world whose foundations he knows and recognizes as those of his own existence and of all common human existence. The doctor who confronts such a guilt in the living memory of his patient must enter into that situation; he must lay his hand in the wound of the other and learn: this concerns you. But then it may strike him that the orientation of the psychologist and the treatment of the therapist have changed unawares and that, if he wishes to persist as a healer, he must take upon himself a burden he had not expected to bear.

One could protest that an existential guilt is only the exception and that it is not proper to frighten the already overburdened therapist with the image of such borderline cases. But what I call existential guilt is only an intensification of what is found in some measure wherever an authentic guilt feeling burns, and the authentic guilt feeling is very often inextricably mingled with the problematic, the "neurotic," the "groundless." The therapist's methods, naturally, do not willingly concern themselves with the authentic guilt feeling which, in general, is of a strictly personal character and does not easily allow itself to be imprisoned in general propositions. It lies essentially nearer to the doctrine and practice to occupy itself with the effects of repressed childhood wishes or youthful lusts gone astray, than with the inner consequences of a man's betrayal of his friend or his cause. And for the patient it is a great relief to be diverted from his authentic guilt feeling to an unambiguous neurotic one that, favored within this category by the school of his doctor, allows itself to be discovered in the microcosmos of his dreams or in the stream of his free associations. To all this the genuine doctor of souls stands opposed with the postulative awareness that he should act here as at once bound and unbound. He does not, of course, desist from any of his methods, which have, in fact, become adaptable. But where, as here, he becomes aware of a reality between man and man, between man and the world, a reality inaccessible to any of the psychological categories, he recognizes the limits that are set here for his methods and recognizes that the goal of healing has been transformed in this case because the context of the sickness, the place of the sickness in being, has been transformed. If the therapist recognizes this, then all that he is obliged to do becomes more difficult, much more difficult— and all becomes more real, radically real.

2

I shall clarify this statement through the example of a life history that I have already made use of before, although all too briefly.[9] I select it from among those at my disposal because I was a witness, sometimes more distant, sometimes nearer, to the happenings, and I have followed their sequence. The life course I have in mind is that of a woman—let us call her Melanie—of more intellectual than truly spiritual gifts, with a scientific education, but without the capacity for independent mastery of her knowledge. Melanie possessed a remarkable talent for good comradeship which expressed itself, at least from her side, in more or less erotically tinged friendships that left unsatisfied her more impetuous than passionate need for love. She made the acquaintance of a man who was on the point of marriage with another, strikingly ugly, but remarkable woman. Melanie succeeded without difficulty in breaking up the engagement and marrying the man. Her rival tried to kill herself. Melanie soon afterwards accused her, certainly unjustly, of feigning her attempt at suicide. After a few years Melanie herself was supplanted by another woman. Soon afterwards she fell ill with a neurosis linked with disturbances of the vision. To friends who took her in at the time, she confessed her guilt without glossing over the fact that it had arisen not out of a passion, but out of a fixed will.

Later she gave herself into the care of a well-known psycho-analyst. This man was able to liberate her in a short while from both her feelings of disappointment and of guilt and to bring her to the conviction that she was a "genius of friendship" and would find in this sphere the compensation that was due her. The conversion succeeded, and Melanie devoted herself to a rich sociality which she experienced as a world of friendship. In contrast to this, she associated in general with the men with whom she had to deal in her professional "welfare work" not as persons needing her understanding and even her consolation, but as objects to be seen through and directed by her. The guilt feelings were no longer in evidence; the apparatus that had been installed in place of the paining and admonishing heart func-tioned in model fashion.

Now that is certainly no extraordinary fate. We recognize again the all too usual distress of human action and suffering, and there can be no talk here of existential guilt in the great sense of the term. And yet, the guilt feeling that grew up at that time in the illness and that so fused with the illness that no one could say which of the two was the cause and which the effect, had throughout an authentic character. With the silencing of the guilt feeling there disappeared for Melanie the possibility of recon-ciliation through a newly won genuine relationship to her en-vironment in which her best qualities could at the same time unfold. The price paid for the annihilation of the sting was the final annihilation of the chance to become the being that this created person was destined to become through her highest disposition.

Again one may raise the objection that it cannot be the affair of the psychotherapist to concern himself about this kind of thing.

His task is to investigate malady and to heal it, or rather to help it toward healing, and it is just this that the doctor who had been called in had done. But here lies an important problem. Stated generally, one can formulate it somewhat as follows: Shall a man who is called upon to help another in a specific manner merely give the help for which he is summoned or shall he also give the other help that, according to the doctor's knowledge of him, this man objectively needs?

However, what is the meaning here of the help that one objectively needs? Clearly this, that his being follows other laws than his consciousness. But also quite other ones than his "unconscious." The unconscious is still far less concerned than the conscious about whether the essence of this man thrives. Essence—by this I mean that for which a person is peculiarly intended, what he is called to become. The conscious, with its planning and its weighing, concerns itself with it only occasionally; the unconscious, with its wishes and contradictions, hardly ever. Those are great moments of existence when a man discovers his essence or rediscovers it on a higher plane; when he decides and decides anew to become what he is and, as one who is becoming this, to establish a genuine relation to the world; when he heroically maintains his discovery and decision against his everyday consciousness and against his unconscious. Should the helper, can the helper, may the helper now enter into an alliance with the essence of him who summoned him, across this person's conscious and unconscious will, provided that he has really reliably recognized the need of this essence? Is something of this sort at all his office? Can it be his office? Particularly where the helping profession is so exactly circumscribed by principles and methods as in modern psychotherapy? Does not the danger threaten here of a pseudo-intuitive dilettantism that dissolves all fixed norms?

An important psychologist and doctor of our time, the late Viktor von Weizsaecker, laid down, in very precise language, a sober admonition on this point. There the "treatment of the essential in man" is simply excluded from the realm of psychotherapy. "Just the final destiny of man," he writes, "must not be the subject of therapy."[10] And my lay insight must concur with this declaration. But there is an exceptional case—the case where the glance of the doctor, the perceiving glance that makes him a doctor and to which all his methods stand in a serving relation, extends into the sphere of the essence, where he perceives essential lapse and essential need. There, to be sure, it is still denied him to treat "the essential" in his patients, but he may and should guide it to where an essential help of the self, a help till now neither willed nor anticipated, can begin. It is neither given the therapist nor allowed to him to indicate a way that leads onward from here. But from the watchtower to which the patient has been conducted, he can manage to see a way that is right for him and that he can walk, a way that it is not granted the doctor to see. For at this high station all becomes personal in the strictest sense.

The psychotherapist is no pastor of souls and no substitute for one. It is never his task to mediate a salvation; his task is always only to further a healing. But it is not merely incumbent upon him to interest himself in that need of the patient that has become symptomatically manifest in his sickness—to interest himself in it as far as the analysis conducted according to the therapist's method discloses to him the genesis of this illness. That need is also confided to him that first allows itself to be recognized in the immediacy of the partnership between the patient who is having recourse to the doctor and the doctor who is concerned about the recovery of the patient—although occasionally this need remains veiled, even then.

I have already pointed to the fact that the doctor, in order to be able to do this adequately, must for the time being lift himself off the firm ground of principles and methods on which he has learned to walk. One must not, of course, understand this to mean that he now soars in the free ether of an unrestrained "intuition." Now too, and only now really, he is obliged to think consistently and to work exactly. And if he may now surrender himself to a more direct vision, it can still only be one that realizes its individual norms in each of its insights—norms that cannot be translated into general propositions. In this sphere of action, too, even though it seems left to his independent direction, the man of the intellectual profession learns that a true work is an affair of a listening obedience.

But in order that the therapist be able to do this, he must

recognize just one thing steadfastly and recognize it ever again: there exists real guilt, fundamentally different from all the anxiety-induced bugbears that are generated in the cavern of the unconscious. Personal guilt, whose reality some schools of psychoanalysis contest and others ignore, does not permit itself to be reduced to the trespass against a powerful taboo.

We cannot now content ourselves, however, with allowing this knowledge, which was long under a ban, to be conveyed to us by this or that tradition which is holy to us. It must arise anew from the historical and biographical self-experience of the generation living today. We who are living today know in what measure we have become historically and biographically guilty. That is no feeling and no sum of feelings. It is, no matter how manifoldly concealed and denied, a real knowledge about a reality. Under the schooling of this knowledge, which is becoming ever more irresistible, we learn anew that guilt exists.

In order to understand this properly we must call to mind one fact, no accessory fact but a basic one. Each man stands in an objective relationship to others; the totality of this relationship constitutes his life as one that factually participates in the being of the world. It is this relationship, in fact, that first makes it at all possible for him to expand his environment (*Umwelt*) into a world (*Welt*). It is his share in the human order of being, the share for which he bears responsibility. An objective relationship in which two men stand to one another can rise, by means of the existential participation of the two, to a personal relation; it can be merely tolerated; it can be neglected; it can be injured. Injuring a relationship means that at this place the human order of being is injured. No one other than he who inflicted the wound can heal it. He who knows the fact of his guilt and is a helper can help him try to heal the wound.

3

One last clarification is still necessary.

When the therapist recognizes an existential guilt of his patient, he cannot—that we have seen—show him the way to the

world, which the latter must rather seek and find as his own
personal law. The doctor can only conduct him to the point from
which he can glimpse his personal way or at least its beginning.
But in order that the doctor shall be able to do this, he must also
know about the general nature of the way, common to all great
acts of conscience, and about the connection that exists between
the nature of existential guilt and the nature of this way.

In order not to fall into any error here, however, we must bear
in mind that there are three different spheres in which the reconciliation of guilt can fulfill itself and between which noteworthy
relations often establish themselves. Only one of these spheres,
that which we shall designate as the middle one, directly concerns the therapist whom I have in mind.

The first sphere is that of the law of the society. The action
begins here with the demand, actually named or latent, which
society places on the guilty man according to its laws. The event
of fulfillment is called confession of guilt. It is followed by
penalty and indemnification. With this sphere the therapist, naturally, has nothing to do. As doctor, an opinion is not even accorded him as to whether the demand of the society is right or
not. His patient, the guilty man, may be guilty toward the society
or he may not be; its judgment over him may be just or it may not
be. This does not concern the doctor as doctor; he is incompetent here. In his relation to the patient this problematic theme
can find no admission, with the exception of the unavoidable
occupation with the anxiety of the patient in the face of the
punishments, the censure, the boycotts of society.

But the third and highest sphere, that of faith, also cannot be
his affair. Here the action commences within the relation between the guilty man and his God and remains therein. It is
likewise consummated in three events which correspond to the
three of the first sphere, but are connected with each other in an
entirely different manner. These are the confession of sin, repentance, and penance in its various forms. The doctor as such may
not touch on this sphere even when he and the patient stand in
the same community of faith. Here no man can speak, unless it
be one whom the guilty man acknowledges as a hearer and
speaker who represents the transcendence believed in by the

guilty man. Also when the therapist encounters the problem of faith in the anxiety concerning divine punishment that is disclosed in the patient's analysis, he cannot interfere here—even if he possesses great spiritual gifts—without falling into a dangerous dilettantism.

The middle sphere, as we have said is one to the sight of which the therapist may lead—up to it, but no farther. This sphere, about which he must *know* for this purpose, we may call that of conscience, with a qualification which I shall shortly discuss. The action demanded by the conscience also fulfills itself in three events, which I call self-illumination, perseverance, and reconciliation, and which I shall define more exactly still.

Conscience means to us the capacity and tendency of man radically to distinguish between those of his past and future actions which should be approved and those which should be disapproved. The disapproval, in general, receives far stronger emotional stress, whereas the approval of past actions at times passes over with shocking ease into a most questionable self-satisfaction. Conscience can, naturally, distinguish and, if necessary, condemn in such a manner not merely deeds but also omissions, not merely decisions but also failures to decide, indeed even images and wishes that have just arisen or are remembered.

In order to understand this capacity and tendency more exactly, one must bear in mind that among all living beings known to us man alone is able to set at a distance not only his environment,[11] but also himself. As a result, he becomes for himself a detached object about which he can not only "reflect," but which he can, from time to time, confirm as well as condemn. The content of conscience is in many ways determined, of course, by the commands and prohibitions of the society to which its bearer belongs or those of the tradition of faith to which he is bound. But conscience itself cannot be understood as an introjection of either the one authority or the other, neither ontogenetically nor phylogenetically. The table of shalts and shalt-nots under which this man has grown up and lives determines only the conceptions which prevail in the realm of the conscience, but not its existence itself, which is grounded in just that distancing and distinguishing—primal qualities of the human race. The more or less hidden criteria that the conscience employs in its acceptances and rejections only rarely fully coincide with a standard received from the society or community. Connected with that is the fact that the guilt feeling can hardly ever be wholly traced to a transgression against a taboo of a family or of society. The totality of the order that a man knows to be injured or injurable by him transcends to some degree the totality of the parental and social taboos that bind him. The depth of the guilt feeling is not seldom connected with just that part of the guilt that cannot be ascribed to the taboo-offense, hence with the existential guilt.

The qualification of which I spoke, accordingly, is that our subject is the relation of the conscience to existential guilt. Its relation to the trespassing of taboos concerns us here only in so far as a guilty man understands this trespassing more strongly or weakly as real existential guilt which arises out of his being and for which he cannot take responsibility without being responsible to his relationship to his own being.

The vulgar conscience that knows admirably well how to torment and harass, but cannot arrive at the ground and abyss of guilt, is incapable, to be sure, of summoning to such responsibility. For this summoning a greater conscience is needed, one that has become wholly personal, one that does not shy away from the glance into the depths and that already in admonishing envisages the way that leads across it. But this in no way means that this personal conscience is reserved for some type of "higher" man. This conscience is possessed by every simple man who gathers himself into himself in order to venture the breakthrough out of the entanglement in guilt. And it is a great, not yet sufficiently recognized, task of education to elevate the conscience from its lower common form to conscience-vision and conscience-courage. For it is innate to the conscience of man that it can elevate itself.

From what has been said it already follows with sufficient clarity that the primeval concept of conscience, if only it is understood as a dynamic one rather than as a static, judging one,

is more realistic than the modern structural concept of the superego. The concept of the superego attains only an orienting significance and one, moreover, which easily orients the novice falsely.

If we now wish to speak of actions in the sphere of conscience
in this high and strict sense, we do not mean thereby the well-
known synthesis out of the internalization of censure, torment,
and punishment that one customarily regards as the proper factual concept of conscience—that pressuring and oppressing influence of an inner high court on an "ego" that is more or less
subject to it. Rather this tormenting complex has, for our consideration, only the character of an angelic-demonic intermezzo on
which the high dramatic or tragicomic act of neurosis may follow,
and the whole affair may end with a therapy that passes for
successful. What concerns us here is another possibility, whether
it be the true process of healing after the neurosis, or whether it
be without a neurosis preceding it. It is that possible moment
when the whole person who has become awake and unafraid
ascends from the anguishing lowland of the conscience to its
heights and independently masters the material delivered to him
by it.

From this position a man can undertake the threefold action to
which I have referred: first, to illuminate the darkness that still
weaves itself about the guilt despite all previous action of the
conscience—not to illuminate it with spotlights but with a broad
and enduring wave of light; second, to persevere, no matter how
high he may have ascended in his present life above that station
of guilt—to persevere in that newly won humble knowledge of
the identity of the present person with the person of that time;
and third, in his place and according to his capacity, in the given
historical and biographical situations, to restore the order-of-
being injured by him through the relation of an active devotion to
the world—for the wounds of the order-of-being can be healed in
infinitely many other places than those at which they were inflicted.

In order that this may succeed in that measure that is at all
attainable by this man, he must gather the forces and elements of
his being and ever again protect the unity that is thus won from
the cleavage and contradiction that threaten it. For, to quote

myself, one cannot do evil with his whole soul, one can do good only with the whole soul.[12] What one must wrest from himself, first, is not yet the good; only when he has first attained his own self does the good thrive through him.

4

The event of illumination corresponds on the plane of the law to the legal confession of guilt, on the plane of faith to the confession of sin. As a social concept, confession of guilt is naturally the most familiar of the three; what takes place here takes place in public in the legal institutions of society.

The confession of sin is spoken by a man when, seeking reconciliation with God, he directly or indirectly steps before the absolute judgment. That may happen in the chorus of the community, as at the Jewish Day of Atonement, or in the whispers of the confessing man into the ear of the confessor, or even in solitude by those who feel themselves as standing before God and their speech as addressing God: the confessing one is always removed from the anonymous publicity of society, but by no means referred to himself. He has one over against him who receives his confession, answers it, "forgives" him—for the Jews, in a significant cooperation with him toward whom the confessing one has become guilty.

The matter is otherwise with the first of the three events in the action of the great conscience, the event of illumination. Here a man ventures to illuminate the depths of a guilt which he has, certainly, recognized as what it is, but not yet in its essence and its meaning for his life. What he is now obliged to do cannot be accomplished in any other place than in the abyss of I-with-me, and it is just this abyss that must be illuminated.

Legal confession of guilt means a dialogue with the representatives of society who rejoin as judges according to the penal law. Religious confession means a dialogue with the absolute divine person who replies in mysterious fashion out of his mystery. As for the illumination of essence, it is in its realest moments not even a monologue, much less a real conversation between an "ego" and a "superego"; all speech is exhausted, what takes place here is the mute shudder of self-being. But without this powerful wave of light which illuminates the abyss of mortality, the legal confession of guilt remains without substance in the inner life of the guilty man, no matter how weighty its consequences may be, and the religious confession is only a pathetic prattle that no one hears.

We must not fail to recognize that it has become more difficult for the man of our age than any earlier one to venture self-illumination with awake and unafraid spirit, although he imagines that he knows more about himself than did the man of any earlier time. The inner resistance which shows itself here—a deeper one than all that discloses itself to the genetic investigation of the analyst—has found so valid a representation in two of the characteristic forms of the epic literatures of the nineteenth and twentieth centuries that we cannot do better than to turn to them in order to supplement our understanding of the problem. I mean Nikolai Stavrogin in Dostoevski's novel *The Possessed* and Joseph K in Kafka's narrative *The Trial*. In our discussion of this subject, the second of these books, as little as it is comparable to the first in artistic power, must still be the more important because in it the present stage of the human problem of guilt has found expression. But in order to see how this later stage is connected with that which preceded it, we must turn our attention first to Dostoevski.

For our formulation of the question it is necessary to proceed from the complete text of the novel, that which contains the chapter of Stavrogin's confession, later expunged by the author on external grounds, with some related material.

Stavrogin was thought of by Dostoevski as the man on the outermost rim of the age who dissolves the meaning of existence through denying it and who manages to destroy himself through the destruction of all over whom he gets power. In the omitted chapter it is told how Stavrogin visits a holy man and brings to him the record of a confession which he declares he wishes to publish. In it he confesses how he raped a little girl. Later he disavows the confession, evidently because he knows from the reaction of the priest as soon as it has been made that it is not able to accomplish what he has expected it to. The content of the confession is true, but the act of making it is fictitious. It has nothing at all to do with Stavrogin's self-illumination, with persevering self-identification, with reconciling renewed relationship with the world. Thus even his "unfeigned need for a public execution" (as Dostoevski states in explanation) is permeated with the fictitious. What Stavrogin desires is "the leap." A fragmentary sketch by Dostoevski informs us unambiguously about this. It says, clearly in this connection, that the priest opposed Stavrogin's intention to publish the confession: "The high priest pointed out that a leap was not necessary, that the man must rather set himself to rights from within—through long work; only then could he complete the leap." "And would it be impossible to do it suddenly?" Stavrogin asks. "Impossible?" rejoins the priest. "From the work of an angel it would become the work of a devil." "Ah," exclaims Stavrogin, "that I already knew myself."

Stavrogin "commits" the confession as he commits his crimes: as an attempt to snatch the genuine existence which he does not possess, but which—nihilist in practice but (in anticipation) existentialist in views—he has recognized as the true good. He is full of "ideas" (Dostoevski even lends him his own!), full of "spirit," but he does not exist. Only after Dostoevski's time, only in our own, will this type of man discover the basic nihilism in existential form after he has learned that he cannot attain to existence by the ways corresponding to his kind of person. Only this is now left to him: to proclaim the spiritual *nihil* as existence and himself as the new man. Stavrogin is not yet so "advanced." All he can do is to kill himself, after all the "demonic" game with ideas, crimes, and confessions—this game that has a goal—has proved itself powerless. The decisive moment—excised in the usual version of the novel as abridged by the author—is precisely the failure of the confession: Stavrogin has wanted the holy man to believe in its existential character and thereby help him, Stavrogin, to existence. But existential confession is possible only as a breaking-through to the great action of the high conscience in self-illumination, persevering self-identification, and a reconciling relationship to the world. This possibility, however, is in Stavrogin's eyes one of two things: either essentially not accorded to him or destroyed by him through his life-game. In Dostoevski's own eyes, however, man is redeemable when he wills redemption *as such* and thereby also his share in it—the great act of the high conscience.

5

The Possessed was written in 1870, Kafka's *Trial* in 1915. The two books represent two basically different but closely connected situations of human history from which their authors suffered: the one the uncanny negative certainty, "Human values are beginning to shatter," and the other the still more uncanny uncertainty, "Do world-meaning and world-order still have any connection at all with this nonsense and this disorder of the human world?"—an uncertainty that appears to have arisen out of that negative certainty.

Everything in Kafka's book is intended to be uncertain and indefinite, at times to the point of an absurdity, which always remains artistically mastered. This court of justice before which Joseph K is unexpectedly cited because of an unnamed and to him unknown guilt is at once prosaically real and of ghostly indefiniteness, wild, crude, and senselessly disordered through and through. But Joseph K is himself, in all his actions, of hardly less indefiniteness—merely a different kind—as, charged with guilt, he confusedly carries on day after day a life as directionless as before. Directionless, that is, except for the one aim he now pursues, sometimes busily, sometimes incidentally, namely, that of getting free of the court. To this end he occupies himself with indefinite advocates, indefinite women, and other indefinite human instruments in order that they may provide him, in the face of the peculiar ways of this peculiar court, with the protection that he imagines is all he needs. The indefinite guilt with which he is charged occupies him only in so far as he thinks from time to time of composing a written defense in the form of a short description of his life which will explain, in connection with each more important event, on what grounds he then acted thus and not otherwise, and whether he now approves or condemns his manner of acting at that time. Finally there happens what is reported in an unfinished chapter: "From then on K forgot the court."

All this is not to be called chaotic, for in a chaos is hidden a world that shall emerge out of it; here there is no trace of a cosmos that wills to come into being. But one may well call all this taken together—the court, the accused, and the people around him—labyrinthine. The disorder, mounting to absurdity, points toward a secret order, one, however, which nowhere shows itself except by way of a hint, which apparently would first become manifest only if Joseph K did what until the end he does not do—make "the confession" that is demanded of him. But he cannot, as he says, discover the least guilt on account of which one could accuse him. Indeed he ends later—clearly without quite knowing what he is saying—by uttering the presumptuous words that are not proper to any human mouth: "I am completely guiltless." The threat that leads out of the labyrinth is not to be found in the book; rather this thread exists only when just that happens which did not happen, the "confession of guilt."

But what can be meant here, under the given presuppositions, by making a confession? This question hovers in a strange, altogether intentional paradox. A well-informed young woman says to Joseph K, leaning on his shoulder, "One cannot, in fact, defend oneself against this court; one must make the confession. Make it therefore at the first opportunity. Only then is there any possibility of escaping." And he answers, "You understand much about this court and about the deceit that is necessary here." Since Kafka himself says nothing like this, it can only mean that Joseph, who holds himself, in fact, to be "entirely guiltless," understands that he should make a false confession, and at this moment he does not seem disinclined to do so. Later, however, a painter, who is likewise, as we hear, well-acquainted with the ways of this court, advises him thus: "Since you are guiltless, it is really possible for you to rely on your innocence." Note well: In the same speech the same speaker declares that he has never yet witnessed a single acquittal, but immediately afterwards he says that the decisions of the court were not published, that there exist, however, "legends" of actual acquittals, and that these legends probably contain "a certain truth."

In this atmosphere the action moves forward, and it clearly seems as though the accusation and with it the encouragement to confession are a senseless absurdity, as Joseph K has declared them to be in his speech before the court: "And the meaning of this great organization, gentlemen? It consists in the fact that innocent persons are arrested, and against them a senseless and for the most part, as in my case, inconsequential proceedings are instituted." Some Kafka interpreters take these words to express the essential message of the book. This position is refuted through the further course of the action and through notes in Kafka's diaries relating to it.

I have in mind the chapter, "In the Cathedral," in which it is told how Joseph K comes by accident into a church and is here addressed by name by a clergyman unknown to him, the prison chaplain, who also belongs to the organization of the court but does not act by order of the court. This chapter corresponds exactly to the one excised by Dostoevski from *The Possessed,* in which Stavrogin hands over his confession to the high priest (a chapter which Kafka, moreover, could have known only in an incomplete version, not including the text of the confession). In both a priest is the antagonist, in both it is a matter of a confession of guilt; however, in Dostoevski it is furnished undemanded while in Kafka it is demanded. For it is this demand that the chaplain wishes to convey by the information that the case is going badly, since the court holds the guilt to be proved. "But I am not guilty," answers K, "it's a misunderstanding. And, if it comes to that, how can any man be called guilty? We are all simply men here, one as much as the other." One must listen closely: what is denied here is the ontic character of guilt, the depths of existential guilt beyond all mere violations of taboos. It is just this that Freud wishes to deny when he undertook to relativize guilt feeling genetically. And to Joseph K's reply the priest answers, "That is true," which means: Indeed we are all men, and should not overestimate the difference between men.

He continues, however, "But that's how all guilty men talk," which means: He who is in question gets off by talking about the others, instead of occupying himself with himself.

Now the priest asks, "What is the next step you propose to take in the matter?" "I'm going to seek more help," answers K. "You cast about too much for outside help," he now hears. And when he still will not understand, the chaplain shrieks at him, "Can't you see two steps in front of you?" He speaks like one who sees a man who still stands there before him as already fallen. What he wants to say with his words, without directly saying it, is that the verdict, "Into which the proceedings gradually pass over," now stands at hand, and the verdict itself already means death.

And now, as the last and most extreme effort, the chaplain tells the man, for whose soul and destiny he wrestles in one, that parable of the doorkeeper who stands, as one of countless men, "before the Law," before one of the countless doors leading into the interior of the Law, and of the man who desires entrance here. This man is frightened by the difficulties that await him who dares entrance, according to the information imparted to him by the doorkeeper. He now passes days and years, the entire remainder of his life, sitting sideways before this one out of innumerably many doors, until shortly before his end the keeper discloses to him that this doorway was destined for him alone and now is going to be shut. Joseph K listens to the parable and does not understand it: what then could the man have done to manage to get in? The clergyman does not tell him. Kafka himself, as he records in his diaries, first understood the significance of the story when he read it aloud to his fiancée. On another occasion, he clearly expressed this significance himself in an unforgettable passage in his notebooks: "Confession of guilt, unconditional confession of guilt, door springing open, it appears in the interior of the house of the world whose turbid reflection lay behind walls." The confession is the door springing open. It is the true "break-through," by which word Joseph K is falsely accustomed to describe the aspired-for escape from the law.

What does the legal concept of confession of guilt become here? What is so named here is self-illumination, the first and opening event in the action of the great conscience.

Stavrogin makes a confession in words. He describes therein in horrible detail the course of his crime, but both in remembering it and in recording it he remains incapable of self-illumination. He lacks the small light of humility that alone can illuminate the abyss of the guilty self in broad waves. He seeks for some kind of foothold, no matter how meager; then he gives up and kills himself.

Joseph K makes no confession; he refuses to understand that it is necessary for him to do so. In distinction from Stavrogin he is not proud; unlike the latter, he does not distinguish himself from other men. But by that very fact, with his, "We are all simply men here," he escapes the demand to bear into his inner darkness (of which Kafka speaks in his diaries) the cruel and salutary light. He insists that there is no such thing as personal existential guilt. His innermost being knows otherwise—because Kafka, who is closely connected with this Joseph K, knows otherwise—but he shuns penetrating to this innermost being until it is too late. At this point Franz Kafka and Joseph K seem to have to part company. Kafka had imparted to him something of his own name, he had given him to bear (as he gave to "K" in *The Castle*) his own suffering from a senselessly acting environment; with humorous caricature he had endowed him with his own traits. But now in the decisive hour, according to the logic of the fiction, he lets him say, "How can any man be called guilty?", and lets him lengthily and ingeniously dispute over the story of the doorkeeper, Kafka's most concentrated statement of his life-view, instead of accepting its teaching. As a result, Kafka, who understands the depth of existential guilt, must separate himself at this point from Joseph K.

He attains connection with him again, however, through the fact that soon afterwards, when the executors are already leading Joseph K to his death, Kafka lets him concentrate himself in a strong, although still rational, self-recollection. He lets Joseph, who now knows that and how the trial is going to end, say to himself, "I always wanted to snatch at the world with twenty hands, and not for a very laudable motive, either." Joseph K has recognized that he has projected on the disordered human world only his own disorder. His self-recollection is not, of course, the beginning of a self-illumination, but it is a first step toward it, without the man who does it knowing it. And now, before the end, Kafka may again take the foolish man to his heart, although at the very end, before the knife falls on Joseph K, Kafka lets the old foolish notions of some still forgotten objections come into his mind. Perhaps Kafka meant himself by the man whom Joseph K glimpses at the last standing in a window, "a man faint and insubstantial at that distance and at that height": he wants to help his creature and may not.

It might still be asked how the absurd confusion that rules in the court is to be reconciled with the justice of the accusation and the demand. The question places before us a central problem of Kafka's that we find in the background of this novel and of the related novel *The Castle,* where an inaccessible power governs by means of a slovenly bureaucracy. We can extract the answer from an important note in Kafka's diary, from the time of the genesis of *The Trial,* in which he speaks of being occupied with the Biblical figure of the unjust judges. It reads, "I find, therefore, my opinion, or at least the opinion that I have formerly found in me." The Eighty-second Psalm, of which he is clearly speaking here, has as its subject God's judgment over those "sons of God," or angels, to whom He had entrusted the regimen over the human world and who had vilely misused their office and "judged falsely." The content of this late psalm is connected with that of the Oriental myth, elaborated by the Gnostics, of the astral spirits who fatefully determine the destiny of the world, but from whose power that man may become free who dedicates himself to the concealed highest light and enters into rebirth. I have reason to assume that Kafka also knew this myth at that time.[13] In *The Trial* he modified it, in accord with his own contemplation of the world, through letting the just accusation of an inaccessible highest judgment be conveyed by a disorderly and cruel court. Only that man can escape the arm of this court who, out of his own knowledge, fulfills the demand for confession of guilt according to its truth through executing the primal confession, the self-illumination. Only he enters the interior of the Law.

6

The destiny of both men, that of Stavrogin and that of Joseph K, is determined by their false relationship to their guiltiness.

Stavrogin, of course, plays with the thought of bearing before him like a banner the confession of his most shameful guilt, but he does not bring forth the greater courage to understand in self-illumination his essential being and the origin of his guilt. His feeling, as he says in his last letter is "too weak and too shallow," his wish "too strong; it cannot lead me." He declares himself unable to kill himself, for "vexation and shame can never exist in me, and consequently no despair." But immediately thereafter despair overwhelms him and he gives himself up to death.

Joseph K belongs to another, essentially later, more "advanced" generation. Not merely before the world, but also before himself, he refuses to concern himself with an ostensible state of guilt. He refuses to find and illuminate in himself the cause of this indictment which this questionable society casts on him from somewhere—say, from an invisible, unknowable "highest court." Indeed, it now passes as proved, in this his generation, that no real guilt exists: only guilt-feeling and guilt convention. Until the last moment he refuses to enter through the door that still stands open and is only apparently shut; thus the verdict overtakes him.

Both Stavrogin and Joseph K have not taken the crucial hour of man upon themselves, and now have lost it.

It is the crucial hour of man of which we speak. For, to use Pascal's language, the greatness of man is bound up with his misery.

Man is the being who is capable of becoming guilty and is capable of illuminating his guilt.

I have illustrated through two examples from epic literature the manifold resistance of the human being against self-illumination. But this inner resistance is entirely different from the patient's struggle, well known to the psychoanalyst, against his efforts to convey from the unconscious into the conscious[14] a repressed state of facts of a guilt-like nature. For the guilt which is in question here is not at all repressed into the unconscious. The bearer of existential guilt remains in the realm of conscious existence. This guilt is not one that allows itself to be repressed into the unconscious. It remains in the chamber of memory, out of which it can at any moment penetrate unexpectedly into that of consciousness, without it being possible for any barriers to be erected against this invasion. The memory receives all experiences and actions without the assistance of man. It may, however, retain the ingredients of what is remembered in such a manner that what ascends into the actual remembering does not enter it in its original character. The existential guilt, therefore, does not enter it as such. Only when the human person himself overcomes his inner resistance can he attain to self-illumination.

The "opening door" of self-illumination leads us into no place beyond the law but into the interior of the law. It is the law of man in which we then stand: the law of the identity of the human person as such with himself, the one who recognizes guilt with the one who bears guilt, the one in light with the one in darkness. The hard trial of self-illumination is followed by the still harder, because never-ceasing, trial of persevering in this self-identification. But by this is not meant an ever-renewed scourging of the soul with its knowledge of its abyss understood as something inevitably allotted to it. What is meant is an upright and calm perseverance in the clarity of the great light.

If a man were only guilty toward himself, in order to satisfy the demanding summons that meets him at the height of conscience, he would only need to take this one road from the gate of self-illumination, that of persevering. But a man is always guilty toward other beings as well, toward the world, toward the being that exists over against him. From self-illumination he must, in order to do justice to the summons, take not one road but two roads, of which the second is that of reconciliation. By reconciliation is understood here that action from the height of conscience that corresponds on the plane of the law to the customary act of reparation. In the realm of existential guilt one cannot, of course, "make reparation" in the strict sense—as if the guilt with its consequences could thereby be recalled, as it were. Reconciliation means here, first of all, that I approach the man toward whom I am guilty in the light of my self-illumination—insofar as I can still reach him on earth—acknowledge to his face my existential guilt and help him insofar as possible, to overcome the consequences of my guilty action. But such a deed can be valid here only as reconciliation if it is done not out of a premeditated resolution, but in the unarbitrary working of the existence I have achieved. And this can happen, naturally, only out of the core of a transformed relationship to the world, a new service to the world with the renewed forces of the renewed man.

This is not the place to speak of the events in the sphere of faith that correspond to the events in the sphere of the high conscience that we have just discussed. For the sincere man of faith, the two spheres are so referred to each other in the practice of his life, and most especially when he has gone through existential guilt, that he cannot entrust himself exclusively to either of them. Both, the human faith not less than the human conscience, can err and err again. And knowing about this their erring, both—conscience not less than faith—must place themselves in the hands of grace. It is not for me to speak in general terms of the inner reality of him who refuses to believe in a transcendent being with whom he can communicate. I have only this to report: that I have met many men in the course of my life who have told me how, acting from the high conscience as men who had become guilty, they experienced themselves as seized by a higher power. These men grew into an existential state to which the name of rebirth is due.

With all this, I repeat, the psychotherapist in his medical intercourse with his patients has nothing directly to do, not even when he ventures in a particular case to set for himself the goal of an existential healing. The utmost that can be expected of him, as I have said, is only this: that, reaching out beyond his familiar methods, he conduct the patient, whose existential guilt he has recognized, to where an existential help of the self can begin. But to do this, he must know about the reality toward which I have tried to point in this essay.

Translated by Maurice S. Friedman

Notes

1. *Proceedings of the International Conference on Medical Psychotherapy,* Vol. III; International Conference of Mental Health, London, 1948; New York, Columbia Univ. Press, 1948.
2. Freud himself described psychoanalysts as "incorrigible mechanists and materialists" (Sigmund Freud, "Pyscho-analysis and Telepathy," in *The Standard Edition of the Complete Psychological Works of Sigmund Freud* 18: 177–193; London, Hogarth Press, 1955).
3. See, for example, "A Philosophy of Life," Ch. 7 in Freud, *New Introductory Lectures on Psycho-Analysis,* New York, Norton, 1933.
4. Freud, "The Economic Problem in Masochism," in *Collected Papers* 2: 255–268; London, Hogarth Press, 1948.
5. Reference footnote 4; p. 267.
6. Carl Jung, *Von den Wurzeln des Bewusstseins,* Psychologische Abhandlungen, Vol. 9; Zurich, Rascher, 1954; p. 296 f.
7. *Ibid.* Reference footnote 6; p. 300.
8. For a fuller analysis of Jung, see Martin Buber, *Eclipse of God,* Section 2, "Religion and Modern Thinking," and "Supplement: Reply to C. G. Jung," translated by Maurice S. Friedman; New York, Harper, 1952.
9. See my Preface to Hans Trüb's posthumous work, *Heilung aus der Begegnung: Eine Auseinandersetzung mit der Psychologie C. G. Jungs,* edited by Ernst Michel and Arie Sborowitz; Stuttgart, Ernst Klett Verlag, 1952. This Preface appeared in English as "Healing Through Meeting" in Martin Buber, *Pointing the Way: Collected Essays,* edited and translated by Maurice S. Friedman; New York, Harper & Brothers, 1957.
10. Viktor von Weizsaecker, *Herzliche Fragen;* 1934; p. 9.
11. See "Distance and Relation," pp. 97–104. *Psychiatry* (1957, no. 2).

12. Martin Buber, *Good and Evil: Two Interpretations;* New York, Scribner's 1953; p. 130.

13. I refer to a question concerning this myth that Kafka put to me at the time of his visit to my house in Berlin in 1911 or 1912.

14. Freud, *A General Introduction to Psychoanalysis;* New York, Liveright, 1935; see Lecture 19.

The Meaning and Value of Atheism Today

Jean Lacroix as much as any other French Roman Catholic philosopher synthesized Marxism and existentialism to develop a Christian personalism engaged with the processes of society in history. His contributions to Cross Currents—*"Religious Conscience and Political Conscience" (Fall 1952) and "The Notion of Work" (Spring-Summer 1954)—reflect his concerns as a philosopher engagé. His discovery in this excerpt of value at the heart of disbelief does more than challenge philosophical theists to purify their arguments for the existence of God; the ultimate question is one of meaning, lived meaning, on both the personal and the social levels. The theist ultimately must value the saint without God whose life incarnates meaning, as the atheist must value believers whose holiness embodies their faith.*

It is difficult and perhaps impossible to speak about atheism without hypocrisy. "When we talk about God, it is not God we speak of," Gabriel Marcel has written. In the same way, when we talk about atheism, we are not always speaking of a rejection of God. A facile apologetics wins a cheap victory by declaring that there are no absolute negations and that every atheist is really a believer who just doesn't know it. This formula is both false and dangerous. First, because it tends to ignore the seriousness of another man's affirmation. We do not easily shake off atheism by immediately refusing to see any meaning in it; it has a meaning and a value which has varied in the course of time. We are concerned with discovering the precise significance of atheism in the modern world.

This problem is supremely ambiguous: there is a good and bad kind of belief, as there is a good and a bad disbelief. The consequence of this is that there is no authentic and valuable belief which is not accompanied in fact—and rightly—by a partial disbelief. We must distinguish intellectually, and perhaps in every attitude and every action as well, between *representation* and *aspiration*. Every image of God is worked out by means of inadequate representations. Thus in any belief there is a partial anthropomorphism and idolatry which cannot be eliminated. "If God has created man in his image, man has certainly returned the favor," Voltaire said. We need not be surprised or scandalized: man cannot know anything without representing it to himself and his representation necessarily takes on a human form. But we must not confuse the representation of an object with the object itself.

We are not putting atheism on trial here, but trying to understand and explain it. The purpose of this study is to locate some landmarks: to try to clarify the meaning of contemporary atheism. Thus, many forms of causes (the problem of evil, etc.) will be left aside; we will retain only those aspects of traditional atheism which throw light on today's atheism by resemblance or contrast.

1

"Atheism, a sign of mental strength, but only up to a certain point," Pascal said. This mental strength, if we try to take it into consideration in terms of the development of humanity and reflect on it, appears essentially as an effort at liberation. This liberation had originally a specifically intellectual meaning and now assumes a more political significance.

Intellectual atheism—under what we may call its methodological aspect—has been the most vigorous and efficacious means of criticizing anthropomorphism. Historically, such criticism has perhaps given us the feeling of a truth that is independent of us, which is not the work of our hands or made in our image. In antiquity this is the criticism made by Xenophanes: Men give themselves gods in their image, but "the Ethiopians say that theirs are flat-nosed and black, and Thracians say that they have blue eyes and black hair." "If cattle and horses had hands and knew how to paint, the cattle would paint figures of gods that were like cattle, the horses and lions would make their gods resemble them." Such an atheism, which we may call an atheism of representation, is indeed only methodological, since the same Xenophanes, looking at the heavens, knows how to read in them the unity of God. Likewise Epicurus says: "The impious man is not the one who destroys belief in the gods of the mob, but the man who attributes to the gods the characteristics which the opinions of the mob lend them." Such criticism is not truly atheism, but is easily mistaken for it. Actually, it can only deny a particular representation of God in the name of a more elevated representation. But often it does not analyze its implications and presents itself as atheism, confusing a particular image of God with every possible representation of him.

Outside of revelation we commonly distinguish three sources of the idea of God: the sociological, the rational, and the mystical. There is the God of the group and of tradition, the God of reason which is the ultimate response to problems concerning the world and man, and finally the God of interior dialogue, prayer and mystical experience. The philosophic mind exercises its criticism in all three areas, especially against the social God, which is often the most gross; but it also denounces the sophisms which use God to give a final explanation, and by applying intellectual criteria make even the discerning of mystical experience very difficult. Every religion can degenerate into superstition, every representation of God which is not purified by atheist criticism becomes idolatrous. Against a Joseph de Maistre who affirmed that we must "defend superstition as an advance-post of religion," Pascal had written two centuries previously that "to defend religion to the point of superstition is to destroy it." That is why every philosophy which is not contested and which is not on trial has very little value because it does not fill its role. This is a constantly renewed value of atheism which it is well to remember, even if it is not of the highest level of importance.

Nevertheless, there is at least one form under which this atheism is of great importance and significance in modern civilization—its scientific form. We might be able to express this idea schematically by saying that if philosophy allows the *God of reflection* to continue to exist, science has destroyed the *God of explanation*. And the general movement of philosophy has confirmed and deepened this destruction by science. If we sometimes still meet the easy apologetics which attempts to utilize the science of the day in order to prove the existence of God or even establish the value of the faith, this is more apt to be among scientists than among philosophers. Meditation on the scientific spirit and its very requirements should be enough to make every believer avoid demonstrating the existence of God by a calculation of probabilities in the manner of Lecomte de Nouy.

We must go further and recognize that atheism today has become that form of the spirit which always refuses God as a principle of explanation. This does not necessarily mean that one cannot go to God by starting out from a reflection on the insufficiency of being in this world, which might be called a "systematic deception"—at least we should recognize that in modern philosophy the question remains open—but in no case would one be able to arrive at God by starting out from a scientific knowledge of the universe. For the scientist as such, what is real by definition is that which we can take into possession, and an affirmation is true only when he can establish it according to his own methods. Science assumes the world as given to her, and limits herself to it, by principle. Her immanentism, if we may so speak of it, is radical.

This new form of methodological atheism has historically played—and continues to play—an immense role of liberation and purification. It safeguards the very possibility of an authentic knowledge of God: *whatever science finds, it is that which we refuse to call God.* Science thus forces Christians to a sort of continual spiritualization of what are rather awkwardly called the proofs of the existence of God—those habitual proofs which

Pascal called too complicated, and of which Kierkegaard said that they implied a kind of disbelief. In a general way, from Lucretius to Marx, atheism appears as the void left by an insufficient representation of God, as the other face of a purely natural, i.e. pagan, affirmation of God. It is in this sense that the atheism of believers is an essential source of the atheism of non-believers. Proudhon has said it in an unforgettable formula: *Man becomes an atheist when he feels that he is better than his God.* This is also the valid significance of the affirmation of Brunschvig: *The God of religion would not know how to be the God of the wars of religion.*

From what we have said it is not necessary to conclude that all the blame and responsibility falls upon Christians. It is not true— or, at any rate, it is no longer true for the modern scientific spirit—that science and faith move in two absolutely distinct domains. We must be courageous and recognize that if science cannot be atheistic, there is in it a certain tendency to develop an atheistic manner of thought and life. By its stricter and stricter alliance with technique, not simply in fact but in right, it can go on developing a sort of spiritual state both of the explanation and of the conquest of the world, which may be called, in a sense, very humanist but does not easily merge with other current forms of humanism. The conditions of application or of practice are from now on incorporated into the essence of theory. A concept is scientific to the degree that it is technical, i.e. to the degree that it is accompanied by a technique of realization. Modern science is destructive of the contemplative mentality, and replaces it with an attitude of conquering explanation.

By penetrating into what Bacon called the secret plans of nature, the human mind does not prove that God does not exist, but ceases to feel the need of him. The scientist does not *contemplate* the intelligibility of God; he *constructs* that of a world. Precisely in virtue of its rigorous honesty, this method of knowledge risks depreciating the other modes of knowing, especially philosophical reflection and religious faith, which easily seem to it to be vague, subjective and almost dishonest. If we recognize that the scientific spirit is widely diffused and popularized everywhere as the very foundation of our civilization, we will understand how important it is for the problem of God. Today it is science more than philosophy, and perhaps more than religion, which has the privilege of requiring the whole of humanity to present collectively to itself the question of its being and destiny. In this way the essential ambiguity of atheism is again evident: science is both that which obliges us to purify our conception of God, and also that which tempts us to bypass the problem.

However intellectualist, this critical atheism is bound to produce political consequences. Belief in God—more often in gods—has for a long time been considered as the essential of the social tie. To deny God would be to withdraw more or less from the constraint of society, to secede. Thus there is in this resistance of the atheist to received belief the mark of a will to the affirmation of self, a protest, an independence of judgment. It was inevitable that those who wished to liberate themselves from the established power were led to liberate themselves from God.

Such, for example, is the meaning of anarchy in Proudhon. For him it is impossible to destroy power and revolutionize society without attacking its foundation, which is God: atheism becomes anti-theism. *Whoever talks to me about God wants my money or my life!* he exclaimed. This means that the affirmation of the liberty of man implies the negation of the existence of God. In order to affirm his own existence, to give his life meaning and value, man believed himself forced to deny God. Aristocratic atheism here becomes democratic; from an intellectual attitude, it becomes, in the strongest sense of the term, political. The problem of God has been democratized; it no longer arises from the science of ideas, aristocratic metaphysics, but from the science of human needs, democratic political economy. From now on, man will make his final choices, including the religious, in relation to his material and social life.

Aristocratic atheism was slowly able to produce political consequences. In principle it aimed only at a liberation of intelligence, valid above all for an elite. But its direction changed during the 19th century. Due especially to Marxism, after being aristocratic and intellectual, it has become democratic and social. In its most radical sense, the problem of atheism from now on has become that of humanism. Contemporary atheism appears as an immense effort of man to liberate man, an extraordinary attempt at the total recovery of man by man.

Atheism is often tied today to human hopes, while belief in God is readily accompanied by a criticism of the idea of progress. Too often theologies of history are presented only as a negation of a philosophy of history. Thus we see the two currents rejoin and reinforce each other: a current of intellectual liberation, and a current of political and social liberation, which has always existed among the oppressed, but only arrives at maturity and becomes fully conscious of itself in a naturally atheistic proletariat which believes it discovers in the denial of God the necessary condition of human advancement. The problem of atheism appears as the most up-to-the-minute expression of the eternal problem of freedom. It is significant that among many of our contemporaries this term is being replaced by that of liberation, ultimately a revolt against alienation. To say that man is free is to affirm at the same time that he possesses his humanity because of himself, not by virtue of another, whomever that might be. In spite of otherwise essential differences, here is a common theme in both Marxism and atheist existentialism: one must choose between the freedom of man and the existence of God.

Atheism is not a super-structure of Marxism, but is profoundly essential to it. We find two reasons for this, of unequal profundity, when we study Marx's work. The first—the best known—remains a little exterior and sociological. For Marx religion is "the opium of the people," a formula that we forget to cite in its context: *Religious poverty is, on one hand, the expression of a real poverty and, on the other hand, a protest against real poverty. Religion is the sigh of the creature that has been crushed, the heart of a heartless world, just as it is the spirit of an age without spirit. It is the opium of the people.* It is because this world does not suffice to assure man his full subsistence, his total accomplishment, his integral development, that he in some way compensates by imagining another world. Religious alienation has its source in economic alienation; suppress the latter, and you will destroy the former. The second reason for Marxism's atheism does this by identifying atheism and freedom, or rather liberation. In fact, atheism is definitely grounded in Marx on his conception of work. It is because man is the demiurge of man—that is, because man makes himself human in his battle against nature—that he could not be made by another, by a god. The atheism of Marx is the necessary obverse side of his positive definition of man as essentially a worker who conquers his humanity by transforming his world by his work.

Ultimately, freedom is aseity: to be free is to owe one's being only to oneself. Consequently, either man has been created by another man on whom he depends, and is not free; or he owes his humanity only to himself, that is to say, he is free, but then God does not exist. The problem of atheism appears then as that of the ultimate meaning of that freedom which Marx called *the eternal aristocracy of human nature*. "No one is independent in his own eyes unless he is sufficient to himself and this condition is reached if he owes his existence only to himself. A man who lives thanks to another man considers himself as a dependent being. . . . For socialist man, on the other hand, since the whole of human history is nothing but the procreation of man by human labor, the becoming of man's nature, he possesses the visible and irrefutable proof of his self-production, the process of his creation."

From his first work the young Marx had taken up the Promethean challenge: "Philosophy cannot keep it secret It makes its own the profession of faith of Prometheus: briefly, I hate all the gods! And philosophy opposes this motto to all the gods of heaven and earth who do not recognize the human conscience as the supreme divinity!" This is Marx's thought at the time when he was still a *philosophical liberal*. But his whole mature work, on this point, terminates in a double and complementary demonstration: the more man is religious, the less he is man; the more man will be man, the less will he be religious. What particularly interests us here, since it gives modern atheism its special mark, is the link between the religious problem and economics and politics. God is not contested in himself, but his foundation in human existence is laid bare and overthrown. Perhaps the greatest originality of Marx is to have maintained that human truth is neither natural nor metaphysical, but in the strongest sense of the term, political—that is to say mediated by society and history. Truth is dialectical, that is historical, since politics as Marxism understands it is the highest dimension of man. At the same time that humanity suppresses private property, which separates the bourgeois from the proletarian, it suppresses God, which separates man from man. "Atheism," Marx wrote, "is humanism mediated by the suppression of religion, and communism is humanism mediated by the suppression of private property." In such a perspective, atheism is no longer presented as the consequence of an intellectual reasoning, but rather as the preliminary condition of freedom, and if it is possible to use the phrase, the humanity of man.

In quite a different context, atheistic existentialism has a kindred meaning. For it the past becomes that from which one is freed, and the ambiguity of history does not allow us to see any general meaning in it but only to give each instant whatever emerges from my engagement in the problems of the present. This existentialism also presents itself as a humanism which takes as its own the motto of Lequier: *To do, and in the doing to make oneself.* Freedom is at the heart of Sartre's thought: it is its very definition. But that we *are* free does not dispense us from *making* ourselves freed. Out of this freedom to which we are condemned we must make our freedom. Man is not, he ought to create himself; free, it is necessary for him to liberate himself; human, he must humanize himself. But this postulate of freedom, if properly understood, requires the rejection of God: between the existence of God and the affirmation of his liberty, each man must choose.

Ultimately, if God exists, he can only limit the freedom of man. To admit the existence of God is to present man as a creature. But if God creates man, he must create him in accordance with the idea he has of man. We must then say that man has a nature, an "essence", and that this essence precedes and determines his existence. Predestination would ultimately be the only logical attitude for a man who admits God. To accept liberty, on the other hand, is to recognize that existence precedes essence; in its foundations existentialism is simply the affirmation of absolute human freedom, and for this reason it is atheist. Man for Sartre is the Cartesian God, creator even of the values which are called eternal.

Although Sartre's freedom does not refer to the eternal but to nothingness, it is also understood as a deliverance, a liberation from the past. For Sartre, freedom must be creative, productive, constitutive, or it is not freedom. In fact, this affirmation, "If man is free, God does not exist," would be identical in Sartre's thought with "If man is free, he is mortal." A being which would never escape from the Supreme Being, could never escape its destiny; it would be determined once and for all by the place that it occupies in the Cosmos. If man were immortal, he could never withdraw from the omnipotence of God. For Sartre freedom is fundamentally tied to mortality, which certainly seems Hegelian. "By the possibility of death," Hegel writes, "the subject shows that he is free and absolutely raised above all restraint." To take up another formula of Hegel, dying is linked up "with the appearance of pure freedom." For Sartre as for Hegel, death and freedom are two aspects of negativity; it is because man is a being through whom nothingness enters the world that he is free and is mortal. Sartre denies immortality as he denies God, because he affirms liberty, and in a sense we may even say that he denies God because he denies immortality. We must refuse to turn to an eternity which is nothing but the opposite of time, precisely because it will deter us from accomplishing our work in time. If God exists, man is nothing; but if man chooses to exist, it is God who becomes nothing.

Our purpose was not to analyze Marxism and existentialism for themselves, but to discern the influence of their atheism on the contemporary mentality. But in one sense this double influence, otherwise so diverse and even contrary, is here convergent. In both cases it is a question of giving man back to himself, of overthrowing the obstacles that he meets on his path, and of permitting him to take up his destiny, even though the latter is understood from quite different points of view. Perhaps the idea of God had, in the course of time, been more or less linked to a contemplative approach to humanity. But today it is a new man who is born, who forges his own destiny, who creates truth by his battle with nature as well as by his relations with other men; who no longer seeks a guarantee in divinity since he no longer wishes any other manager but himself; and who perhaps no longer believes in the idea of God simply because he no longer believes in ideas. The precise significance of modern atheism, under its many forms, is the abandonment of the heaven of ideas for the earth of men.

2

If this description is at least schematically correct, the sharpest problem of the day is for Christianity and atheism to *confront* each other honestly. By this we do not mean abstract opposition, or a choice between two contraries, but the confronting of two attitudes of thought and life, being careful to recognize the positive values that atheism conceals under its negation. Many problems are here raised, which are common to both "Christian" and "secular" thought. On one hand, what is Christianity in today's civilization, and what have Christians become, that atheism should appear in fact to millions of men as a value and even as the supreme value? On the other hand, what is there in the modern world which opposes Christian values but which is also obscurely in accordance with them? Without encroaching on future studies, perhaps it will not be useless, by way of conclusion, to sketch out a few lines of research.

The importance given to history and to philosophies of history tends to dissolve our notion of an absolute. For the man who considers things *sub specie aeternitatis,* God appears to be evident; when we begin to consider them *sub specie temporis,* God seems to be dissolved in a process of becoming. But perhaps the habit of linking God with the heaven of ideas is an inheritance of Greek thought rather than a requirement of faith. In any case a particularly important and difficult work waits to be accomplished by Christian philosophy: to think out the relation between eternity and time more adequately. Under the pretense of defending God, are we not often defending an idealist conception of philosophy? Christ has not come among concepts, but among men, and the negation of the heaven of ideas does not permanently exile him.

It is true that the affirmation of man's earth aims at the exclusively human. What, asks Camus, can give birth to charity except atheism? If the individual is a reflection of God, what does it matter to him that here on earth he is deprived of men's love, since he will one day find love in its fullness? But if he is a blind creature, wandering in darkness, and the human condition is cruel and limited, he has need of equals and of their perishable love. Thus what is serious for the believer is life before God, but for the unbeliever it is a life which refuses to be mystified and to feed on illusion, a life-without-God, a life before man. For Nietzsche the absence of God gives a stimulant to existence, just as the presence of God does for Kierkegaard. At least they are in agreement in recognizing that the only authentic problem is that of existence: do we realize the plenitude of existence before God or before man? In other terms, we might say that the confrontation of Christianity and atheism is the confrontation of supernatural *hope* and earthly *hopes*. Christians ought at least to know that it will be by the way in which they reconcile both of these hopes that they will be judged. The question posed is no longer their conception of God, but their conception of man. It is up to those who call themselves Christians to show that their authentic humanism implies God on the level of both thought and action.

First, on the level of thought. The value of intellectual atheism is far from being exhausted. There is—and there always will be—an element of idolatry in our conception of God. Thus we cannot exaggerate the importance of the negative dialectic which attacks the grosser aspects of our conception of God. In a more general way, we must rediscover the negative tradition of theology, and especially of philosophy. For there is an implicit and natural faith in God in the midst of which philosophical progress takes place by a kind of dialectic of doubt and affirmation; there is also a supernatural faith in which there is a dialectic of belief and disbelief. This process goes on within; the dialectic of belief and disbelief is asserted in the very heart of faith, of which it is an internal requirement, which can become more conscious of itself through contact with outside criticism.

This work of spiritual purification is never finished and the weakness of Christians makes it necessary for them to make frequent use of the criticism of non-believers, which is all the stronger for taking the place of that which Christians themselves should have offered. To take but one example, what Christian would not be overwhelmed by those fiery pages of *Capital* where Marx reveals the deepest idolatry of modern times and denounces the fetishism of economic goods, synthesized in the fetishism of gold? The spirit, as Spinoza has recognized, lives in a climate of affirmation. This means that ultimately affirmation alone has ontological value, and negation has methodological value; the act of faith is well named, since in every meaning of the term it is the very act of the spirit. Negative thought should always persist, necessarily present in every affirmation of God, which can escape idolatry only by a continuous effort at poverty of spirit.

It is obvious that we ourselves in no way consider what are called "the proofs" of the existence of God outmoded, and have often said that the intelligence also ought to bear witness, but this testimony must constantly purify itself in order to take into consideration the progress of scientific, moral, and philosophical demands. What should always be guarded against in such proofs is the temptation for the believer to feel that he has become in some way the master of God, possessing him by possessing the idea of him. Fortunately, atheism is there to recall to us constantly that our knowledge of God is always precarious and obscure. If we understood better that in order to find God we obviously must set out for him, we would surely speak less of knowing God than of recognizing him—and we would study further the intellectual and spiritual conditions of this *recognition*. This would not involve narrowing the quest for God, but enlarging it. In fact, the knowledge of the idea of God is not all the knowledge that man may have of God. Perhaps even the idea is less a knowing about God than about man, a sort of demand that proceeds in all dimensions. If there is a uniquely negative atheism, there is another form of it which remains open and makes necessary a wider and more rigorous search.

But this is only the minimum. Another task is to penetrate even the most enclosed atheism in order to respond to its implicit requests. To take but one example, Marx has perceived dialectical ties between man and nature, which suppose and explain the primacy of mind over the world. The truth, instead of being found in an intellectual logic, was to be discovered only in a spiritual dialectic—in a battle, ideal or real. The truth of man and nature is not ready-made; it ought to be conquered; it must be earned, like bread, by the sweat of our brow. In the end it is through work, that man meets man, becomes human and conquers his objective being, truly becomes human. This idea is not at all the same as that of proletarian pseudo-science, which exalts itself through a class subjectivity; it means simply that the truth about man is ultimately the truth of his relations with nature and other men. This attitude is ambiguous, and in Marxism it remains tied to a denial of God which is essential to the system. But outside of its context, we are able to employ it as a valid method which will allow us to recognize that the truth of our relations with the world and with others implies the truth of our relations with God.

We are today at a turning-point for philosophy. If for the ancients Ideas are beyond the soul, for Christians the soul is above Ideas. Consequently, the truth itself must be earned. This at least means that it could not be an abstraction contemplated in purity by a separated and detached intelligence, but is inseparable from the total situation of the human person. *We make ourselves an idol even of truth,* Pascal wrote; *truth apart from Charity is not God.* A purely abstract truth, without any relation to the concrete totality of humanity, is not literally true. The problem of the nature of truth is inseparable from that of communication, which rebounds against it and transforms it. An essential philosophical problem becomes that of mutual recognition; the question of truth is that of reciprocity. *Verum facere se ipsum:* this formula of St. Augustine states that we are not in truth unless we realize at each moment exactly what are our relations with the other man. There is no more theology outside the communion of the Church than there is philosophy outside the community of men. The problem of God has become a political one, that human truth is political by nature, since it is mediated by humanity, i.e., by history. We understand nothing of the significance of modern atheism unless we see that it is linked to the meaning of the advancement of political economy—and we cannot completely detach one from the other.

Intellectual atheism makes us understand better that there is a certain theoretical use of God that we ought to abandon, but this *use* of God—if we may call it that—is still more intolerable on the practical level. Formerly, belief in God was a total engagement, and atheism was a sort of intellectual withdrawal and abstraction. Things have changed. Too often today it is atheism which has become a true commitment of one's whole self, while theism is a respectable opinion, vague and without efficacy. Through centuries of bourgeois thought and behavior, God has been "compromised". And a lived atheism is that which eliminates, in an ambiguous manner, these compromises.

The attitude of the Christian is particularly difficult. Denying all false gods, and first of all those that he bears within himself, in the very interior of his belief, he also affirms the true God. It is precisely here that the confrontation of Christianity and atheism is situated. Its place of honor is that which has been called the experience of the priest-workers. Their essential problem was not Marxism: it was atheism. Their profound experience, which was overwhelming, was in meeting with atheist values and their genuine significance. It would seem that no Christian of our time can escape this problem. To what extent does the Catholic, by refusing everything that modern atheism presents him, place himself outside of reality and protect simply an idea of God, with neither content nor truth? In what degree, on the other hand, by participating in the values of atheism, does he risk compromising the purity of his faith and all its requirements? No intellectual solution, divorced from experimentation, can answer a dramatic question. What is certainly sure is that, on one hand, no Christian can postpone till tomorrow bearing witness to Christ, and that on the other hand he must discover new forms of witness that have not been compromised, which will require the most difficult self-abnegation. Perhaps it will be possible to find here a practical application to the distinction that we made at the outset between *representation* and *aspiration*. Testimony cannot be absent, but sometimes it is even in the silence of words and gestures that its presence should manifest itself, more luminously than ever.

JÜRGEN MOLTMANN

Hoping and Planning

Jürgen Moltmann, whose Theology of Hope *is a landmark in the revival of Christian eschatology, is in many ways the theologian of historical surprise. The scriptural God of covenants does not betray his promises, Moltmann maintains, but those promises are kept in novel and unexpected ways. The scientific and technological world of the twentieth century prefers planning to hope, and so condemns itself to organizing the future on the basis of what is now perceived as possible, blinding itself to the emergence of the new, on which the great prophets waited. Moltmann applies his insights most specifically to socio-historical liberation, to changing the world rather than interpreting it. (See Walter H. Capps, "An Assessment of the Theological Side of the School of Hope," Cross Currents, Summer 1968, 327.) They may equally apply to the future of human consciousness and human action as they may be reborn through the dynamic of convergence.*

Hoping and planning both have to do with the future; but they are not identical with one another. They actualize the future in different ways; but they are not separate from one another. They are active with and for one another: if hope is not alive, there is no stimulation for planning; if there are not definite goals of hope, there is no optimal decision in the possibilities of planning; but if there is no planning, there is no realistic hope.

Hoping and planning both have their basis in suffering from the insufficiency of the present. However, whereas planning ap-

109

pears only in the theory of action, hope embraces the perception and acceptance of suffering. Moreover, both seek paths into another future and consequently have their basis in the fact that the reality of human life is history, in which things present and possible can merge with one another, and in which the possible can be realized and the new can be made possible. *Futurum* has a special meaning for both. This is not to be taken for granted; for there are cultures and religions without a sense for the future. This sense first must be awakened in them through Christianity or industrialization. Furthermore, in both hoping and planning the freedom of man in relation to a changeable world comes into play. Through "future" the field of hoping and planning is outlined historically; through "possibility" it is outlined ontologically; and through "freedom," anthropologically.

By planning, we shall understand the "advance disposition for the future." The greater the abundance of scientific-technological possibilities becomes and consequently the more social conditions are involved in change, the more important it becomes to plan in order not "to fall back-first into the future." (Paul Valéry) Such advance dispositions can, by means of *deterministic systems*, convert what is future and possible into necessities. In the network of cause and effect these kinds of dispositions are possible in the case of limited and automated things. They can also convert what is future and possible into probabilities by means of *probabilistic systems*. Such dispositions are appropriate when it is not only a question of causes, but also of people who cause and who do not have the delightful regularity of the stars in their courses. Finally, such dispositions are yet again possible when it is a question not only of causes and effects nor of people who cause and their coincidental interactions, but of competitors, antagonists and rivals. Having been developed out of the *Theory of Social Games*, actions and reactions can be meaningfully calculated with the aid of plan games and simulators. The goal which is to be attained can then be led systematically into the path of realization not only by means of calculable laws and not only through calculations of probability: it must happen agonally, i.e., through the estimation of the possible counteractions of others.

Planning is thus only at its lowest and most primitive stage the prediction and divination of that which is going to come in any case. When related to larger and more complex realities, planning always stands in a dialectical relationship to history: a foreseeable, historical development necessitates the making of plans in order to adjust itself to them; but in their turn, advance dispositions urge history to develop toward definite goals. Dispositions and prognoses also influence disposed and prognosticized history by their very publication. Thus, one must plan into the plan the influence on history of one's own planning; for there is also *self-destroying prophecy* (as is to be seen in the case of the prophet Jonah, and as it occurs especially in the case of negative predictions). Finally, the dialectical relationship between planning and history raises the question of valuation in goals and purposes: which goal should one pursue when many are possible? What is urgent and what can be renounced for the time being? "The God of physics exists in order to give us what we wish, but not to tell us what we ought to wish" (Santillana). In the final analysis, planning is always reduced to the question of what men actually want, hope for and seek; and this question is always raised in the context of that from which men suffer, experience dissatisfaction and become needy. If indigence and thus suffering cease, so too do wishes and hopes. Then the future—and planning—lose their meaning.

Hope, on the other hand, is harder to define. By hope one can understand a subjective feeling: to hope and never to lose heart. One can demand hope where advance dispositions become uncertain and by so doing mean the strength to assume risks. But then hope would depend on those remnants of fate and accident which are left over on the periphery of plans for the future. Then hope would only come into consideration in our household budgets under the heading of "for unforeseen events": it would be the human attitude in the face of the unmanageable element in what is to be managed of the unplannable in our plans. It would refer to factors in history which are incalculable and cannot be included in a plan. After all, dispositions for the future presuppose that there is a definite future for me to arrange and they extend only so far as the future now appears arrangeable.

However, the word "hope" probably stems more from the interpersonal realm. One does not like to arrange another person and does not readily allow oneself to be arranged. In personal relationships hope presupposes the otherness of the other and his freedom and it becomes a hoping trust when another person is one's security for the future. Hope then refers less to the future which is at one's disposal by virtue of one's own power than it does to that future which another puts at my disposal through promises and in which he puts himself at my disposal. This does not mean that I can know nothing about this future. Also, hope leads neither to fatalism nor to irrationalism, for such a future of the other or such another future reveals real-objective possibilities to me, a new environment, new freedom and an open field for activities in which indeed there are plans. To make a comparison: one will only with difficulty be able to plan when one will marry someone. However, in such a case plan-making begins with the mutual promise of marriage.

When, in the face of *planned future,* we speak of *hoped-for future,* there is always involved the factor of the otherness of the future in comparison to the present. It is therefore a question of how we can more closely characterize the factor of otherness. If by this we mean the factors of fate (*fatum*) and chance (*contingentia*) in the future of history, these factors will have to be excluded to as great an extent as possible through planning, for planning is the elevation of fate and chance, of the irrational game of chance of bare decision, to the conscious and thereby solely responsible establishment of the future through man. The factor of the otherness of the future can never really be called fate and chance, for both the latter have nothing in common with "future" if "future" has to mean "possibility" ontologically and "freedom" anthropologically. The fascinating factor of the otherness of the future lies much more in the "new" which it perhaps brings. Something is new when the impossible becomes possible, when the unthought is thought and when the unfound is found and invented. In this sense only the new is the making possible of possibilities, the stipulation of the future (*Zukunft*) that is impending (*zu-kommt*) and the revelation of freedom.

What does planning have to do with such a *novum* of the

future? If planning is advance disposition, it depends on the determination of possibilities and represents perception which is directed toward the future and the achievement of the generically different, unfamiliar new. What does hope have to do with such a *novum* of the future? In my opinion, everything. For hope always arises out of the coming into view of the new. It perceives the latter's approach, reaches for it in open expectation, and both internally and externally leaves behind what is old and insufficient. In the moment when hope awakens because of the new, the suffering and dissatisfaction because of the old comes into life as well. On the other hand, hope has absolutely nothing to do with "fate" and "chance." Hope is the opposite of fatalism and situation-decisionism. For that reason it is intent on the removal of the irrational factors in history, for it likes to plan to the advantage of the new, upon which it is kindled.

For the Greeks, hope was an evil out of Pandora's box, poured out to confuse the human mind so that men would not become overbearing. For the Greeks, meaning and truth could lie only in the constant, timeless, always-being and eternally-present, but not in history and in the mutable. By contrast, for the Israelite and Christian mind the truth resides in the approach of the new which has been promised by God. Its relationship to the truth, for this reason, is one of hope. Changes in history and changes of history have meaning only because the promised new has to be expected historically.

The catch-word of hope, for the prophets as well as the apostles, always refers to the "new." Thus the Old Testament speaks of a "new exodus," "new possessing of land," "new Zion," "new Heaven," and "new earth." Thus the New Testament speaks of the "new covenant," the "new life," the "new commandment," etc. Even the simple fact that the basic writings of Christianity contain the antithesis of "Old" and "New" Testaments has engraved into our awareness of history that tension of "old" and "new" whereby the priority of significance is given to the "new." But even if hope is kindled on this tension of "old" and "new," this does not make the stream of time into a medium of transitoriness, but instead cuts into it with the judgment "old" and "new," thus directing it "historically" toward the future. The fulfillment of hope, the fulfillment of time, is precisely not the eternity which is immutable, and which is equally near and far from every moment; instead, the fulfillment evokes a temporal understanding for realities from which one distances oneself or which have approached closely.

Only when Christian hope recollects its own unique basis—the God of the Promise, the God of the Exodus in the Old and the God of the Resurrection in the New Testament—can it become a critical and active partner of the contemporary planning mentality. To this end, however, it must distinguish itself as sharply as possible from the storm-God of history, the God of fate and chance. Theologically, this means that one must again learn to distinguish between God's promise and God's providence. The decline of Christian hope began in theological and intellectual history with the dissolution of God's promise, which makes history into the general providence of God regarding history. Not until this levelling process did the transference of what has been revered as "providence" into prognostic planning systems become possible. The "promise" became the mere expression of the divine mentality of planning for history. The human spirit of planning could be understood as its likeness and this provided the occasion for the understandable inversion according to which "providence" was only a hypostasized ideal of the still underdeveloped human ability to make advance dispositions.

1

It has been said that in our contemporary planning systems we are dealing with a conquest and expansion of time analogous to the conquest and expansion of space. This correspondence did not arise only today. It derives from the Enlightenment. To that well-known movement of mathematical-natural-scientific Enlightenment of space and its laws from Galileo to Newton there corresponded parallel movements of a historical and prognostic Enlightenment of history and its laws. The one movement was looking for divine wisdom in creation, "the book of nature," and found it in geometry. The other sought divine wisdom in history and found in the books of the Bible, that message of the divine historical plan. At the beginning of this Enlightenment there stands Luther's statement that history is the impenetrable masquerade of God. At its end stands the conviction of the systematic development of history toward the predetermined goal. How did this transformation come about?

Even the 17th Century, the age of the Counter Reformation and of Absolutism, experienced a remarkable spring of apocalyptic and chiliastic thought in Protestant theology. It began in Holland and England and came to full blossom in Würtemburg and Saxony. In the middle of this a-historical, indeed, anti-historical orthodoxy a new historical sense arose. One no longer sought divine doctrines *(doctrina coelestis)* in the Bible, but began to question it for its testimony about past and future history. Beyond the "law" of the Old and the "gospel" of the New Testament a third genus was discovered: prophecy as the revelation of divine providence. If the Apocalypse of John had been an inaccessible book for the Reformers, now it was called the "Princess among the Scriptures." With this the investigation of the "series temporum" became the great theme of "prophetic theology" in the 17th and 18th Centuries. "Prophetia est quasi rerum futurarum historia," declared Johann Coccejus. All prophecy is "antecipata historia."

Out of this arose for Johann Albrecht Bengel and the Elders of Schwabia a "system of hope" which runs through all epochs. It is the "plan for the divine kingdom," the progressive realization of which was believed to have been discovered. Since the promise and providence of God coincide, history itself becomes the progressive perfection of the Kingdom, the *procursus regni Dei*. For Christian August Crusius, the Pietistic philosopher in Leipzig, this "system of hope" changes into a "systema moralitatis" which rules progressively the history of man.

With this development, all the necessary transformations in theology have taken place so that subsequently Lessing and Kant can substitute for those systems of hope based on faith the systems of a planned education of the human race. The pious Enlightenment of God's providence according to final goal and plan was itself already deistic through and through. "God" faded to a mere decoration of a thoroughly understood plan to which history was corresponding and was going to correspond. If prophecy is nothing other than anticipated history, then it is also prognosis. In place of the eschaton of fulfillment, which on the basis of the promise has to be sought with hope, there appears a finale of history which through the passage of time is to appear. Out of a historical theology and a historically acting faith arises a theology of history and a belief in history. It is strange that this Christian Enlightenment of Christianity and an apocalyptic surpassing of faith took the place of an apocalypse of faith.

When providence and the intelligible historical plan emerge as a mediating element between God and Man, there also arises out of this mediating factor that which is mediated and in which the emphasis is on what is ascertainable by man. This change, offered by theology, was taken up by the series: Vico-Kant-Hegel-Marx. Vico's "Scienza Nuova" of 1725 expresses the aforementioned principle of the belief "in history." What has come into being is true, *verum et factum convertuntur*. His philosophy of history claims to present eternal, ideal history according to the principle that by necessity it had to happen as it has happened. "According to our first, unquestionable principle the historical world is quite certainly made by us men and for this reason can be found again in the modifications of our own minds. There can never be greater certainty than where he who creates things also tells about them." This insight gives to him who understands history "divine pleasure, for in God knowledge and action are the same thing." This last statement elevates the historical knowledge of human history to participation in the divine knowledge of divine history, while at the same time putting a limitation on it. In God knowledge and action are one. The *intellectus originarius* creates the world by thinking it. It can also predict history, for it can also make it. However, man can know his history only after he has made it. For Vico God has foresight while man has always, as it were, only hindsight. Man can become the knowing participant in divine providence, but only in retrospect, for what is true is what has come into being and providence coincides with the actual course of history.

When today we still ask why things had to happen as they

happened we are continuing to make this presupposition uncon-
sciously. The advance view of history is possible, according to
Vico, in the final analysis, because and to the extent that historical processes repeat themselves cyclically so that one can recognize what is typical. These limits of human historical
knowledge disappear (1) when the regularity of the assumed
cyclical structure of the direction of history is interrupted by the
expectation of a final fulfillment of time; and (2) when the ideal
prototype of a divine *intellectus originarius* for the human intellect is abandoned. In both cases reason is no longer capable of
reproducing future conditions merely according to the models of
past conditions. It must become prospective and inventive. It
then demands a new epistemological substantiation of its prognostic achievement.

Kant took up precisely this problem with the question "How
is a historical a priori possible?" He answered: "When the man
making the prediction himself makes and arranges the events
which he proclaims in advance." For this he cites three ironically
intended examples. The Jewish prophets had a good time making
prophecies, for they themselves were the authors of their fate.
Our politicians say that one must take people "as they are." But
the "as they are" should read "what these politicians have made
them by means of unjust coercion." Churchmen gladly predict
the decline of religion while they themselves are doing precisely
those things which are necessary in order to initiate the decline.
Thus, men are the prospectors of history to the extent that they
are subjects of history. Man can recognize and predict history to
the extent that he can elevate himself to its subject. However, for
Kant this humanly projected and created world remains embed-
ded in a presupposed, large, inclusive context: "One can consider the history of the human race at large as the execution of a
hidden plan of nature in order to bring about an internally—and
for this purpose externally as well—perfect polity as being the
sole condition in which it can fully develop all of its potentials."
"One sees," says Kant in this connection, "that philosophy too
could have its chiliasm." It is only a question whether experience can discover something of such an intention on the part of
nature for the human race, for the "prophesying history of the

human race must after all be connected to some experience."
Kant found such an event in the French Revolution, which, he
claimed, had found even in wishful participation a response
which could have nothing other than a moral potential in mankind as its cause.

Thus, according to Kant, history is possible a priori when and
to the extent the predictor makes the events himself which he
proclaims in advance. But what he predicts and what sort of
history he is supposed to create is founded, according to Kant, in
a presupposed hope which knows itself to be at one with the
intention and the over-all plan of nature and which sees these
revealed in a revolutionary event, a "historical sign," as Kant
says, that is no longer forgotten. Thus mankind is a subject of
history and, nonetheless, is not one, because human history
gains its meaning only from a tendency of divine providence or of
nature itself. History is makeable, plannable, and predictable, but
this planning and making is subject to a higher insight into the
over-all tendency of nature.

The next step will now lie in basing this dualism of natural
tendency and human history on a dialectic. For whatever was
presupposed as providence or natural intention has effect on the
making of history only through prospective determinations.
These presuppositions can also be understood actively as the
disposition of the spirit which produces history according to its
own projection. Planning and acting then not only correspond to
values, they also produce values. Only then the knowledge of
history emerges out of *theoria* and is no longer insight into what
is fundamental but instead is the production of the new. It produces because it prospects. It does not make facts or potentials
appear, but brings the human *facere* into play. Prognosis is then
no longer anticipated *fatum,* but rather the anticipated *praxis*
of man.

In this sense, for Karl Marx, the significance of history is to be
recognized theoretically to the extent that men make themselves
ready to perceive this significance practically, with their will and
consciousness. The makeability of history itself becomes the
goal of the making of history. "To the same extent that history
actually becomes more makeable in this way, the self-awareness

of enlightenment, of learning how to control history rationally, grows as well." In this establishment of goals, however, there lie anticipatory moves and general concepts which cannot be substantiated in a purely pragmatic manner. The goal of the universal and communal makeability of history and the general development of essential human abilities which is to be attained in the process has a "historical sign" for itself as well: it is not only the French Revolution, as it was for Kant, but also the Industrial Revolution. It is understood as a *signum prognosticum* for a possible realization of the humanistic ideals of the Enlightenment and German Classicism. The inner progressiveness of industrial growth which had been accepted without question becomes the proof of the traditional belief in progress.

These historical signs give testimony of an encompassing vista of makeable, human history, namely of the desired unification of the human race. As it was said, what was seen only ideally in Christianity by means of the mission "to all peoples" and in Humanism by means of universal understanding and tolerance, can now be realized through economic integration and universal interdependence. For the first time, through the connection of industrial communications men become what they were always claiming to be but what they never were: men in one humanity. Thus history, which previously had progressed only in the histories of peoples, groups and classes, is unified for the first time into the one history of the one world. The singularization of the world and its history which emerges here is the precondition for a common planning of one history.

If one is clear about these implications, a series of critical questions arises:

1) History becomes possible a priori when the predictor makes the events himself which he proclaims in advance. The limits of significance of this plannable and makeable history lay for the entire Enlightenment down until Marx in what Kant called "philosophical chiliasm," according to which the general development of the human race is supposed to be realized and the kingdom of freedom and self-realization is supposed to be impending. This chiliasm can be historically relativized very easily: man did not become such a subject of history until re-

cently; only now does he find himself developing into such a subject. The categories of the unity of the human race and of the one history which are now necessary are not valid timelessly and absolutely, but only by epoch and hypothetically. One cannot cast the net of universal historical connections (which had not been woven until just recently) over history after the fact and declare all history to be "prehistory" as though since the origin of man history had had its eye only on the present conditions. It is always the error of chiliasm to assume a particular epoch of history as the "end of history." If, however, the modern world is not the end of history up until now, but only an epoch, then it is also not at the end with itself; on the contrary, open history stands before it. Through such a historical criticism the systems of modern history-planning and history-making lose their air of promulgation of the end of time and their utopian narrowness. Through this criticism that difference is again discovered which these systems discovered for themselves: the difference between the hopes with which they began and the conditions which they created; between the history which can be planned and made by them and the history of this history.

2) This can be made clear from still another point of view. In every departure into a new, unknown future for which all historical models are insufficient, more lies latent for man than the subsequently experienced arrival can provide. This is a painful experience of difference which Israel suffered in her history: from the Exodus out of Egypt to the land of Canaan where milk and honey were not exactly "flowing," from the return out of exile to the destroyed homeland. This experience extends all the way through the history of western revolutions. It will also be repeated in an industrial planning society of tomorrow. "What disappoints in truth is the experienced or foreboded human existence itself as it emerges or will emerge out of the industrial society. . . . As long as socialism is being erected it can preserve the magic of a genuine transcendence. To the extent that it is created, it loses this spell. "But," asks Raymond Aron, "can man live without any transcendence after the transcendence of the future, after the transcendence of God has been eliminated?" In the highly industrialized countries there are increasing signs that

the accepted category "future" is expiring. Once progressive, utopian thought is passé. In place of the once necessary investments for a future which was to be obtained, there appears a consumer's attitude which has absolutely nothing to do with the future. Out of a thus foreboded disappointment all of those critical questions against great plans and models of a world of tomorrow have arisen: Does planning make man into the free master of his fate or does it lead him into an organized adaption to empty executions of plans? Does planning awaken a new consciousness of the future or does it defuturize the future? Will we, as Günther Anders formulates it so pregnantly, "in the future see the future no longer as the future"? Does planning bring about the elevation of blind fate to the level of responsibility for man? Or does man become the fatalist of his own calendar of events of a thoroughly planned life?

The foreboded human existence is not so unambiguous as was promised in the initial impetus. For example, what did the program of the shortened working day promise? An increase of leisure time and freedom and self-realization. Why doesn't this occur? Apparently, non-identity remains man's good fortune and his torment. *Horror vacui* exerts itself when people "don't know what to do with themselves." One must indeed know about these differences of man in order not to undertake too much and in order not to produce disappointments the consequences of which cannot be foreseen.

2

If by "feedback" one understands the continual control of the impulse on the effect and of the effect on the impulse, then a fruitful relationship of planning and hoping can perhaps be thus described. The impulses of hope have to be measured on the effect of the planning, and this on the intentions of the hope. If definite hopes—as they become active in the face of revolutionary historical signs and as they perceive new realms of the possible—are transformed into plans, they are exhausted as soon as all of these new possibilities are exhausted. But when the discrepancies between hoped-for and planned future is a motive force of history, planning must always keep in mind its original source arising out of hope and must be aware of the head start of hope. If it puts itself in the place of hope, it loses the latter's transcendent impetus—and by so doing it loses itself in the long run.

Through planning, the historical transition from the possible into the real and from the future into the present is made and executed consciously. In comparison to this, hope has primarily nothing to do with the historical transition from the real to the new; instead it is kindled by the new, by which the possible is made possible and is invented in the first place. It places itself in an evolutionary contradiction to the present reality not merely in the name of the possible; it is not only, as Kierkegaard claims, the "passion for the possible." Faced with the historically possible, hope reaches beyond and can actually be characterized as the "passion for the impossible," for the not-yet possible.

But that would be too formal a definition. Let us consider more concretely Christian hope, which has its origins in the event of the revival of the crucified Christ. Christ's suffering reveals for Christian hope what is really bad in the world—the torment of creation, the unsaved condition of the world and its immersion in nothingness. For this reason hope is always kindled anew on Christ's resurrection. When this hope comes into a human life a deep discrepancy arises between what one believes and hopes and what one sees and experiences. The individual falls into a contradiction with himself and with his environment and begins to suffer from the environment. But it is not only a suffering from earthly distress, but still more a suffering from the distress of the earthly, of the entire "waiting creation," which has been discovered, taken up and put into words by the hope of resurrection. Not in apocalyptic phantasies does this hope exhibit its power, but in patience and in the contradiction to the character of the world as it is.

Let us attempt to describe even more precisely the manner in which this hope has an effect on the present.

1) Suffering presupposes love. Whoever doesn't love anything, doesn't suffer either. One can avoid suffering by not making

attachments to anything and by rendering oneself insensitive in the face of happiness and pain. In this way, all things, situations, and relationships in life become interchangeable and substitutable. If one attempts to overcome suffering by creating a culture consisting exclusively of loose connections which can be broken at any time (and a consumer supply of the substitutability of all things), then, to be sure, pain can be avoided. But there arises a frustration of living emptiness and boredom. Hope keeps love alive. For it gives love the freedom to renounce itself completely and to take upon itself pain and suffering, and thus it loses itself when it makes a connection with something else. Neither the loosening of all relationships nor the substitutability of all things is able to cope with the pain of transitoriness, but only love which gains its ability to suffer and its endurance from the hope for the conquest of death.

2) This hope places the thus beloved life into an intentional vista which extends beyond all types of fulfillment which are possible and thinkable here into that realm of freedom from death. One is not pacified by the given circumstances and also not by what has been conceived and produced. One anticipates a future in hope: a future which reaches beyond this, and which for this reason also extends through the history which can be planned for the future. Out of this there arises the permanent discrepancy between the achieved and the plannable existence— as it is here and as it can be made possible here—and that which is actually important in existence. This discrepancy, which is kept awake and made conscious, has the effect of a permanent revolution, of a continual iconoclasm. This discrepancy is the motive force, the main spring, the torment of history, for, by reference to what was actually wanted and sought with hope, it shows the perennial inconclusiveness of what has come and is coming into being. It thus evokes realistic visions which involve value judgments and according to which certain historical possibilities are to be sought after and others to be left alone—but without this hope itself being completely subsumed by such realistic visions.

3) The reverse side of this intentional vista of hope is suffering and dissatisfaction with the present in which man cannot be man

in the manner in which it can be hoped. It is suffering from earthly distress and human non-freedom which is recognized by the love which wishes happiness for the poor and freedom for the suppressed. These are not adverse conditions which are perceptible to everyone, such as traffic congestion, shortage of living space and hospitals, etc., which can be alleviated by means of planning and investments. Even more urgent are those perils which will descend upon mankind during famines resulting from over-population. What is lacking in order to encounter these perils is the consciousness of human solidarity which does not close its eyes in the face of others' distress, but which accepts them as one's own. This is also true in the case of the non-freedom of others. One cannot discard one's hope for the future in order to consume one's attained good fortune as long as the majority of other people have not even attained this future. The value of renunciation of consumption for the reason of self-preservation through asceticism is not particularly apparent for everyone. However, it is apparent by reason of the necessity of investment for the future of others. Christian hope must encourage this if it does not want to be a private hope for the hereafter, but instead the vista of hope of love and solidarity with all other similarly suffering creatures.

We see the manner in which hope is effective (1) in the intentional vista which it extends over one's lifetime—through this vista the motive "additional value" of the actual future over the planned future is perceived; and (2) in the emotion of love which awakens hope. If this is correct, then we can further say that this hope of man leads to the origin of the freedom of the future and of the possible.

Christian hope should not make the future taboo in a fatalistic manner. It also should not think that it can have done with the future with the help of its faith. But it should strive so that men can "keep their heads up" in a world which is extremely involved, that they can recognize meaningful goals and find the courage to make human as well as material investments for this purpose.

Translated by William R. White

EVERETT E. HAGEN

Are Some Things Valued by All Men?

Everett E. Hagen is an anthropologist. His essay was part of the symposium "For White America: Perspectives on Development and Social Change" (edited by James J. Lamb, Cross Currents, Fall 1968). Hagen centers his attention on a question central to progress in the growth of well being: what values, if any, are common to all humankind? His answer is a single word: respect. And, Hagen suggests, on the foundation of respect can be built sound structures of development and change. A Chinese philosopher called respect that which makes the seed sprout and the cherry tree blossom. Hagen's insight, if applied not just to human societies but to the cosmos itself, to the very processes of the earth and the universe, forms one basis for an ecological ethic more hope-filled than than any morality derived from warnings of future doom.

The Center for the Study of Development and Social Change has a bias in its research—a bias in favor of human welfare. Not the welfare of Americans or of Africans or of Asians, but the welfare of all men considered of equal importance. To make this bias effective, and avoid the bias of some cultural viewpoint, it is necessary to ask, Is there an ultimate way of stating the source of human happiness that is applicable to men everywhere? What is it that men want? Are the things that will maximize the welfare of Americans different from those that will maximize the welfare of Europeans or Africans or Asians? Until the answer to this question is clear, it is not possible to know whether one is studying human welfare or only, say, Brazilian welfare or Algerian welfare or Indian welfare.

A thoughtful American, asked what it is that will make a man content, may say freedom and economic sufficiency. He may add that an increase in economic affluence adds to contentment. Except for some difference of opinion as to whether affluence adds to happiness, many persons in many countries would agree with these statements. It is the central contention of this essay that they are wrong, at least in part. I shall argue that in any simple definition of the word freedom the desire for freedom is not universal, and that an increase in the level of income in a country does not tend to increase contentment.

1

Suppose that the word "freedom" is defined to mean freedom from control by a government whose policies the individual has not had a voice in determining. Freedom, that is, means self-government. If that is the definition, many peoples do not want freedom. For it is clear that in a number of countries that obtained their independence from colonial rule after World War II, after obtaining that independence the people of the country did not seek to participate in the determination of governmental policies. Rather, they enthusiastically installed an individual as the leader of the country and asked him to make the decisions. They chose an authoritarian form of government. If a reader objects to this term, on the ground that their governments are thereby being called evil, I would note that the evil is not in the form of government but in the reader's or the citizen's view of it. I see no reason to regard an authoritarian form of government as inferior to a democratic form, if the former is what the mass of the people of a society desire. The leader of one such country said to a friend of mine, a few years ago, somewhat despairingly, "I spend my days trying to teach my people democracy, but they want me to be God."

The point I am making is that desire for democracy is not

universal. The facts cited above make that point, but the facts merit further discussion. To the Western liberal who states that desire for democracy ought to be universal, I would ask why he thinks his scale of values should be imposed on other persons. He may answer that individuals favor authoritarian government only if they are uninformed. This is incorrect; clearly a majority of Germans supported Hitler's authoritarian regime in the late 1930's; and the Germans were a highly educated people. However this is not the type of authoritarian regime I have in mind.

The majority of people—and probably virtually all people—in a number of countries do not prefer a voice in broader governmental decisions. I think that the reason is as follows. For virtually every man, there is a sphere of activity within which he feels competent, and within which he finds the opportunity to use his skill and his judgment stimulating. He likes the process of problem-solving or decision-making within that sphere. Thus, for example, when a peasant plants and cultivates his crop, he does not do so simply in a traditional way without using any judgment of his own. He has much more skill than a person not acquainted with his craft appreciates. He knows what to do if the season is early or if it is wet, or if he is planting on a south slope as distinguished from a north slope, and so on. Similarly, a fisherman who goes out in a small boat or a canoe exercises great skill both in the rowing or sailing and in locating schools of fish and catching them.

But many individuals find this stimulating only within a very narrow sphere of activity in which they have had experience from childhood. In broader areas, facing the necessity of making decisions creates anxiety. It is as though the individual said, "I do not believe that I have good judgment in this area. If I try to make a decision here, I will probably fail. The possibility makes me anxious. Let someone else do it." Thus, if peasants or fishermen in many societies are asked what should be done about problems of their region, problems of relationships among villages or national problems, they are likely to say, "What? I, a mere peasant?" They cannot conceive of themselves as having judgment in the wider spheres, and they flee the threat of facing such a decision as they would the plague.

The anxiety created by facing decisions in areas outside of the sphere in which one feels competent can easily be avoided in a hierarchical and authoritarian society. Faced with a question beyond what one feels is one's competence, one can refer it to the person of a social status above one, who is supposed to be able to answer it. And the decision he gives will be right, not by an operational test, but because he has given it. A successive set of layers of status, rising in a pyramid to the top central authority, is comfortable and seems right to the persons of many countries. Hierarchical and authoritarian social relations seem right to many persons for other reasons as well, but this one reason is the one that concerns us here.

I am not suggesting that the people of one country as a group all differ from those of another country in this respect. Rather, I believe that the situation is somewhat as follows: If within any society say 5% of the adults of the society find it stimulating and satisfying to exercise their judgment concerning the broader economic, social and political affairs of the country, then there will be individuals scattered throughout the villages, towns, and cities of the country who like to be leaders. They express viewpoints, other voters turn to them, and democracy will work well and be satisfying even though facing decisions in broad areas makes nineteen persons out of twenty anxious. But if the number of persons who feel stimulus and satisfaction in facing the use of their judgment in broader areas is only, say, one-fourth of one percent rather than five percent, then an authoritarian hierarchical social order will seem preferable and right.

Social-clinical psychologists today know something about the causes of one or the other attitude. They know that it is rather little affected by information or by the substance of formal education, though it may be affected by the relationship between a student and his teacher. Much the most important single cause, however, is the home environment in which the infant and child spends the first half dozen years of his life. From the attitudes of parents soon after birth, and continuing thereafter—their anxiety, their nurturance, their reassurance to him in a thousand ways that the great mysterious world is a safe place, or absence of such assurance; their support for and pleasure at his explorations or on the contrary the fact that he must follow their arbitrary orders if he is to gain their approval—from all these factors the very young child makes generalizations about the nature of the safest and most rewarding behavior. And "as the twig is bent so the tree inclines"; these generalizations, which the child quickly buries in his unconscious thought processes, influence him all his life. And although later influences may counter them, the early impressions are especially influential.

Hence formal education is of *relatively* little importance in this respect. To make this point most vividly, it is plausible that if the tensions of modern life create home environments in which somewhat anxious and preoccupied parents treat their infants and children in authoritarian ways, then—for example—highly educated United States citizens might gradually become authoritarian during the coming half century. This is not a prediction, but only a way of emphasizing an important point. That point is that the desire to be free from control by policies decreed by others is not universal. *In certain circumstances* an authoritarian and hierarchical political and social structure is preferred. Those circumstances are discussed below. It cannot be taken for granted that a movement toward democracy will increase human welfare.

2

Let me ask next whether affluence increases happiness. Almost any person will answer, Yes. He is reasonably sure that if he had more income, other conditions remaining the same, he would be happier.

Yet, paradoxically, there is historical evidence to the contrary. Consider first the United States. If one reads historical accounts of the first decade of this century, and asks oneself whether the average American is happier now than he was sixty years ago, one will have no persuasive reason to answer that he is.

It is possible to argue that this is because conditions other than economic ones have changed. However, consider a broader historical comparison. In Western Europe, the present average level of income and of consumption per family is six to ten times as high as it was before the Industrial Revolution. In the United States, it is more than ten times as high as in Western Europe before the Industrial Revolution. Moreover, it is no more unequally distributed now than it was then. On the contrary, it is probably more equally distributed. The rich today are probably less rich (after paying taxes) than they were in 1500, relative to the low-income classes.

Yet who would claim that people are happier today than they were in the later Middle Ages? Some persons would. They have an image of the Middle Ages as a period when life was "nasty, brutish, and short," to use Hobbes's phrase, an image of people spending their lives in great misery.

However, if one reads the historical literature, one does not find support for this image. Contemporary accounts describe peasants' festive times on the village green, sketch fairs in the towns and ceremonies at the manors in which all classes found enjoyment, give an occasional glimpse of satisfying family life. In one of her novels, Willa Cather has one of her characters argue eloquently that people living on manors in the Middle Ages were fully as happy as they have ever been since. The case is well made.

It is true that the death rate was high. Perhaps half of the children born died before the age of ten, and certainly half died before they reached adulthood. Of course parents loved their children, and of course they felt sorrow when a child died. But they did not carry this sorrow with them throughout their lives. They turned their love and attention to the children who lived. Moreover, their level of living did not seem minimal and meager. It was what they expected, and it seemed adequate. I repeat that there is no warrant whatever in the historical literature for assuming that they were not normally content with their lives, or that the percentage of them who felt a sense of deprivation on the average in any year was greater than the percentage of persons in the most affluent society in the world today, the United States, who feel a sense of deprivation.

The scanty records of ancient Egypt, ancient Greece, and

other countries of the ancient world do not offer evidence to contradict the assertion that the same statement applies to these times and places. The flavor of life in ancient Greece is well presented in the novels of Mary Renault, and no one who reads those novels thoughtfully will feel that they present a picture of lack of happiness. The image of near-universal unhappiness in former times arises in part from the conception that people must have been held under authoritarian rule by brute force— whereas, as suggested above, except when an insensitive ruler made cruel demands, people probably found satisfaction in the anxiety-relieving hierarchical system.

It is true, of course, that during the periods when the Pharaohs ruthlessly recruited workers to build the great pyramids, there may have been great misery. The Khmer rulers may have dragooned peasants to construct the great temples at Angkor. The Bourbons had lost all sense of any responsibility for the welfare of the people of France, and the people responded by hating them. Many other acts that may have brought misery could be cited. But this evidence concerns not the low economic level, but the disregard of man for man. Paradoxical and contrary to commonly accepted assumptions though the statement is, there is no hard historical evidence to suggest that the peoples of times past felt that their level of living was low or deprivational. That it was is a projection which we make into the past from our condition of affluence.

Again, it would be hazardous to maintain today that the average person in England, or Japan, or even India, was less happy than the average person in the United States. Indeed, it is a fair guess that if the people of those countries were polled on the question, their image of the United States is such that they would vote overwhelmingly that they are happier. (If one cited items of evidence concerning violence or unrest in India to the contrary, consider for one horrible moment the contrary items of evidence concerning the United States.)

A final illustrative example: the average American who lives in a small town has income that is a small fraction of that of the persons who live in Hollywood, or of the persons who make the movies associated with the name Hollywood. Would anyone maintain that the ratio of his happiness to theirs is the same as the ratio of his income to theirs, or that he is less happy at all?

The fact seems to be that the level of income needed for contentment above a certain physiological minimum is a matter of one's conception of what is a reasonable income. If other classes in one's society have higher incomes but this is regarded as normal, then it may leave one contented. If one's income falls below the income one has had previously, one is likely to feel unhappy. If one lives in a society in which income is steadily increasing, so that one has become accustomed to expect one's income to increase from each five-year period to the next, then if it does not increase one may feel a sense of deprivation. But one does not feel a sense of deprivation merely because one has less income than fabulously wealthy persons whom one knows in fantasy, as one knows the inhabitants of moving pictures.

I suggest, as a corollary to this principle, that the peoples of the low-income countries of the world do not feel a sense of deprivation merely because they have lower income than the fabulously wealthy Westerners whom they know only in what is really a fantasy. There are millions of people in many countries of the world today, who have inadequate diets. I believe that the more affluent peoples of the world have a moral duty to help them. But I also believe that the concept of many Americans that the general population of the low-income countries are miserable because they are poor is a figment of the American imagination, a result of guilt feelings, rather than a fact of life. Many of them are unhappy today. The cause, I think, lies deeper. I shall suggest it below.

3

I believe there is something which is valued universally, and which is the source of happiness or its lack the source of unhappiness of people everywhere. This, to put it in its simplest form, is the sense that one is respected. More precisely, what is needed for happiness is the sense that others are not using one as a tool to attain their purposes, without any regard for one's own purposes.

Half a century ago, the French sociologist Marcel Mauss, in an essay entitled "Essay on the Gift," reviewed all anthropological literature up to that time and argued that a principle of reciprocity seems to prevail in human affairs in all societies and communities. Where reciprocity does truly prevail, then each person feels that the other person respects his aims and purposes in life and therefore respects him. This perception that one is being treated as an individual who has worth, rather than as a tool for the satisfaction of the other individual's purposes, is, I think, the basic source of human contentment.

Hierarchical social structure causes pain and anger, I suggest, where it is felt that the persons above one use one for their purposes without regard to one's own. Low income creates misery and resentment when it is felt that it exists because others have no regard for one's welfare. (Many urban American families now classed as impoverished have radios, TV sets, and old automobiles—items that were luxuries a generation or so ago. Their poverty is no less real, but for the families who have such items the situation is not one of deprivation in any absolute sense.)

A friend of mine who has worked in Nepal is fond of telling of the Nepalese anthropologist who has said to many Westerners when he first met them: "Look around you. If you see three Nepalese, one thing you can be sure is that they are not equal. Each of them is either the superior or the inferior of each other." My friend also says that even though the Nepalese peasant can borrow money from a government organization at a far lower rate of interest than from the local landlord, he prefers to borrow from the landlord. It is true that the reason in part is that there is delay in getting the money from the government organization. But my friend says that he believes the main reason is that when the peasant is in trouble, for example if his wife is sick in the middle of the night, he can rush to the landlord and he will get help. There is an old French saying: "Noblesse oblige," that is, being a member of the nobility carries obligations. Where the spirit of "noblesse oblige" prevails in even a moderate degree, and where very few people find stimulus rather than anxiety in facing broad problems, authoritarian hierarchical government is probably the most satisfying. The first of these conditions prevails in few places today, but this is probably because the tensions of modern life have disrupted traditional hierarchical relationships, not because men inherently prefer democracy and political participation.

A peasant takes for granted that he is a social inferior of the local landlord, the teacher, the head man in his village. But in the days when traditional societies were functioning more effectively than they are now, the relationship between peasant and landlord or other important villager was probably more reciprocal than it is today. The peasant provided services and rent; the landlord or other leader provided ceremonial leadership on religious occasions and other occasions of emotional importance, provided the use of his influence if the peasant's clever son wanted schooling, and provided aid in sickness and misfortune. Where he performed such functions, hierarchical political and social structures were probably satisfying. And this probably has been true throughout most of human history. "Happy the land that has no history," a philosopher has said. The converse of that statement is that the times of a nation's trouble are the times that are recorded in history. The great blank spaces of history may have been the times of relatively satisfying life.

The low-income societies today are also the less powerful societies. They are the societies in which the elite groups of the society, having been humiliated by their weakness in the face of small groups of Western intruders, have vented their frustration on the lower socio-economic groups of their own societies. I think it is a reasonable speculation that before the Western intrusions the inter-class relations in those societies were characterized by a much greater degree of reciprocity than at present. I suggest that the perception at present by the members of the lower socio-economic groups of those societies that they are not looked upon by the elites above them as having worth but rather are merely instruments by which those more elite groups and intruders from outside seek to satisfy their own insensitive desires, is the fundamental source of present social discontent,

political instability, and physical turmoil in many of those societies. The members of the lower groups must step in the gutter,
take what is offered them, whether equitable or not, hide their
valuables and their daughters from the landlord, the tax collector,
the police, and the army. I suggest that this, not their poverty, is
the source of their present unhappiness and bitterness. I doubt
that in these circumstances they would feel happy if they had
twice or thrice their present income; and if they were treated
with respect I suspect that they would be contented even with
their present income.

This does not imply that all present social turmoil is to be
accounted for by objective observation of relationships among
adults. It is also true that in the circumstances described, parents
must be more anxious, more preoccupied with their own worries, than in happier circumstances, and that therefore infants
and children acquire from the earliest days of life a sense that the
important persons around them do not care for them. It is a well-
known human trait to deny to oneself that this perception derives
from the early behavior of one's own parents. This perception is
too painful and dangerous to bear. It is therefore the common
human practice to attribute one's feelings, later in life, to the
behavior of other persons around one. Persons who grew up in
such circumstances therefore have a great sensitivity, a sort of
allergy, to inconsiderate treatment by more powerful figures in
the society, and react with an intensity with which they would not
if their own infancy and childhood had been more satisfying.

If the argument presented above is correct, it does not provide
us with an infallible key to the most desirable social structure. It
may lead us to a dilemma. Let us suppose that in a given society
the large majority of persons find satisfaction in a hierarchical
and authoritarian social-political structure, and a small minority
find it in a social structure in which all share in the making of
decisions. Let us suppose that the happiness of the majority will
be achieved only if they are able to dominate the small minority
which I have mentioned. The conditions for the happiness of the
two groups will be inconsistent. In a sense, each can attain
happiness within the society only by imposing on the other. For
if it is true that a man who desires control must impose on a

second to attain happiness, then it is also true that if the second insists on participating in decisions, he in a sense is imposing on the first. But the principle of the equal moral worth of all men, a principle which from a detached philosophical basis is hardly disputable, suggests that as a minimum the majority has no moral right to dominate the minority. For it can arrange within its own group the hierarchy which is satisfying, and the most that could reasonably be required of the minority group is that it should detach itself from the larger society, and form its own. Whether hardships would thereby be involved, so that some other solution is more equitable, is a complexity that need not be argued here.

There is an added reason for favoring egalitarian social structure. For reasons that have not been presented above, it seems more likely that an authoritarian hierarchical society will attempt to impose its will on its neighbors than that an egalitarian one will. The rationalization by which the internally democratic American society has attempted to impose its will in Vietnam must make one hesitate to announce this as a general principle; yet I think it can be defended as generally true.

Hence there is strong empirical presumption that if problem-solving personality were generously sprinkled among all peoples, the level of human happiness could be maximized. Concerning men's relations to each other, the basic commandment of the Christian religion is, "Thou shalt love thy neighbor as thyself." This includes all of the other commandments concerning human relationships. But men cannot love their neighbors as themselves merely by wiling to do so. They will do so only if they understand themselves—understand that their aggression, anxieties, sadnesses, and joys have inner roots, not merely external causes—and thereby can understand the aggressions and anxieties of other men and reach accommodations with them. In this case, society would be egalitarian and all would share in its decisions (even though income and social-political roles were unequal). But if we must accept men as they are, then we cannot make a general argument for either egalitarianism or affluence as means to maximum human welfare.

Whatever the empirical complexities, in principle the *sum-*

mum bonum is clear: it is respect for the dignity of every man. This, I think, is the only universal. The social and economic structures which it should lead men of good will to advocate are, I think, relative matters, depending on the personalities that the conditions of life have produced in each society.

MARY B. MAHOWALD

Feminism, Socialism, and Christianity

Mary B. Mahowald is a philosopher at Case-Western Reserve University in Cleveland, Ohio. Her thought here and elsewhere begins with the rejection of individualism and the embrace of communalism, in which the self "is comprised within the concept of the ever-widening community." Just as Everett Hagen maintains that humanity values respect more universally than it values freedom, so Mahowald suggests that freedom itself should be socialized—"that social dependence or interdependence is desirable"—and that equality does not eradicate differences but requires that "No individual, because of his/her differences [be] regarded or treated better (or worse) than another." The convergence of feminism, socialism, and Christianity that she envisions does not melt the three realities into one another; rather, it envisions making each more itself, and more clearly a movement in service of human solidarity.

I deologically, I consider myself feminist, socialist and Christian. I recognize, however, that there are concepts of feminism, socialism and Christianity which are different from mine, while consistent with each other. The difference, I believe, occurs for the most part because of essentially opposite emphases—in one case, individualistic; in the other communalistic. As I here use the terms, "individualistic emphasis" means primarily a self-interest, whether the self be one or many; "communalistic emphasis" refers to a primary concern for an ever-widening community, an orientation that is essentially outward and open-ended. Within the context of either emphasis, meanings of the three ideologies overlap or are related, and the consistency of the overall position depends upon that context. In this article I want to examine both contexts, and to consider feminism, socialism and Christianity in light of their differing emphases. My aim is to elaborate a basis for assessing the consistency of ideas and practices within the three ideologies, and for determining which of their interpretations is more viable. In the last section I will briefly describe my own ideological perspective.

1

Historically, most ideologies originate in a concern about individuals as such. This focus may be obscured by the fact that many individuals profess the same ideology, and come together as a kind of pressure group to achieve their ends. If the group's perspective is individualistic, the "community" they form exists solely for the sake of its members or of a specifically limited number of beneficiaries.[1] Whether others are affected adversely or positively is immaterial to the community's *raison d'être*.

Underlying an ideological concern for the individual is the concept of freedom. While the reality of freedom may be questioned or ignored, diverse concepts of freedom continue to give rise to different ideological emphases. Among these, the meaning of freedom implied by a consistent individualistic ideology is a demandingly existential concept, which I shall hereafter refer to as "raw freedom." In effect, this concept entails rejection of all paternalistic "help" or influence, assumption of full responsibility for one's own life, and presumption of opportunities for the achievement of one's full potential as a person. The locus of such freedom is the lone individual. To the extent that its specific expressions are extrinsically prescribed or proscribed (by law, custom, etc.), its individualistic basis is betrayed. Both conceptually and practically, the essential assumption of raw freedom is that individuals exist or can exist independently of one another. Ideally, it entails the notion that this should be the case.

Feminism, socialism and Christianity all affirm equality between persons as a desirable social goal. But just what "equality" entails is not so clear. Obviously an individualistic context does not imply that equality means sameness among individuals. On the contrary, the equality implied by a pure individualism is one which preserves and reinforces the uniqueness of persons through a thoroughly *laissez-faire* approach. Each person, regardless of his/her distinct capabilities and achievements, is entitled to the same quality and quantity of public assistance. Since practices such as compensation for the disadvantaged or gradation of taxes according to income constitute interference with the natural development of the individual, these measures are inconsistent with an individualistic orientation. In that context, given their natural differences and freedom, individuals should be left free to regress as well as progress, when measured by any extrinsic standard.

Within the context described above, feminism is an ideology which defines the liberation of women as its primary goal. Although the concept of sex equality is also affirmed, what this means in practice is promotion of women's interests, not men's. The emancipation idealized is raw freedom for every woman as an individual. This implies the capability and desirability of women's independence from men, and possibly from one another.

Individualistic interpretations of feminism have occurred among both moderate and radical feminists.[2] The most obvious example of the former group is the National Organization of Women, which describes itself as

a new civil rights organization pledged to work actively to bring women into full participation in the mainstream of American society NOW, exercising all the privileges and responsibilities thereof IN TRULY EQUAL PARTNERSHIPS WITH MEN.[3]

To participate fully "in the mainstream of American society" as it exists today implies an endorsement of the individualistic ethic which predominates in that society. In other words, the concern of NOW is to see that women as individuals obtain the civil rights to which they are entitled within the American system.

That the goals of NOW are moderate rather than radical is evident through its overall adherence to basic structures and institutions such as marriage and the family. NOW's efforts in behalf of sex equity or women's liberation substantially reinforce the principles presently governing a male-dominated society because they simply promote female domination in its place. Consider, for example, the admission of Betty Friedan, NOW's founder: "I want to get women into positions of power."[4] Since the meaning and reality of power is basic to American individualism, Friedan thus aims to reform rather than radically alter the American system.

The specific issue in which the individualist thrust of NOW and other feminist groups is most apparent is that of abortion. In publications and actions, legalized abortion has been supported with the argument that a woman should have exclusive rights over her own body.[5] Logically, this argument precludes a legal responsibility to respect the rights of others affected by one's body. The problem of course is that, in varying degrees, others besides the mother and the fetus—e.g., the father, and the rest of society—are inevitably affected by every decision for or against abortion. If the general argument were applied to all persons, it would legally justify acts of self-mutilation or suicide. Ironically, such a defense of abortion rights lends strength to the chauvinistic attitudes of men who consider themselves removed from responsibility for embryonic and fetal life.[6]

Other positions held by moderate feminists are not as clearly consistent with the pure individualism indicated by the preceding argument. With regard to child care, for example, Friedan insists

we must challenge the idea that woman is primarily responsible for raising children. Man and society have to be educated to accept their responsibility for that role as well.[7]

Such an understanding of responsibility may or may not be individualistic—depending upon whether the welfare of others besides the mother is the reason for its advocacy. What the overall position clearly advocates, however, is that women alone have the right to choose parenthood, while responsibility for children is to be shared by both parents and society as a whole. Radical as well as moderate feminists tend to concur on both of these points.

In contrast with moderate feminism, however, radical feminists propose to alter the basic principles and structure of society. Although their numbers are relatively small (especially in contrast with the membership of NOW), radical feminist organizations have sometimes compensated for this by greater ardor. In fact, membership may be restricted so as to insure that ardor. One group, for example, not only excludes men from its membership but stipulates that no more than one-third of its members be married. To permit even that number to be married is actually inconsistent with its specified reasons for defining such a quota, viz.,

> Because THE FEMINISTS consider the institution of marriage inherently inequitable . . .
>
> Because we consider this institution a primary formalization of the persecution of women, and
>
> Because we consider the rejection of this institution both in theory *and in practice* a primary mark of the radical feminist.[8]

Such selectivity regarding membership suggests a form of individualism within the women's movement itself.

Not surprisingly, some radical feminist groups have originated in reaction to NOW's positions. For example, Ti-Grace Atkinson helped to found The Feminists after resigning her presidency of the New York Chapter of NOW, because of "irreconcilable ideological conflicts" within the organization.[9] The main conflict, according to Atkinson, concerned power. In contrast to those calling for reformation of society through the establishment of "Woman Power," Atkinson and her supporters purposed "to destroy the positions of power." Admitting dissatisfaction "about the unequal power relationships between men and women," she insisted that "[t]o change that relationship requires a redefinition of humanity, of all the relationships within humanity."[10]

As a radical feminist, Atkinson's own redefinition of humanity is based on the notion of class. Historically, she maintains, class distinction between the sexes arose because men took advantage of the social disability imposed upon women through their role in reproduction. The motivation for this continuing "metaphysical cannibalism" (i.e., appropriating another human being to the substance of oneself), is the universal desire to overcome the insecurity and frustration evoked through the realization of human limitation.[11] Since this desire is universal, however, Atkinson's account suggests a rather dim view of women as well as men: if men were the bearers of children, women might be the metaphysical cannibals. In either case, the reality of politics is born of an inevitable conflict between the sexes.

Accordingly, radical feminism may be defined as a class action on behalf of women, i.e., all women. Its ideology thus stands in specific opposition to the class enemy of women, viz., men. Combatting this enemy requires destruction of other "institutions" besides that of marriage—e.g., "love" and "heterosexual sex."[12] An additional goal to be achieved is the development of extra-uterine means of reproduction—so that women as a class may be fully delivered from the social disability caused by their participation in this process.

Through its emphasis on class, radical feminism is individualistic because its primary concern is for a self that is many.[13] The ideology of most radical feminist organizations includes some of the same individualistic elements of moderate feminism (e.g., in their pro abortion stance), even while rather rigidly prescribing the attitudes towards their situation that individual women ought to have. Although generally the theory purports to deplore power, it is difficult to see how class action does not depend precisely on that: obtaining and using one kind of power (woman power) in order to supplant another.

In a sense, by so defining women, radical feminism gathers all individual women into one individual Woman, and by defining men as the enemy, implies that Woman's wants and needs are primary in relationship to man's. A (supposedly) liberated and fulfilled Womankind, rather than a liberated and fulfilled Humankind, is the ideal to be achieved. Since the more limited ideal may be more readily realizable, it is not without pragmatic justification. Similar justification may be offered for restricting the goals of societal groups such as families or labor unions. Within such situations, attitudes or concepts become individualistic to the extent that they confine their concern and sense of responsibility to a single group, even at the expense of other groups or classes.

As the ideology which has dominated modern efforts to relieve oppression, socialism is logically related to feminism. Although individualism is generally construed as its opposite, individualistic interpretations of socialism occur wherever only the needs and rights of the oppressed group or class are considered, and where responsibilities peculiar to that group are ignored or disowned. Such deliberate limitation of perspective exemplifies the class form of individualism promoted by radical feminism. Yet moderate as well as radical feminists are socialistic in that they call upon the state to respond to the peculiar needs of women.

A text often quoted to define socialism is Marx's statement of its guiding principle in the *Critique of the Gotha Programme:* "From each according to his ability, to each according to his needs."[14] Certainly, to so state an ideal indicates a strong sense of the individual. Nonetheless, the emphasis is communalistic rather than individualistic, because a societal orientation is implied by the context. The fuller statement might read: "From each to society (i.e., to others) according to his ability; to each from society (i.e., from others) according to his needs." Ultimately, the ideal of a classless society means to promote and maintain the interests of all individuals. Since such an ideal is essentially communalistic, we must look elsewhere for an individualistic emphasis within socialism.

The meaning of socialism which appears individualistic through an exclusive concern about a particular class is the first phase of communism, which Marx characterized as a "political transition period in which the State can be nothing but the revolutionary dictatorship of the proletariat."[15]

In other words, the class individualism of capitalism has here been reversed, for the proletariat dominate the bourgeoisie. Marx considers such a dictatorship benevolent in that it seeks to overcome oppression as much for the sake of the oppressor as for that of the oppressed; and he considers it more democratic than nominally democratic capitalism because in the latter case the moneyed interests of a minority actually control the majority.

But Marx also admits the limitations of the proletarian dictatorship. "[D]efects are inevitable in the first phase of communist society," he writes, "as it is when it has just emerged after prolonged birth-pangs from capitalist society."[16] Obviously it takes time to accomplish the transformation of consciousness which is essential for a freely egalitarian society. Just how long the dictatorship is to be exercised has been a crucial and much-debated point among Marxists. On the practical level, however, perhaps a more crucial issue is *how* individual consciousnesses are to be transformed. If means of persuasion are coercive (and certainly the term "dictatorship" suggests this) rather than educative, Marx's concern for individual freedom seems to have been violated. It can be argued of course that all education is, to some extent, coercive. But a socratic process of education, which trusts the student to think for him/herself, may be possible if the "dictatorship" permits an increasingly democratic participation by the bourgeoisie.

Present instances of supposed adherence to Marx's principles generally exemplify the class individualism of communism's first phase. Unfortunately, however, their totalitarian dictatorships are exercised not by the proletarian or peasant masses, but by a revolutionary elite who pursue their own ends for all of the people. Lenin attempted to justify this departure from Marx's doctrine by observing that

> the wider the masses spontaneously drawn into the struggle, forming the basis of the movement and participating in it, the more urgent the need of such an organization [i.e., the ruling revolutionary elite], and the more solid this organization must be (for it is much easier for demagogues to sidetrack the more backward sections of the masses).[17]

Like radical feminists, Lenin conceived of membership in the revolutionary elite as restricted to those who had already been both theoretically and practically radicalized. "Such an organization," he wrote,

> must consist chiefly of people professionally engaged in revolutionary activity; . . . the more we *confine* the membership of such an organization to people who are professionally trained in the art of combating the political police, the more difficult will it be to wipe out such an organization.[18]

The elitism of such a position is certainly interpretable as individualistic. Totalitarian socialism or communism thus sustains an inhibition of the freedom of the masses while imposing on them the will of an elitist minority. In such a situation it can well be argued that socialism becomes precisely what it accuses capitalism of being: imperialistic. Either system instances an extended form of individualism.

The popular version of Marx's critique of religion is well known: religion is the opium of the people. The critique was aimed especially at Christianity as Marx understood it, since this was the religion which predominated in his culture. Consequently, many Marxists and Christians find it disconcerting to observe the number of scholars and religious leaders who claim important points of congruence or coincidence between Marxist and Christian principles. Similarly, recent feminist criticism draws attention to the part which religion plays with regard to the oppression of women.[19]

For Christianity, as for feminism and socialism, an individualistic interpretation is both available and defensible. In fact, that interpretation arises from the most fundamental datum of Christian faith, viz., redemption, or salvation through Christ. Contemporary liberation theology focuses on this datum in explaining that the essential right and responsibility of the individual Christian is to live freely and to facilitate the freedom of others.[20] Ample references from Scripture support this focus; for example, the epistle to the Galatians tells us: "You were called, as you know, to liberty," and "when Christ freed us, he meant us to remain free."[21] So strong an emphasis on freedom implies an emphasis on the individual; it is not so certain, however, that such emphasis is individualistic.

Perhaps the most poignant modern parable of freedom is Ivan's account of the Grand Inquisitor in *The Brothers Karamazov*. Dostoevsky describes alternative repositories of freedom: every individual, or their elitist leadership. In the former situation, Christ is the dispenser of a liberation which provokes anxiety through individual responsibility; in the latter case, the Cardinal and his church assume the burden of freedom so that Christians may be happily secure through their submission to authority. Thus, Christian redemption, as expressed through Ivan, implies raw freedom for every Christian, and possibly for every person. The ecclesial hierarchy, on the other hand, suggests comparison with Lenin's revolutionary elite, reserving raw freedom to itself for supposedly altruistic reasons. Either of Dostoevsky's alternatives represents an individualistic interpretation of Christianity.

Another plausible source of individualistic emphasis in Christianity is the fathers of the church. For example, Augustine's concept of the primacy of love entails the possibility of a situation ethics, i.e., an ethics which rejects absolute normative principles, insisting that none can be sufficient to the uniqueness of individuals and the circumstances affecting their moral decisions. While it is true that the famous dictum "Love and do what you will" is actually a very demanding counsel when considered in its Augustinian context, it is also true that the stress on love may be interpreted individualistically.[22]

Aquinas may also be invoked as an advocate of individual freedom for the sake of moral behavior. Since virtue and vice are habits arising from human acts (not merely acts of man), their morality or immorality depend upon each person's rational participation. Hence, virtue is subjectively meritorious because it involves an individual's free choice of an apprehended good. On the other hand, an act or habit devoid of freedom is subjectively amoral, regardless of its objective moral status. For example, to simply conform to the expectations or requirements of one's church without intelligent, free decision to do so is to act in a morally neutral manner, even if such conformity constitutes ostensibly saintly behavior. Individual freedom implies individual responsibility, making both indispensable to Christian morality. Both Aquinas and Augustine thus stress the individual, even as Marx did. And if that stress is sustained to the point that one's own spiritual ideal or destiny becomes all important, no matter what the cost to others, then Christianity is ultimately individualistic.

Historically, Christian asceticism has contributed a large dose of individualistic emphasis to Christianity. Whether living as hermits (often the ideal) or in communities (religious or otherwise), Christians have persistently been counseled that each one's primary concern ought to be the salvation of her/his own soul. For "[w]hat will a man gain if he wins the whole world and ruins his life?"[23] Protestant Christianity has also stressed the interests of the individual over those that are universal. In the colonizing of America, such religious individualism reinforced the ideal of rugged individualism to meet the demands of frontier life. Ironically, this individualistic interpretation of Christianity provided a religious rationale for assessing ethical worth through material success. It is an interpretation which continues to strengthen the underlying theory of capitalism.

In *Beyond God the Father,* Mary Daly analyzes an extended form of religious individualism. Categorizing the sex-based division of society as a caste (rather than class) system, Daly describes how patriarchal religion has consistently supported the oppression of the low caste, women. "The priestly or quasi-priestly caste," she writes,

> . . . speaks with prestige and authority, guiding women to see the folly of rebellion against the destiny designed by "God" and/or anatomy. . . . Thus an elitism is perpetuated . . . that keeps control in the hands of a few, perpetuating the dichotomy between 'agent' and 'patient' and reflecting a condition of society in which power is divorced from real love.[24]

According to Daly, this male "elitism" arises from the most fundamental doctrine of Christianity, since "the idea of salvation uniquely by a male savior perpetuates the problem of patriarchal oppression."[25] A "call for the castration of sexist religion" is the logical upshot of Daly's radically insightful criticism. If Christianity is a religion of "real love" towards all persons, ecclesial sexism opposes its essential purpose. It remains problematic whether Christianity can be stripped of sexism—either doctrinally or practically. Since Daly believes it cannot, she has moved beyond God the Father and Christ in her philosophy of women's liberation. Even if sexism were eliminated, however, an individualistic interpretation of Christianity is still possible.

2

While communities are formed where ideologies are shared (or ideologies are shared where communities are formed), communities are not necessarily communalistic. In fact the term "communalistic," like "individualistic," may describe an individual as well as a group or class. The essential mark of a communalistic community is that the interests of its members, as members, stretch beyond themselves to those of the wider community. In contrast to an individualistic community (whose goal could simply be that of self-perpetuation), a communalistic community necessarily idealizes a community embodying the universal fulfillment of individual interests. Short of that ideal, communalistic communities exist as means towards its achievement. Their orientation is not to be confused with an altruism which excludes concern for self. Rather, the self, whether one or many, is comprised within the concept of the ever-widening community.

Within this context, raw freedom is an ideal whose uninhibited exercise is restricted to those whose primary interests are already universal or general rather than particular or individual. In effect, then, members are not free to act in a way that would harm another, even oneself. The good of the entire community, which necessarily encompasses a good for every member, justifies the limitation of freedom for an individual or group. In view of such real or possible restrictions, the concept of freedom which underlies communalistic ideologies is one of socialized or limited freedom.

On practical as well as theoretical levels, an essential assumption of socialized or limited freedom is that individuals do not and cannot exist independently of one another. Ideally, the assumption entails the notion that social dependence or interdependence is desirable. Only in such a situation can individuals fully develop their uniqueness, and the reality of freedom be equitably sustained.

Equality, from a communalistic perspective, is a principle of distribution through which differences in abilities on all levels (physical, mental, emotional, etc.), are accommodated to differences in the needs and interests of individuals. In other words, since all persons are not born equal, they are made equal through the application of an ideology which construes their being made equal (as far as possible) a matter of social justice. The radical nature of this concept lies in its implied critique of an extremely pervasive tendency to evaluate persons on the basis of their quantitative or qualitative differences. For example, some of the most "liberal" among us may esteem those who are intellectually or artistically accomplished more highly than those who are not; we also may judge those with more material advantages (e.g., money, looks, athletic talent) as better persons that those who lack them. A communalistic interpretation of equality draws an important distinction between such differences among persons and the persons themselves. No individual, because of his/her differences, is regarded or treated better (or worse) than another.

Within the context described above, feminism is an ideology which defines human liberation as its primary goal, and women's liberation as the means to be pursued towards that end. The liberation sought for both sexes is one which takes into account real differences between them, whether these be purely biological, or psychological and/or cultural as well. Hence, women's liberation minimally entails social adjustment to the needs and capabilities of women as women. Since society depends upon some women fulfilling a reproductive function that curtails their availability for other social functions, justice requires that men and women not participating in this function perform a greater share of other works. Human liberation thus means limited freedom for individuals of both sexes, who are equal or equalized according to their differentiated participation in society.

A communalistic perspective recognizes that differences between individuals may be greater than those between the sexes. Hence, its implied concept of sex equality is contained within the broader notion of equality as a principle of distribution through which capabilities and needs are to be shared among all individuals. To define needs peculiar to some women qua women as actual needs of all women is to miss the concern for every individual which is essential to a communalistic ideology. Accordingly, the ideology is betrayed through a class emphasis, such as exists through laws or practices in which restrictions or privileges are based on gender rather than an objective differences between individuals.

Just as the American system suffers many exceptions to its individualistic bias, NOW has advocated measures which appear communalistic both in theory and in practice. For example, taking issue with radical feminist opposition to marriage and family, Friedan maintains that

> It is a perversion of the new feminism for some to exhort those who would join this revolution to cleanse themselves of sex and the need for love or to refuse to have children. . . . To enable *all* women, not just the exceptional few, to participate in society we must confront the fact of life—as a temporary fact of most women's lives today—that women do give birth to children.[26]

To confront this "fact of life" entails realization that children are a social and not merely parental responsibility. Accordingly, the revolution that Friedan talks about "has got to be for everybody."[27]

Another indication of NOW's communalism is that its membership is open to men. "Man is not the enemy," Friedan writes, "but the fellow victim of the present half-equality."[28] Explicitly affirming a relationship between women's liberation and men's liberation, she insists that

> [m]en will only be truly liberated, to love women and to be fully themselves, when women are liberated to be full people.[29]

Similar affirmations have been made by more radical feminists. In *The Female Eunuch*, for example, Germaine Greer observes that

> The first significant discovery we shall make as we racket along our female road to freedom is that men are not free, . . . that slaves enslave their masters, and by securing our own manumission we may show men the way they could follow when they jumped off their own treadmill.[30]

Of course to merely assert a relationship between women's liberation and men's liberation is not necessarily to be primarily concerned about human liberation. Still, the assertion may express a communalistic rather than individualistic orientation, and to the extent that it does, women's liberation is a means rather than an end in itself. Feminism, from such a perspective, seeks its own demise, and the hope of the women's movement is to achieve its own irrevelance.

A communalistic interpretation of socialism focuses on the ideal of *Kommunismus* elaborated by Marx. This is the second or "higher phase of communist society," which Marx thought attainable when a universal transformation of consciousness has been effected through the dictatorship of the proletariat.[31] The community enabled and intended to enjoy the ideal's realization is quite unlike previous communities, for it is one in which

> the enslaving subordination of the individual to the division of labour, and with it the antithesis between mental and physical labour has vanished; . . . labour is no longer merely a means of life but has become life's principal need; . . . the productive forces have also increased with the all-round development of the individual, and all the springs of cooperative wealth flow more abundantly.[32]

A key element here is the connection between the increase of "productive forces" and "the all-round development of the individual." Recently, Michael Harrington has argued that true socialism is possible now as never before because the world's productive capability is for the first time adequate to the needs of everyone.[33] As Marx had written, "Right can never be higher than the economic structure of society and the cultural development conditioned by it."[34] In others words, concern for the exigencies of life must cease to be a primary or predominant worry for anyone if the all-round development of *all* individuals is to be achieved. Harrington's argument thus provides a credible explanation for socialism's past failures and present hopes.

Rather optimistically, Marx construed the second phase of communism as "the true solution of the conflict between freedom and necessity, between individual and species."[35] Since he thought this goal achievable, he viewed human nature as capable of progressing from the egoism or "passion of greed" which motivates capitalism to a kind of passion for others' welfare.[36] The socialism or communism he foresaw was one where no person would want to live purely for her/himself but would prefer to use her/his energies for the common good. In the absence of private property and societal classes, all individuals would be considered and treated as equals by taking account of their differing needs and talents.

Present-day socialist regimes obviously fail to implement the principle of equality demanded by Marx's ideal. With regard to women, for example, Hilda Scott has pointed out that their "equal" right to work entails a quite unequal distribution of labor.[37] Under socialism women generally continue to work in the home as well as outside of it, while their male counterparts average several more hours of free time per day than they.[38] Totalitarian regimes also violate the principle of equality by preventing the democratic participation which Marx considered essential to socialism. Except for the Israeli kibbutzim, the only recent instance of democratic socialism was Chile under Allende. China, Cuba, Russia, and other nominally socialist or communist countries exemplify instead what Harrington calls anti-socialist socialism or communism.

In contrast with Marx, Harrington admits that "what socialism ultimately is . . . will never come to pass in its ideal form."[39] His implied view of human nature is thus less optimistic than Marx's. Nonetheless, Harrington insists on the practical necessity of detailing "the dream in order to better design each approximation of it," and thus outlines his vision of socialism as follows:

> It is the idea of an utterly new society in which some of the fundamental limitations of human existence have been transcended. Its most basic premise is that man's battle with nature has been completely won and there is therefore more than enough of material goods for everyone. As a result of this unprecedented change in the environment, a psychic mutation takes place: invidious competition is no longer programmed into the life by the necessity of a struggle for scarce resources; cooperation, fraternity and equality become natural. In such a world man's social productivity will reach such heights that compulsory work will no longer be necessary. And as more and more things are provided free, money, that universal equivalent by means of which necessities are rationed, will disappear.[40]

Clearly, for society to so devalue work and money would be "utterly new"; and to eliminate these from life would require drastic psychic mutations in most of humankind.

A term which may best describe the communalistic nature of Christianity is "church"—i.e., if church means "people of God," rather than an institution or hierarchical structure which exists apart from or regardless of Christians themselves.[41] As people of God, the church is necessarily comprised by a group of individuals whose primary interest extends beyond themselves and their own lives. Since the human Christ was one whose life was lived for others, Christians are called to emulate his spirit by living similarly. The primary interest of the Christian church is thus the entire community of humankind.

That entire community, according to Christian belief, is the work of a Creator God. But to believe in the existence of a Creator is to accept the Creator's effective definition of human nature. Sartre put the relevant argument quite logically: if God exists, then human beings are determined, and there is no absolute freedom. Accordingly, belief in creation is incompatible with a concept of raw or absolute freedom.

Other Christian beliefs imply a limitation to human freedom— for example, the doctrine of sin and punishment for sin. As

Augustine (among others) has pointed out, human beings are free to sin but not to avoid the consequences of sin. Further, since to be human is to be an *imago Dei,* one is only "free" to be human by sustaining the resemblance through avoidance of sin. "By abusing free choice," Augustine claims, "man loses both it and himself."[42] On a more philosophical level, Aquinas distinguishes between free choice and the necessitated will. "[S]ince choice is not of the end, but of the means," he writes, . . . "it is not of the perfect good. . . . Therefore, man chooses, not of necessity, but freely." On the other hand, "if the will be offered an object which is good universally and from every point of view [i.e., God], the will tends to it of necessity. . . ."[43] Ultimately, then, a Christian interpretation of freedom is limited through beliefs in creation, a final end, and the inevitable consequences of moral decisions.

To assert that Christian freedom is limited, however, does not imply that Christianity is communalistic. For a communalistic concept of freedom, the letter to the Galatians again provides a helpful source. According to Paul, the liberty to which Christians are called by Christ is essentially a freedom for service to others. "Be careful," he warns,

> or this liberty will provide an opening for self-indulgence. Serve one another, rather, in works of love, since the whole of the Law is summarized in a single command: Love your neighbor as yourself.[44]

In other words, love is the core of the gospel and of Christian life, but freedom is the precondition for love even as it is for sin. To use freedom to serve others lovingly is necessarily to build community, since love involves a dynamic and open-ended relationship between persons. Even as Plato described it in the *Symposium,* love is essentially life-giving, and non-exclusive. Love is thus communalistic rather than individualistic.

Unlike Marx, Christians acknowledge, through the doctrine of original sin, that human beings are naturally inclined towards selfishness. Nonetheless, their doctrine of grace provides a basis for faith that egoism can be overcome and replaced by a truly communalistic spirit. Since grace is a sharing in God's life, graced

Christians become one in a life which is essentially communalistic. Their initial and continuing participation in that life
always occurs in a communal setting. The priesthood in which all
Christians share is a call to build community in order to mediate
the presence of the Lord to his people. "Where two or three meet
in my name," Christ said, "I shall be there with them."[45] The
most effective sign of Christ's presence is Eucharist, where the
being-for-others of Christ is recalled and relived as Christians are
strengthened to be-for-others also.

By virtue of their belief in creation, original sin and grace,
Christians affirm a communalistic concept of equality. A question of Paul evokes realization of creaturely equality: "What do
you have that was not given to you?"[46] Since each one's needs
and talents are God's gift, there is obviously no justification for
regarding or treating one person as better than another. Then,
too, there is the example of Christ who loved the sinner even
while despising his/her sin. A recognition of equality is also
reinforced by the eschatological dimension of Christianity, since
the same finality applies to all, regardless of their natural differences. Only moral differences, based on each one's freedom,
affect differences in eternal destinies.

My use of the terms individualistic and communalistic in the
preceding account may be criticized as an oversimplification of
an extremely complex and almost unlimited range of meanings
which attach to three important ideologies. To some extent,
however, oversimplification is an inevitable aspect of our thinking
about things. Recognizing this, we may justifiably continue to
think about them so long as we avoid what Whitehead calls the
fallacy of misplaced concreteness.[47] Moreover, even while the
gap between concepts and reality perdures, our concepts do
influence real behavior. Accordingly, clarification and criticism
of the ideologies which affect our lives is not only justified but
morally demanded.

It may also be argued that purely individualistic or communalistic versions of the three ideologies ought not to be idealized
because the best justified ideal combines elements of both. There
should thus be a third context, which, as both individualistic and
communalistic, provides the only adequate rationale for the way

we live our lives. It is doubtful, however, that an even balance between individualistic and communalistic ideological components is either possible or justifiable. In the final analysis, one or the other emphasis predominates in ideologies as in practical decisions. While the emphasis may shift, individuals are free to determine the predominant thrust of their ideological allegiance.

In this article, while focusing on specifically individualistic and communalistic elements within feminism, socialism and Christianity, I have not buried my own ideological preferences. Since ideologies are not ultimately provable, these preferences are a matter of belief rather than of certain knowledge. More explicitly, then, I believe that a communalistic emphasis is essential to feminism, socialism and Christianity, and that certain individualistic goals can and should be achieved precisely because of a communalistic orientation. In other words, one is related to the other as means to end. Women's liberation, the dictatorship of the proletariat and the grace of Christ may all be viewed as individualistic means through which the communalistic ends of feminism, socialism and Christianity are to be procured. The communalistic end of feminism is human liberation: of socialism, the equitable distribution of the goods of production; of Christianity, a universal brother/sisterhood sustained through love. If equality is prerequisite to liberation, feminism requires socialism to achieve its purpose; and if freedom is a condition for loving, Christians must also be feminists in order to move towards their communalistic end. In light of that end, the three ideologies necessarily intersect.

A communalistic context also provides a criterion according to which individualistic goals may be evaluated. Basically, measures intended to promote the good of an individual person or group may be undertaken with the broader aim of benefitting everyone. If achievement of separate goods in any way impedes the welfare of others, their pursuit may not justifiably be sustained as means towards a communalistic end. In light of that end, then, ideological principles and practices ought continually to be reassessed.

With regard to feminism, for example, the argument favoring abortion on the basis of a pregnant women's exclusive right to decide the fate of the fetus is an argument that resists any communalistic interpretation. From the latter perspective, however, feminists may argue that abortion is permissible in some circumstances for the good of the wider community (including the fetus). Or, as Sydney Callahan has maintained, that societal responsibility for every individual (including fetuses) is directly proportionate to the need of each. In either case, the morality of individual decisions depends upon their communalistic orientation.

With regard to socialism, individualistic measures can only be justified insofar as they contribute to a growing communalistic emphasis within society. Such growth of spirit is clearly impossible in a situation where individual freedom is dictatorially suppressed, but growth may be facilitated through an equitable distribution of goods and labor, and through efforts to teach both bourgeoisie and proletariat to overcome their natural tendency towards selfishness. If society, however, merely reinforces that tendency—e.g., through an emphasis on competition, a communalistic orientation can only be impeded.

For Christians, the grace that is given to individuals to enable them to procure their own salvation is thwarted if its purpose is not interpreted communalistically. Paradoxically, only the person who is willing to lose his/her life for others will ever find it.[48] Christians who primarily pursue their own freedom or equality, whether as individuals or as a group, fail in both pursuits because such goals can only be fully achieved for some by being achieved for all. The goal of ordination for women is an example of an individualistic means that is justifiable by reason of its essential relationship to a wider community. But since the right and responsibility of building community belongs to all Christians, it is also arguable that priesthood should not be limited to some women and men but available to all the people of God.

In the context of an errant human nature, the communalistic ideal of universal liberation, equity and love admittedly constitutes an impossible dream. Nevertheless, such ends may not even be approximated except through their being consciously and energetically pursued. Realistically, then, a communalistic emphasis within feminism, socialism and Christianity gives hope for practical progress towards the dream's realization.

Notes

1. I am using the term "community" here as it is used in ordinary language—i.e., to signify a group of individuals who share a common goal or interest. Elsewhere I have elaborated a more detailed and demanding concept of community; e.g., in "Community in Royce: An Interpretation," *Transactions of the Charles S. Peirce Society* V, 4 (Fall 1969), 224–242, and in "Marx's *Gemeinschaft:* Another Interpretation," *Philosophy and Phenomenological Research* XXXIII, 4 (June 1973), 472–488.

2. What I mean by "radical" and "moderate" feminism will be indicated as the essay progresses. Others have elaborated various feminist positions more fully, sometimes using different labels; e.g., Juliet Mitchell, *Woman's Estate* (Baltimore: Penguin Books, 1966), William T. Blackstone, "Freedom and Women," *Ethics* 85, 3 (April 1975), 243–245, and Beverly Wildung Harrison, "The New Consciousness of Women: A Socio-political Resource," this journal XXIV, 4 (Winter 1975), 460, n. 1. I do not here attempt a comprehensive critical categorization of the diverse strains of feminism (which are certainly more than two), but simply to provide examples of individualistic and communalistic emphases found within its range of variant interpretations.

3. From an informational brochure distributed by the Philadelphia Chapter of the National Organization of Women (P.O. Box 15505, Pa. 19131).

4. Quoted by Ti-Grace Atkinson in *Amazon Odyssey* (New York: Links Books, 1974), 10.

5. Cf. item VIII of NOW's founding *Bill of Rights* (1967): "The right of women to control their own reproductive lives by repealing penal laws governing abortion." Cited in Robin Morgan (ed.), *Sisterhood Is Powerful* (New York: Vintage Books, 1970), 514. Also, the "true right to life" is "that of being able to control one's own body." (*NOW News*, Bloomington, Indiana, April 1974). The claim that a pregnant woman has an exclusive "right to choice" regarding the fate of the fetus illustrates the concept of raw freedom implied by a pure individualism.

6. A group of feminists who have accordingly rejected NOW's position as anti-feminist are called "Feminists for Life."

7. "Our Revolution Is Unique," in M. L. Thompson (ed.), *Voices of the New Feminism* (Boston: Beacon Press, 1970), 40.

8. Manifesto of "The Feminists: A Political Organization to Annihilate Sex Roles," in S. Firestone (ed.), *Notes from the Second Year: Women's Liberation* (New York: P.O. Box AA, Old Chelsea Station), 116.

9. *Amazon Odyssey*, 9.

10. Ibid., 10.

11. Ibid., 57–63.

12. According to The Feminists, the "institution of love" is a "self-defense developed by the female to prevent her from seeing her powerless situation. . . . Heterosexual love is a delusion in yet another sense: it is a means of escape from the role system by way of approval from and identification with the man, who has defined himself as humanity (beyond role). . . ." *Notes from the Second Year*, 117.

13. I might have used the term "collectivistic" to describe an ideological stress on class. But this would suggest a third orientation, and there are really only two: one that is essentially inward with limited goals (which I have called individualistic whether the self be one or many), and one that is essentially outward and open-ended. A "collectivistic emphasis" could conceivably focus in either direction.

14. "Critique of the Gotha Programme" (1875), trans. by T. B. Bottomore in *Karl Marx Selected Writings in Sociology and Social Philosophy* (New York: McGraw-Hill Book Company, 1964), 258.

15. Ibid., 256.

16. Ibid., 258.

17. Cited by Robert V. Daniels in *The Nature of Communism* (New York: Random House, 1961), 87.

18. Ibid.

19. E.g., Nancy van Vuuren, *The Subversion of Women* (Philadelphia: The Westminster Press, 1973), Letty M. Russell, *Human Liberation in a Feminist Perspective—a Theology* (Philadelphia: The Westminster Press, 1974), and Mary Daly, *Beyond God the Father* (Boston: Beacon Press, 1973). Among those who have elaborated connections between Marxist and Christian principles are Quentin Lauer and Roger Garaudy, *A Christian-Communist Dialogue* (Garden City: Doubleday and Company, Inc., 1968) and Joseph M. Petulla, *Christian Political Theology, A Marxian Guide* (New York: Orbis Books, 1972).

20. Liberation theology also provides a link between feminism and

socialism. Two recent works pertinent to such connections are Rene Laurentin, *Liberation, Development and Salvation* (New York: Orbis Books, 1972), and Rosemary Ruether, *Liberation Theology* (New York: Paulist Press, 1972).

21. 5:13, 1. All citations from Scripture are from *The Jerusalem Bible*.

22. *Ep. Joan.*, vii, 5 (PL 35, 2033), cited by Joseph Fletcher, *Situation Ethics* (Philadelphia: The Westminster Press, 1966), 79. Fletcher translates the original text ("Dilege, et quod vis fac") as "Love with care and *then* what you will, do."

23. Matt. 16:26.

24. 161.

25. "A Call for the Castration of Sexist Religion," in Alice L. Hageman (ed.), *Sexist Religion and Women in the Church* (New York: Association Press, 1974), 138.

26. Thompson, 40.

27. Ibid., 41.

28. Ibid., 32.

29. Ibid., 36.

30. (New York: McGraw-Hill Book Company, 1971), 328–329.

31. Bottomore, 258.

32. Ibid.

33. Cf. *Socialism* (New York: Saturday Review Press, 1970).

34. Bottomore, 258.

35. Ibid., 244.

36. *Cf.* Robert Tucker, *Philosophy and Myth in Karl Marx* (New York: Cambridge University Press, 1961), 213.

37. *Does Socialism Liberate Women?* (Boston: Beacon Press, 1974). Scott elaborates her negative answer to the book's title through a focus on the Czechoslovak experience.

38. Ibid., 106.

39. Harrington, 344.

40. Ibid.

41. Cf. Chapter II, "Dogmatic Constitution on the Church," W. M. Abbott (ed.), *The Documents of Vatican II* (New York: America Press, 1966), 24–37.

42. *Enchrididion,* XXX (PL 40, 246), cited by Aquinas in *Basic Writings of Saint Thomas Aquinas,* Vol. One, ed. by A. Pegis (New York: Random House, 1945), 788.

43. *Summa Theologica I-II, Ibid.,* Vol. Two, 262, 285.

44. 5:13–15.

45. Matt. 18:20.

46. I Cor. 4:7.

47. Cf. Alfred North Whitehead, *Process and Reality* (New York: Harper Torchbooks, 1960), 11. According to Whitehead, "[t]his fallacy consists in neglecting the degree of abstraction involved when an actual entity is considered merely so far as it exemplifies certain categories of thought. . . . The aim at generalization is sound, but the estimate of success is exaggerated."

48. Cf. Matt. 16:25.

LEONARDO BOFF

The Need for Political Saints

Leonardo Boff, O.F.M., divides his time between teaching and writing and pastoral work with base communities of the Brazilian poor. His Jesus Christ Liberator *and* Passion of Christ, Passion of the World *are classics of liberation theology, while his* Trinity and Society *offers a new understanding of traditional trinitarian teaching. Religious custom, and not only Christian religious custom, has tended to recognize holiness primarily in those set apart—in monastic men and women, for example, rather than in a husband and wife who work their farm and, exhausted at day's end, turn to the holy as best they can. As a result, religions have largely developed spiritual ways suited to a consecrated minority, ways that are then adapted—watered down—to meet the needs of the rest of the community. Boff here proposes a different way, where prayer is "materialized in action" and expresses the liberating community, where liturgy celebrates life, and the place of political sanctity is made clear.*

I n recent years the Latin American church has been increasingly aware of the responsibility of faith for social changes that would promote greater justice and participation for the masses of the poor. In the light of faith, and in evangelical solidarity with the neediest, numerous and significant church groups, even entire episcopates, are trying more and more to live and teach the Christian faith in a way that would make it a driving force for integral human liberation. Thus, an extensive and well-articulated liberation process is underway in the midst of Christian communities, a process rooted in the unity of faith and life. In addition, a corresponding critical discourse has been developed, called "liberation theology," a theology developed in the interests of integral liberation, particularly of the most oppressed sectors of society. However, what sustains this liberating theory (theology) and practice is a spiritual encounter with the Lord amidst the poor.[1] Behind all innovative practice within the church, at the root of every genuinely new theology, there lies hidden a typical religious experience, which constitutes the word-source; everything else proceeds from that all-encompassing experience, trying to work out a translation within the framework of a historically determined reality. Only by starting from this presupposition can we understand the great syntheses of past theologians such as St. Augustine, St. Anselm, St. Thomas, St. Bonaventure, and Suarez, or of present day theologians such as Rahner and other spiritual masters.

All spiritual experience means an encounter with a new and challenging face of God that emerges from the great challenges of historical reality. Great socio-historical changes carry within themselves an ultimate meaning, a supreme demand that is identified by religious minds as originating from the mystery of God. God has meaning only when in fact he emerges as that which is radically important within a reality presented in its lights and shadows. In this way, God does not appear as a defined category within a religious framework, but rather as a meaningful event, speaking of hope and an absolute future for the history of men and women. This situation encourages a natural and typical experience of the mystery of God.

What we have emphasized thus far implies the subjective moment of the experience. However, it can also be stated in strictly theological terms: in his desire for self-communication, God reveals himself concretely in history. We perceive a new face of God, because God is revealing himself in this way. He establishes sacramental signs, chooses messengers, fosters the growth of an adequate discourse, and encourages consistent practices. And there will always be attentive spirits capable of identifying the new voice of God and being faithful to his call.

We believe that in recent years there has been a volcanic

eruption of God in our Latin American continent: he has privileged the poor as his sacrament of self-communication. Through
the poor, his demands for solidarity, identity, justice and dignity,
are being heard. And the churches have been obedient (*ob-
audire:* to listen) to God's appeal. Faced with the scandal of
poverty, we are urged to act on behalf of the poor, against poverty
and for justice for all. This activity has a clear dimension of
liberation that emerges as a process of giving historic grounding
to a faith that wishes to be united to the Lord who is present in
the poor. To struggle with the poor and to embody their desires is
to communicate with the poor Christ and to live in his company.
This perspective implies being contemplative while working toward liberation—"contemplativus in liberatione"—and presupposes a new way of seeking sanctity and mystical union with
God. The spiritual encounter with this new manifestation of God
has produced certain traits that are inherent to a spirituality lived
and practiced by many Christians who are committed to the
complete liberation of their brothers and sisters. The shock of
that encounter lies at the roots of liberation theology. Before
attempting to describe that spirituality, however, it would be
useful to situate it within the great spiritual tradition of the
church and also to emphasize its originality. The problem we
need to clarify is how to be contemplative within the liberation
process; how to live out a vivid and concrete encounter with God
in our pastoral practices and in contact with the people.

1

Obviously, the classical formulation of the search for the unity
of faith and life was made by the monastic tradition with its
motto, "ora et labora," pray and work. It is not possible here to
trace the history of that inspiration, but we can grasp its basic
thrust, in which there is a clear predominance of the "pray" over
the "work." This spirituality takes the time of prayer and of
contemplation, alternating with that of work, as the organizational axis of spiritual life. Prayer is the source of all value and is
expressed in liturgy, choral office, devotional exercises, and the

entire range of religious expression. Work, in itself, is not direct
mediation with God, but has value to the extent that it is bathed
in the influence of prayer and contemplation. It means the profane and the purely natural; it constitutes the field of ethical
expression and is that part of human testimony in which meaning
is developed within the context of prayer. In other words, prayer
prolongs itself in work, and makes it sacred as well. The whole
conception implies a type of "spiritual monophysitism": the
unique nature of prayer redeems the creaturely and natural pro-
faneness of work. For this reason, there is the persistence of a
parallelism that is never entirely overcome: on the one hand,
prayer; and on the other hand, work. The conjunction "and" is
indicative of this theological bilingualism. In any case, this spirituality fills the work of many Christians with prayer and elevation, and has provided religious signs for every area of life that
was considered profane.

Socio-historical developments led to a relative autonomy of
the profane and a culture of words.[2] Functionality and efficiency
are the axes of the new culture, the ultimate expression of which
is found today in the combined scientific-technological enterprise. The motto is inverted: "labora et ora," work and pray. The
divine and Christ-like character of work, as a form of human
collaboration with divine creation, has been discovered. God did
not leave us a finished world as a gift, but wished to associate us
with his transforming task. Work possesses its own dignity and
sacredness, not because it is baptized by prayer or as a result of
supernaturalizing good intentions, but rather because of its own
creative nature, inserted into the christological project. What
matters is the work done in its own legitimate order, directed to
the construction of the earthly city intended by God, in anticipation of the heavenly city. It is especially the work of justice,
committed to the needs of the poor, that achieves what all prayer
seeks—contact with God. The prophetic tradition is explicit with
regard to this (cf. Is. 1:10–20; Jr. 22:16) and Jesus refers to it
directly (Mk 7:6–8). It is not preaching but practice that is our
guarantee of salvation (Mt. 25, 31–46). Prayer continues to have
its place, but its truthfulness is measured by its expression in
genuine and ethically correct practice. In its most radical form,

this spirituality of the divine character of matter, and of the work performed on it, leads to an emptiness of prayer and of liturgical and devotional expression.

This perspective emphasizes the objective character of prayer, which pervades all spheres and is not restricted to the field of awareness and explicitness. In other words, the presence of God is not attained automatically nor exclusively wherever God is spoken of or his memory is worshipped, but always and objectively wherever a correct practice of truth and justice occurs in history, even if an explicit awareness of God does not exist. However, the predominance of work, religiously lived, over prayer, may create a new type of "spiritual monophysitism"; prayer becomes another form of work and of practice, losing its specific character as prayer. We are still speaking of work "and" prayer, and have not yet reached the unity of faith-life, action-prayer.

The synthesis that needs to be made and that is in gestation in Latin America is that of prayer *in* action, *within* action and *with* action. It is not a question of keeping prayer and action in separate compartments, nor of prayer outside of a concrete commitment to the liberation of the oppressed, but rather of prayer inserted in the process of liberation, living out an encounter with God "in" the encounter with our brothers and sisters. We may say that every great saint achieved that vital and concrete synthesis, which always constituted the secret of all authentically Christian life.

In Latin America, however, we are called to live in a somewhat new situation, or at least one with very distinctive tones. The problem does not lie merely in the prayer-action relationship, but in that of prayer-liberation—that is, prayer and political, social, historical, transforming action. In its correct formulation, the matter should be dealt with in terms of mysticism and politics. How can one be radically committed to the liberation of the oppressed and at the same time committed to the source of all liberation, which is God? How can one combine passion for God, which is characteristic of every truly religious person, with passion for the people and their justice, which is the distinctive trait of all political militants? In order to be complete and consistent, this synthesis should make use of all the richness of "ora et labora," of prayer as a privileged encounter with the Lord; it should also make use of all the truth present in "labora et ora," of the value of work and the commitment to achieve justice and fraternity.

It is not a question of achieving a verbal synthesis or a correct correlation of the terms. It is a question of living out a Christian practice that is simultaneously involved with prayer and commitment, so that commitment is born out of prayer, and prayer emerges from the midst of that commitment. How can this be achieved?

2

The experience of a genuine and living faith constitutes the unity of prayer-liberation. However, the experience of faith must be correctly understood. To begin with, faith is a way of experiencing all things in God's light. Faith defines the "from where" and the "towards where" of our existence, which is God and his design of love, that is communicated through, and materialized in, all things. To the person of faith, reality is not profane and sacred in origin, but simply sacramental: it reveals God, it evokes God, it is imbued with the divine reality. For this reason, the faith experience confers unity on life, because it contemplates the reality consolidated by God as the origin and the destiny of all things. As a way of life, the living faith implies a contemplative stance towards the world: it finds the touch of God everywhere. It is not enough, however, for faith to be alive; it is important that it be real. But only a faith transformed into love, truth and justice is real. Those who please God are not those who merely "accept" him, but rather those who build his Kingdom of truth, love and justice. Only such a committed faith is redeeming, and thus real faith. "Faith without deeds is useless" (Jas. 2:20). Demons, too, have pure faith but without deeds. (Jas. 2:19).

Christian faith knows that Christ has a sacramental density among the poor. They not only have needs that should be assisted; they possess a unique and intrinsic richness: privileged carriers of the Lord, principal heirs of the Kingdom, with the potential for evangelizing all nations and the church as a whole (Puebla 1147). The faithful do not simply have a socio-analytical conception of the poor, but identify with their passion and the causes of their impoverishment. Assuming all this,[3] the Christian watches the class of the impoverished with eyes of faith and discovers in them the suffering face of Yahweh's servant. Such an observation is not limited to contemplation, as if one were "using" the poor in order to be united with the Lord. Christ identifies himself with the poor and wishes to be served and received there. This miserable situation produces a fundamental change of heart: "I was hungry. . . ." (Mt. 23:25). One is truly with the Lord when among the poor, when committed to struggle against poverty, since it humiliates people, contradicts the will of God, and is the fruit of exploitative and sinful relations. Faith itself implies and demands a liberating commitment: "and you fed me" (Mt. 25:36). If you do not engage in liberating action, not only do you not love your neighbor, but you do not love God (1 Jo. 3:17). Love must not be merely "of words and talk, but something real and active" (1 Jo. 3:18).

Such a spiritual experience confers unity on the faith-life (or mysticism-politics) relationship. But how can we maintain that unity? How can we nurture it in the face of so many segregating forces? A vision that is both contemplative and liberating does not emerge spontaneously; although it is the most meaningful expression of living faith. But how can one make this faith consistent?

Here two poles emerge: prayer and practice. However, we must avoid remaining within this polarization, for we would then once again fall into one of the "monophysitisms" that we criticized earlier. It is necessary to articulate the two poles dialectically, treating them as two spaces that are open to one another and imply each other. However, one of the two poles of the relationship must be privileged—prayer.

Through prayer, we express the most noble and profound aspect of our existence. We can transcend ourselves and all the greatness of creation and history; we enter an ecstatic condition and in dialogue with the Supreme mystery cry out, "Father!"

With this, we do not leave the Universe but transform it as an offering to God; we free ourselves from all chains, denounce all historical absolutes, and alone and nude, confront the Absolute in order to make history with Him. There God is discovered as the Holy; we are in the face of the most high and the most solemn. Nevertheless, this God, holy as he is, reveals himself as a committed God, who is sensitive to the sorrows of the oppressed. He can say: "I saw the oppression of my people . . . I heard their complaints against the oppressors, I stopped to see their sufferings and I descended to liberate them . . ." (Ex. 3:7–8). Hence, the God who through prayer says to us, "Come!", in that same prayer also says "Go!" The God who calls upon us is the same God who drives us on in a commitment to liberation. He commands us to unite the passion for God with the passion for the oppressed. Better yet, he demands that the passion of God in Jesus Christ be lived out in the passion of our suffering and needy brothers and sisters.

Action in the service of our brothers and sisters and in solidarity with their struggles for liberation grows from within the very midst of the prayer which reaches God's heart. Prayer aids the believer to see the sacramental presence of the Lord in the poor and in every variety of exploited people. Without prayer, rooted in faith, our sight becomes blurred and superficial; it cannot penetrate into that depth of theological mysticism in which it enters in communion with the Lord, who is present among the condemned, humiliated and offended peoples of history.

On the other hand, the pole of liberating practice sends us back to the pole of prayer as the source which sustains our strength in the struggle and guarantees Christian identity in the process of liberation. Christians are concerned that it be a genuine liberation, an anticipation of the Kingdom and the concretization of Jesus' redemption in history. Faith and prayer allow them to consider their efforts (which are often of little relevance) as an historical construction of the Kingdom. Social practice has its concrete and intramundane density, but its significance does not end there; faith unveils its transcendental meaning and its redeeming importance. For someone who understands this per-

spective, the liberating service to our brothers and sisters constitutes a true deaconry to the Lord, an act of association to his
redeeming and liberating task, and a true liturgy to the spirit.
This is what it means to be "contemplativus in liberatione."
Contemplation is not carried out only within the sacred space of
prayer, nor in the sacred precinct of the church; purified, sustained and nurtured by living faith, it also finds its place in
political and social practice.

The fact that those bishops, priests, religious and laity who are
most committed to the cause of the poor (their justice, rights, and
dignity) are also the most committed to prayer is a noble characteristic of our Latin American Church; they unite God and the
neediest neighbor into one movement of love and dedication.

3

How might we identify some of the most meaningful traits of
this contemplation that is lived out in the context of liberation?[4]

a) Prayer materialized in action. Liberating prayer gathers
together all the material of a committed life: the struggles, collective efforts, the errors, and the victories; thanks are given for the
steps that have been taken; one asks, not individualistically but
in terms of a long-range effort, for those who suffer and for those
who cause suffering; in prayer, the strife-torn nature of the liberation process is echoed; the confession of sins is spontaneously
collective; no one hides behind ethereal words but rather opens
one's heart to the most intimate matters. It is a prayer that
reflects the liberation of the heart; one is forced to confront the
incongruity between what is professed and what is practiced,
especially the lack of solidarity and of commitment.

b) Prayer, an expression of the liberating community. Although prayer has its permanent and guaranteed value, among
committed Christians prayer is essentially a sharing of experiences and practices, illuminated and criticized in the light of faith
and of the Gospel. The experience is not limited to a splendid
privacy of the soul with God, but opens itself through listening
and communication. One comforts the other; comments on the

problems of the other; people help each other deal with the problems that are presented; there is no sacred "shame" that hides divine visits and illuminations. The great majority present their souls as an open book, which already reveals the process of liberation in the midst of the community.

c) Liturgy as a celebration of life. A canonical liturgy maintains its bonding character and expresses the catholicity of the expression of our faith. But to the extent that communities unite life and faith, mysticism and politics, they increasingly insert the celebration of life shared by all into the liturgy. A rich creativity grows out of this field, possessing a dignity and sacredness that are guaranteed by the refined idea that the people possess within themselves what is sacred and noble. Meaningful group symbols are utilized, and sometimes genuinely religious dances and plays are produced as expressions of the people themselves.

d) Hetero-critical prayer. Liberating prayer frequently serves as a critical examination of the practices and attitudes of a community's participants. They are able to criticize each other without embarrassment and without wounding each other. What matters are the objective criteria: the Kingdom, liberation, respect for the progress of the people. On the basis of such realities, the practices of pastoral agents are confronted. Genuine assistance is given and true conversions occur because of this sincerity and loyalty.

e) Political sanctity. Christian tradition knows the ascetic saint, master of his or her passions and faithful observer of the laws of God and of the Church. But there are hardly any political and militant saints. In the process of liberation, the conditions were created for another type of sanctity: in addition to struggling against one's passions (a permanent task), one struggles against the mechanisms of exploitation and the forces that tend to destroy the community. Here, more real and difficult virtues emerge: solidarity with one's class, participation in community decisions, loyalty to the solutions that are defined, the overcoming of hatred against those who are agents of the mechanisms of impoverishment, the capacity to see beyond the immediate present and to work for a society that is not yet visible and will perhaps never be enjoyed. This new type of asceticism, if it is to keep the hearts pure and be led by the spirit of the beatitudes, has demands and renunciations of its own.

f) Prophetic courage and historical patience. Many committed Christians have the courage, *sustained by* faith and prayer, to confront the powers of the world by struggling for the causes of the people and their trampled dignity. They show the apostolical self-surrender of risking themselves to the point of suffering persecution, imprisonment, job dismissals, tortures and even physical elimination. In spite of this evangelical courage, they have historical patience for the slow advance of the people; accustomed to repression, militants are sensitive to often hesitant rhythm. However, Christians have faith in the people, in their courage and capacity to struggle, in spite of their limitations, mistakes and intellectual backwardness. Men and women who are committed fervently believe in the strength of the Spirit who acts through the poor and suffering, and in the triumph of their cause and in their right to struggle. This attitude is rooted in a contemplative view of history, of which only God is the Lord.

g) Paschal attitude. Every liberation pays a price; death and resurrection must be accepted with evangelical joy and serenity. Sacrifices, threats, and even martyrdom are not feared, but are simply part of following Jesus. There is a strong sense of the cross as a necessary step toward victory. Resurrection is lived as the moment in which justice triumphs, in which the people win the struggle and make life more worthy of being lived. It is the resurrection of Jesus advancing as an immense liberation process that moves through history. This is celebrated and lived as the strength of the Spirit's presence in history.

We could list more characteristics of this type of prayer, which becomes more and more real within communities that are committed to the liberation of the neediest. The unity of prayer-action, faith-liberation, and the passion for God expressed in passion for the people, always reappears. Each time further new objective possibilities are created that favor the emergence of a new kind of Christian, deeply committed to the earthly city and at the same time to the celestial city, convinced that this depends on the way we insert ourselves in the creation of the former. Heaven is not an enemy of earth; it already begins here on earth;

both draw their life from the liberating action of God, in Jesus Christ.

All this is not academic theology, but the life and mysticism of many Christians today.

Translated by Linde Rivera and Leon King

Notes

1. Some important titles: Frei Betto, *Prayer in Action,* Civilizacão Brasileira, Rio 1977; S. Galilea, *Spirituality of Liberation,* Vozes, Petropolis 1976; Theologians at Puebla, "Spirituality and Evangelization: Towards a Spirituality of Liberation," in SEDOC July/August 1979, pp. 72–79; L. Boff, *Witnesses of God in the Heart of the World,* Instituto Teologico de Vida Religiosa, Madrid 1977.

2. With the culture of work something unprecedented in the history of humankind was created; there was a total activation of productive forces, modifying humanity and its world. It is no longer simply a matter of working, but rather of producing the maximum with the minimum amount of investment. Today, this has a world-wide dimension. The Church has not yet adequately assimilated this revolution. Ethics, spirituality, and theology are still too marked by the world of natural rhythms and by the harmony of the old world. It was an uncontested achievement of the capitalist system—and its great contradiction—to have introduced this qualitative change in history.

3. The Christian militant, accustomed to the complexity of the social reality, which today is extremely sophisticated and can only be understood with the help of scientific tools, must strengthen his faith vision to the maximum in order to grasp the presence or absence of God and his grace in socio-historical mechanisms. Today, more than at any other time in history, there is a need for prayer united with political sagacity, for mystical theology articulated with a critical analysis of reality.

4. One great difficulty of this spirituality of liberation lies in the fact that the history of the church presents few or almost no saints who achieved the synthesis between the mystical and the political as they are understood today. St. Francis of Assisi, St. Bernard of Siena, St. Vincent, and a few others had an attitude which in our judgment was more one of offering help than of liberating. They did not move, nor did

they have the theoretical and practical conditions to do so, within a political framework in which alternatives, at times radical ones, are imposed in the name of faith/or justice. This is the great challenge of our times: to create militants with a truly political holiness. It is important that we be both holy and political, in the full sense of the word.

THOMAS BERRY

Classical Western Spirituality and the American Experience

Thomas Berry, director of the Riverdale Center for Religious Research, has most recently published The Dream of Earth. *His central concern has long been to bring to consciousness "a modern world responsive to the spiritual, a spiritual tradition responsive to the modern world" ("Traditional Religion in the Modern World,"* Cross Currents, *Spring 1972). That concern has in recent years been wedded to his sense that there is emerging a new story of origins, a new cosmology that gives rise to a new spirituality of the ecological age. Berry here contends that identification of the divine and the human as transcendent to the natural world, along with belief in a millennium infallibly to come as the redemptive order unfolds, have unleashed demonic forces in the form of an American compulsion to use, consume, and dominate nature. Classical spirituality has emphasized salvation dynamics at the expense of creation dynamics. At the same time, other elements in its experience should give America a special affinity for the new cosmology and the spirituality to which it gives rise.*

The American experience can be presented in terms of enlightenment philosophy, post-reformation christianity, scientific competence, technological skill, commercial drive and military might; all let loose on what might be the richest, most benign, surely one of the most beautiful and unspoiled of continents. After some four centuries of the American experience we have before us a still beautiful and abundant land but also a land of roads and automobiles and grimy cities, a land of acid rainfall, polluted rivers and endangered species, a land extensively plundered of its forests and its mineral resources, a land with its human inhabitants somewhat bewildered and somewhat rebellious against their role as the great consumer people of earth.

Much has happened in these centuries, glory and wealth and knowledge and power; all these and their opposite. It's too confused a story to tell, the story of the American experience, although it is a story as exciting as any story of a comparable period of time. The Roman story is not greater, nor is the Chinese story, nor the story of any of the great classical ages. Indeed the American story has about it a magnitude and a meaning that baffles all our efforts at understanding. Such power, such ideals of human freedom, such commercial cunning, such a sense of historical destiny, and all brought together in an attempt to bring the entire world into the millennial age.

1

Without judging events as good or evil, looking at America simply as historical drama we can see and contemplate the human venture in one of its most spectacular phases. From the beginning the resources of the continent and the possibilities of life on this continent were to be activated. The land and everything on the land and under land was to be transformed. Nothing was to be left in its primordial state. The view of Francis Bacon that human intelligence had as its primary purpose the understanding and control of nature found its fulfillment here.

Today we can reflect on the causes for this and its meaning and the relation this bears to classical western spirituality of the past and to the emerging spirituality of the future. Strangely enough, perhaps, we might consider the American experience itself as one of the great spiritualities. In this manner we could speak of three spiritualities: the classical western spirituality, the more

recent American spirituality and the emerging spirituality that is
the challenge and the task of our present generation.

I have already referred to the destructive aspect of the American experience largely because public spiritualities generally
have a demonic aspect and I am primarily interested in public
spirituality, which I describe as "the functional values and their
means of attainment in an identifiable human community." This
public spirituality is, I think, much more interesting and much
more significant than the cultivated spirituality of marginal
groups or individuals engaged in intensive prayer and meditation
apart from the dynamics of the larger human community. Their
life and their guidance are of significant import for the human
venture; but the ultimate spiritual issues are those dealt with in
the cruel as well as the compassionate world of active human
existence, in the market place, in the halls of justice and injustice,
in the places where the populace lives and works and suffers and
dies. The glory of an earlier period, as described by Paul Claudel,
was the medieval cathedral that arched over the cross-roads of
the world with all its surging presence of good and evil, whereas
in later times the ideal of religion and spirituality frequently met
with is more that of the withdrawn place of worship, a place
reflecting more boudoir intimacy than market-place turmoil, a
place of undisturbed goodness and divine presence. This is true
even when extensive efforts are made in the evangelical tradition
of mercy and social justice.

But even while we locate the area of our discussion as that of
public spirituality I would like to indicate that any realistic discussion of our subject must take place in the context of the
supreme historical event of recent times, the discovery of a new
origin story, the story of the universe as emergent evolutionary
process over some fifteen billion years, a story that now provides
our sense of where we are in the total context of the universe
development. Our new consciousness of the universe and of the
planet earth can be understood as a revelatory experience of
universal significance for the human community and for every
phase of human activity.

So significant is this new story of the universe that all human
roles, all professions, all programs, are profoundly altered in a

manner somewhat like the manner in which the entire planet earth and its integral functioning were altered when life appeared, or the manner in which the entire human venture was altered when the great religions came into being. This is the order of magnitude of the change that has taken place, although its effect is still delayed and its major impact is still to be recognized throughout most areas of life. This is to be expected of an event so momentous in its significance. We of this generation are caught in a transitional situation; our own experience of the universe as it comes to us through scientific observation and inquiry has given us the power that enables us to journey into space and to visit the moon; that enables us to perform calculations at a rate soon to attain the measure of a billion operations a second; that enables us to pick out of the surrounding air thousands of radio messages; that enables us to hear presently through microwave radiation the sound of the early emergent universe back through some billions of years; all this and much more could be listed including our amazing capacity to understand and even to alter genetic coding. Yet with such a magical world as we have made, or discovered, we have no functional cosmology to guide and discipline our human use of all this knowledge and skill and all these energy resources.

We really do not understand the new story of the universe or its meaning. We have the scientific data. We can perform the magic. But the scientists themselves, until recently, seldom manifested any sense whatsoever of what it all means. To do this has been considered to compromise scientific integrity. Indeed during the great period of scientific inquiry after Newton, cosmology as a study diminished considerably in importance. Analytical processes alone provided true knowledge. Only in recent decades has cosmology come back into the area of serious consideration, and indeed we are still fumbling about with the whole subject just as we are vainly trying to comprehend the historical and human meaning of technology, how it relates to the biosphere, its role in the total earth process. The extent of intellectual paralysis in regard to these critical issues is astounding as this occurs in scientists, technologists and commercial persons. The real tragedy, however, is that religious and spiritual persons themselves remain blissfully unaware of their need to provide for themselves and for the society a more significant evaluation of this larger context of their lives. For the pious to say that God alone suffices is to avoid the issue and to betray God himself by disdaining his creation. On both sides, the scientific and the pietistic, there is a naivete that is ruinous to the human community, to the essential functioning of the biosphere, and eventually disastrous to the earth itself.

Because we have no functional cosmology we have no adequate spirituality; nor in this situation can our inquiry into the spiritualities of the past be of any great significance. We have abundant knowledge of both classical spirituality and the American experience but no adequate interpretation. A context for partial understanding can be obtained by seeing how traditional western spirituality conditioned the American experience or how American experience altered classical western spirituality. Another way of approaching the subject might be to see how both these enter into the larger dimensions of the human-earth process. In this latter case we situate our thinking within the context of the functional cosmic-human process which I am proposing as the context in which the total human venture must now be seen.

2

One important consideration concerning our subject is that classical western spirituality provided the context in which not only the creative but also the destructive aspect of the American experience can be seen. While the positive and creative aspects of western spirituality are present throughout the American experience, there are also the negative, alienating and even destructive aspects of these same spiritual traditions. That traditional western spirituality has not enabled its followers to control, resist or even to understand the terrifying assault of American society on the natural world is evidence of a serious weakness, lack of understanding, or even of a demonic aspect of western spirituality. It might not be too much to say that classical western spirituality not only provided much of the context in which this assault became possible but that it also provided a positive, if often indirect, support for this process. Without this background the course of the American experience might well have been quite different from what it has been. We must, however, be constantly aware that the American experience has resulted from a complex of forces and conditions beyond human calculation. Thus we are not proposing that classical western spirituality is the only force involved, only that it is a pervasive force of great significance in understanding the total process. In evidence of this we might consider the following:

First, there is the identification of the divine as transcendent to the natural world. Thereby we make a direct human-divine relationship possible but also we negate the natural world as the locus for the meeting of the divine and the human. The natural world becomes less capable of communicating divine presence.

A second aspect of classical western spirituality that made the demonic element in the American experience possible is in establishing the human also as transcendent to the natural world. This increased the alienation and isolation of the natural world from the divine and the spiritual and made possible the conception of the natural world as merely external object. A further step in degradation came later, out of the western philosophical tradition when in the philosophy of Descartes not only the divine and the human were taken away from intimate presence to the natural world but when all inner dynamism was taken away, even the life principle. The concept of crass matter emerged as mere extension capable only of external, manipulated and mechanistic activity. This redounded upon the human itself in the 18th century when La Mettrie wrote his book *Man the Machine*.

A third influence of the earlier spirituality on the American experience is in its doctrine of an infra-historical millenial age of bliss to be infallibly attained in the unfolding of the redemptive order. The concept of the millenium is different from the idea of Utopia or Paradise or Arcadia. Utopia is an ideal model for human society that is never expected to be achieved in itself, but is intended simply as an outline of basic forms of human life in order to assist in thinking through how they might best function in the social and personal order. Paradise is that transcendent beatitude expressed in intimate forms of bodily and spiritual delight. Arcadia is a quiet pastoral ideal that comes down to us from Roman times and is associated with a certain serene if poignant sense of existence in a garden apart from the tragic world of time. It is considered the best possibility of restoring an original earthly paradise.

All of these ideals influenced America, but the millenial drive is the strongest. When this millenial age did not appear by divine grace, the American people felt an obligation to raise it up by human effort. This is the original dynamism of American political life. The millenium also provided the deeper inspiration of science and technology, reminding us that the dynamics of science is non-scientific and the dynamism of technology is non-technological; in both cases it is visionary, millenial. In addition to science and technology, American commercial and political life and universal education were understood as the means of achieving a millenial transformation of the earth, the human community and human consciousness. The expectation was that we would enter the sacred world out of a demonic world.

Just as the doctrine of human transcendence left the natural world in a degraded status, so the millenial vision of a blessed future made all present modes of existence also somehow degraded. All things were in an unholy condition; everything needed to be transformed. In the American world this meant that anything unused had to be used if the purpose of its existence was to be realized. Nothing in its natural state was acceptable.

This compulsion to use, to consume, has found its ultimate expression in our times when the ideal is to take the natural resources from the earth, and transform them, by industrial processes, for consumption by a society that lives at an ever-higher consumption rate. That consumption has something sacred about it is obvious from the central position it now occupies; through it we enter the millenial world of the Book of Revelation. This becomes clear when we consider the relentless advertising campaigns to convince society that neither peace nor joy, neither salvation nor paradise can be achieved except through heightened consumption.

A sense of an untouched world, of the primordial wilderness

as divine presence to be left undisturbed by human interference, survived in a few persons such as Henry Thoreau and John Muir, but they were exceptions. Only a few like them were aware that the loss of species is not simply an economic loss, but also a weakening of the entire biosphere, the elimination of a profound psychic experience, the diminishment of imaginative power, and ultimately the loss of a special mode of divine presence. Though Thoreau's and Muir's teachings were read with a certain respect, the American determination to eliminate natural modes of being continued as the dominant attitude of the society.

The instrument for this was a technology that was also transcendent—that is, one for which the natural world had no adequate limiting power. This phase of human technological cunning was too much for nature. The basic law of nature was that every expansive life force should have arrayed over against it limiting powers that would prevent any single force or combination of forces from suffocating the other members of the life community. Such a law, however, could not operate effectively in confrontation with this transcendent technology, even though the natural world might eventually overwhelm the human perpetrator with his own poisons and waste products, leading to the degradation of the quality of human life and possibly to the elimination of the human.

A fourth influence of classical western spirituality on the American experience is its emphasis on salvation dynamics to the neglect of creation dynamics. This is in a direct line with the other influences we have mentioned. The argument of Lynn White that the historical roots of the ecological crisis lie in the deepest sources of western spiritual tradition could be easily criticized if we considered only one or two of the items I have mentioned here. This was the approach of the late René Dubos, who correctly pointed out that all classical religious cultures abused their land and devastated their environment. What must now be recognized, however, is that we have now increased the destruction process to a new order of magnitude. Our new types of destruction disturb the biosphere in a way never before possible. We should also observe that, even while this destruction of nature was taking place in America, there was widespread piety, an extensive advance in spirituality, and revivalist preaching across the nation. The founding of convents, monasteries, retreat houses and houses of prayer took place on an extensive scale. Religious groups set up educational programs covering everything from kindergarten to university in a monumental effort unparalleled in Christian history. In all this there was abundant spirituality and enormous resistance to the secularization of life, atheism, lack of moral discipline, and injustice to the poor. Works of mercy were advanced with extraordinary spiritual dedication.

Few, however, have apparently been able to see that the ultimate difficulty lay in classical western spirituality itself as it has come down to us through the centuries, a situation that could be remedied only by a spirituality more intimately associated with the cosmic-earth-human process itself.

There is no point in arguing that the spirituality being taught was not the real Christian spiritual tradition, that an earlier, more valid and more integral tradition existed in which these defective tendencies did not exist, and that this earlier tradition would in time prevail in a spontaneous purifying reaction. This may be true but it is difficult to accept a pure unspoiled form of any tradition; in this sense, there may be no fixed identifiable religious or spiritual system. By definition any "tradition" is a process, not an established and unchangingly fixed mode of believing, thinking or acting. There is no identifiable fixed Christianity or Hinduism or Buddhism but only an identifiable Christian process, Hindu process, or Buddhist process. The historical reality is the reality of the tradition. All traditions have their grandeur and their limitations, their luminous and their dark aspects, their successes and their failures. These tend to be correlative. The specific mode of grandeur makes possible a corresponding mode of failure. Discipline can generally be associated with indulgence.

What is important here is to recognize that traditions must constantly go beyond any existing expression of themselves to new forms of expression. Today the time has come for the most significant change that western Christian spirituality has yet experienced. But this change is itself part of a much more comprehensive change both in human consciousness and in the entire earth-human process.

To understand the present situation we need to consider the basic dynamics of the earth process as envisaged from the standpoint of the central human event, the central life event, the central earth event of recent centuries. The discovery of the evolutionary process can be considered a moment of supreme significance for the total cosmic-historical process. It is the moment when the universe completed its primordial fourteen billion years quest for a conscious reflection on itself and its developmental sequence in human intelligence through empirical observation and inquiry.

Within this context the human itself needs to be seen as a function or mode of being of the universe, more especially of the earth process, rather than a separate being in the universe or a particular being on the earth.

The earth as a self-emerging, self-sustaining, self-governing, self-healing and self-educating community of living and non-living beings provides its own education, its own inner guidance, its discipline, its intelligibility and its spirituality in the pre-human realm of living beings through genetic coding. This coding provides the basic pattern for activation of the various life forms, leaving little need for additional education or spiritual discipline after birth.

But then came the genius of earth in its genetic coding for transgenetic functioning, now at the level of the human mode of consciousness. The entire range of cultural and spiritual development of the human is genetically coded to take place, but by human invention, by a further self-education process at the conscious level. Genetically coded to speak, the human must invent the modes of speech; genetically coded to a social mode of life, the human must invent the forms; genetically coded to spirituality, the human must invent the spiritual disciplines.

When we refer to this invention process, we must note that the entire earth community and the universe itself participates in all the various inventions whereby the human gives shape to his or her existence as individual and as society, along with the cultural and spiritual expression of itself attained by the society.

Just as the human body took its shape through some fourteen billion years of effort on the part of the universe and through some four and a half billion years of earth existence, so also the human psychic structure and our spirituality have been taking shape over all this time, beginning with the primordial atomic particles which held within themselves the destiny of all that has followed, even the spiritual shaping of the human. The formation of our psychic structure, originating at this mysterious level far beyond rational or empirical penetration, takes further shape in our genetic coding but even more completely in the cultural coding that the human community has established in the fourfold cultural sequence that follows the fourfold cosmic sequence.

This cosmic sequence can be understood in terms of these stages: (1) the emergence of the galactic systems and the elemental structures, (2) the shaping of the planet earth in the solar system, (3) the emergence of life, and (4) the emergence of consciousness at the human level.

At the human level there is a diversity of cultural expressions in different regions of the planet and among different societies, but there exists a certain sequence of major codings, cultural-spiritual phases: (1) the tribal-shamanic culture, (2) the great classical religious cultures, (3) the scientific-technological culture, and now (4) the emerging ecological culture. These four can be considered mutation phases of human development somewhat parallel with species mutation in the biosphere.

After the tribal-shamanic phase, in the period of the great classical religious civilizations, an extraordinary sense of the divine coexisted with a sense of social hierarchy, seen in sacrificial rituals, revelatory experience, and interior spiritual disciplines whereby the human activated the deepest level of its being. This cultural-spiritual phase was so fully developed, so powerful in its coding, so effective in its communication of this coding to successive generations, that any significant change inevitably appeared to be destructive, immoral, heretical, anarchistic. Any significant alteration of the knowing process would be seen as illogical and irrational.

When we look back at the period of classical western spirituality we can now see a kind of a priori necessity for the scientific venture of the next period to appear as a needless destructive process that could only end in a devastating period for the human venture. And it is quite true that this new age, with its emphasis on scientific observation, quantitative measurement, and mathematical reasoning, along with its aversion to hierarchy in favor of democracy, its neglect of faith in favor of reason, its exaltation of technology as the instrument for the conquest of nature, its insistence on individual freedom, has brought with it sufficient devastation to satisfy the advance judgment brought against it.

Once the scientific-technological period established itself, however, the intensity of its dedication to its own objectives took on the characteristics of a religious attitude and of a spiritual discipline parallel with the religious dedication and spiritual discipline of the classical religious cultures that preceded it. This included a new sense of orthodoxy, a new dogmatic integrity not to be challenged by reasonable persons. In other words, as already stated, neither the creators of this new situation nor the dominant spiritual personalities of the period have known how to read the change that has taken place.

Perhaps the full extent of the change escapes us because we have mistaken its order of magnitude. The proposition can be defended that these centuries of science and technology should be considered more as a geological age rather than simply as a historical period since, by means of our technology, we have within a few generations altered the planet in its physical structure and the biosphere in its basic functioning on a scale that formerly took a hundred or two hundred million years. Although much of this change has been destructive, it was, understandably, seen by its human agents as a sublime human-spiritual accomplishment. These agents could, of course, see only what the cultural coding of the scientific-technological age permitted them to see. As is generally the case, cultural coding, like genetic coding, establishes values and patterns of action. Especially in cultural coding the demonic aspect of cultural determination is not seen. In this sense the culture depends on what might be called an altered state of consciousness, a trance state.

Until now such a mode of consciousness has coexisted in our

society, often in the same person, with a traditional spiritual coding in the pattern of western classical spirituality. These patterns cause little trouble to each other because neither the modern scientific mode of consciousness nor the classical spiritual mode of consciousness is concerned with the integral functioning of the earth community. Indeed, both modes of consciousness experience the human as olympian ruler of the planet, the planet as mechanical functioning, and natural resources as objects for unlimited human exploitation.

Today we have begun to realize, however, that the planet earth will not long endure being despised or ignored in its integral being by scientists, technologists or saints; it will not submit forever to the abuse it has had to endure. Already it is taking away the oxygen we breathe, the purity of the rain, our protection from cosmic rays, the careful balance of our climate, the fruitfulness of the soil; this process will continue until finally we begin to recover some form of reverence for the material out of which we were born, the nourishing context that sustains us, the warmth of the wind and the coolness of the water, all of which delight us and purify us, and communicate to us the divine presence. At present this reverent attention hardly exists among us, nor can it exist in any vital mode until the spirituality of the new ecological age begins to function with some efficacy.

3

I propose that the historic role that is now being assigned to America is that of creating, in its main outlines, the spirituality of the ecological age, the fourth great cultural coding that is now taking on its effective form. Of course, all peoples are ultimately involved in this new cultural coding, since the scientific basis of the new origin story is now being accepted as the context for education everywhere on the planet. For the first time in its history the human community has a single origin story.

The greatest single need at present is the completion of the story, as told in its physical dimensions by science, by the more integral account which includes the numinous and consciousness dimensions of the emergent universe from its primordial moment. Only after this is done can a meaningful universe, a functional cosmology, be available as a foundation for the total range of human activities in the ecological age.

America should have a special affinity for this new cultural coding since American society has experienced so extensively the creative possibilities and the limitations of both the classical-religious and the scientific-technological periods. Now is the opportunity to establish a cultural coding grounded in the inter-communion of all the living and non-living components of the universe.

This universe community, but especially the planet earth, is the primary revelation of the divine; it is also the primary educator, primary healer, primary commercial establishment and primary law-giver for all that exists within this community. The basic spirituality communicated by the natural world can also be considered as normative for the future ecological age. This spirituality is grounded in the three characteristics of the universe as manifested from the beginning: differentiation, subjectivity, and communion. These constitute the ultimate basis of a functional spirituality for the human community just as they constitute the functional cosmology of the human community.

Differentiation is primary because this is the immediate expression of primordial reality. In the particular mode of each being set off from every other being we find the articulated reality of created existence. Reality is not homogeneous smudge: this is the first observation to be made about the universe. Each being is unique in its ultimate reality even though there is a constant flux and flow in which articulated realities are constantly being transformed. Each particular being is historically irreplaceable, fulfilling a role that is proper to itself alone.

Subjectivity, the second most significant aspect of reality, indicates the inner form, the radiant intelligibility, that shines forth from the deep mystery of every articulated mode of being. Already the articulated energy of the nuclear structure is a spiritual as well as physical reality of fantastic capacities. At the depth of its being the ultimate mystery of the universe can be experienced as profoundly as anywhere in the world. This subjectivity, while expressed by the scientist in its physical form, cannot be reduced to crass matter, for ultimately there is no such thing as matter independent of intelligible form. This subjectivity increases as complexity increases until it reaches the stages of life and consciousness. There could be no longer consciousness or spirituality or numinous presence if these were not present in the beginning.

Communion is the third most significant aspect of the universe. The relatedness of the universe in its every manifestation is what establishes the unity of the entire world and enables it to be a "universe." Every atomic particle is present to every other atomic particle in an inseparable unity, a unity that enables us to say that the volume of each atom is the volume of the universe.

Communion, too, is the immediate cause for the unfolding of the universe in the full complexity of its living and non-living forms. Without communion nothing would ever happen. In this sense the gravitational attraction which holds every being in its identity and its relatedness finds its fulfillment in the meeting of individuals in the world of the living and in the full expression of affection at the level of human consciousness.

Here, too, we find the sublime expression of the deepest mystery of the universe, the revelation of the divine. To deepen this experience of the divine is the purpose of all spiritual discipline and of all spiritual experience.

This sense of communion at the heart of reality is the central force bringing the ecological age into existence, signalling the birth of a new overwhelming spiritual experience at this moment of earth history.

One further change in human consciousness needed to bring about this new historical age as well as this new spiritual experience is the change from our dominant machine-metaphor of reality to a dominant vital, organic, person-metaphor of reality. Although Sir Isaac Newton advanced our scientific understanding of the universe in a remarkable manner, he left us with a universe of mechanistic forces devoid of vital-emotional-personal content, a universe to be manipulated for human utility or to be contemplated in its abstract mathematical splendor.

While the centuries since Newton have been centuries dedicated to human freedom, justice and personal well-being, these achievements have been sought in a human social order with no essential relationship with a functional cosmology, or if after Darwin some relationship was established with the biological order, this was itself experienced as a random determination of the mechanistic forces of nature.

Throughout these Newtonian centuries the human remained an effort at the domination and exploitation of a natural world despoiled of its numinous qualities, its inner vital principles, its intellectual radiance, and its emotional sensitivities. All these were considered as belonging to a romantic and unrealistic tradition, naively incompetent to deal with the hard realities of the world about us.

In this way, our pragmatic entrepreneurs have taken over, national and multi-national corporations, engineers with their gigantic machines, financiers with their money values: these are the men—it is hardly a coincidence that very few women are in their company—without reverence for the earth, without mercy for the host of living creatures on the earth, without any sense of the divine presence pervading the landscape. These are the practical managers who leave us with polluted air, acid rainfall, toxic rivers and seas, a drastic decline in the genetic diversity of life forms, and a threat to the ozone layer that protects us from cosmic radiation.

To restore a sense of the earth as matrix of the human is a difficult undertaking but one which will inevitably be validated in confrontation with the demonic aspect of our existing mode of cultural coding. The new coding, which we tend to think of as "ecological," might better be designated simply as "functional cosmology." This integration is not simply an ideal put forward as an abstract goal to be sought but a process that is already taking place throughout America. Hundreds and even thousands of movements in this direction are already taking place in every phase of American life—in law and medicine, in agriculture, architecture, commerce, industry, and education. Some awareness of the wide range of activities supporting this new coding for the fourth great cultural age can be obtained by paging through the recent book of Marilyn Ferguson, *The Aquarian*

Conspiracy, a work that surveys the transforming movements already taking place throughout the world but especially in America. While her study is sometimes redundant and journalistic in style, it does convey a sense of the concern being manifested for the integrity of the planetary system as the only context in which the human mode of being can sustain itself and develop in a coherent manner in the future.

Many religious and spiritual persons are beginning to understand the new context of their own future development as members of the planetary community, although most Christian theologians and scripture scholars have so far remained unaffected in their study by the altered context of contemporary existence. Over-attachment to the salvific role of classical western spirituality seems to prevent any serious inquiry into a creation-oriented spirituality within the context of our present mode of experiencing the universe.

Soon, however, we can expect a change. The imperatives of life and thought are too urgent for continuing the present impasse. As the Fathers of the Church gave a new expansiveness to Christianity through their association of Christian belief with Platonic philosophy, as Augustine and Dionysius gave a higher spiritual vision to Christianity by the insights of Neoplatonism, as Thomas gave new vigor to the Christian faith by his interpretation of Aristotle, so now a new vision and a new vigor is available to Christian tradition through our modern understanding of the origin and development of the universe and the emerging ecological age. If creating this new cultural coding of the ecological age is the next phase of the American experience, creating a spirituality integral with this coding should be the next phase of the Christian tradition.

BEATRICE BRUTEAU

Global Spirituality and the Integration of East and West

Beatrice Bruteau, director of the Philosophy Exchange, is author of Worthy Is the World: the Hindu Philosophy of Sri Aurobindo *and* Evolution to Divinity: Teilhard de Chardin and the Hindu Tradition. *She has written that the next revolution in human consciousness will be neo-feminine, "not the paleo-feminine instinct nor the masculine reason, but the next level of advance, an intellectual intuition, or insight. . . . a supreme act of cognition which is simultaneously an act of spiritual sympathy" ("Neo-Feminism and the Next Revolution in Consciousness,"* Cross Currents, Summer 1977). *The present essay takes literally the idea shared by Gandhi and Jesus that human beings are children of God and affirms that their value lies in the act of life itself. The most fully human relatedness, she says, goes beyond I and thou: "What love really wants is to enter into the beloved and coincide with the beloved's own subjectivity. The ultimate relation of love we may therefore call the 'I-I' relation." Bruteau concludes with a meditation on spirituality as the incarnation of creative process, as readiness to answer the call of the future: "Let us go where we have not been before!"*

As astronomer Fred Hoyle predicted in 1948, "Once a photograph of the earth, taken from outside, is available—once the sheer isolation of the earth becomes plain, a new idea as

193

powerful as any in history will be let loose."[1] This powerful idea is that we human beings—better, perhaps, we living beings—constitute one family on a tiny fragile planet in limitless space.

For millions of years, we earth-people have identified and valued ourselves by contrasting our immediate tribe with the tribe next door. The background for having a sense of who *we* are has been "other people." "Other people" were the ground and "we" were the figure. We—whoever we were—were the norm of human being, and others were outsiders, aliens, barbarians, savages, gentiles, pagans, infidels. But when we see Earth from deep space, we know that the only ground against which we can be seen is the emptiness of the abyss.

A fundamental method of organizing our experience has been undermined. The contrast method, by which we perceive figure against ground, sound against silence, by which we conceive one idea in distinction from all others which it is not; by which we value one object above another, one act above another, one person above another—this fundamental method has been shaken because its paradigm, the sense of who *we* are in our tribe as against *them* in their tribe, has been shown to be utterly incommensurate with the reality of our situation.

How shall we say who we are, now that we know we are all one? Since we need a new method of thinking and feeling about ourselves, we also need a new global spirituality for the future. A popular way of putting this has been to speak of an integration of East and West, but even this is now obsolete. What is required is a unitary view that is original and drawn from our experience itself, not something patched together from the materials of the past.

This is not to say that we may overlook the fact that we are descendents from that past and that its genes have shaped our present lives. Indeed, we inherit all the traditions of all the cultures of this planet. None of us is limited to the heredity of one tribe alone. Today, however, as the incumbents of the present age, we must bring to birth a vision of reality in which the features of this global inheritance will be plainly visible, but whose unity, vitality, and thrust toward the future will be its own.

1

"You are gods, children of the Most High, all of you." Ps.
82:6
"Beloved, we are God's children." I John 3:2

That we are all children of God is a familiar idea but it has
never been taken seriously and literally enough. Most traditions
have used this notion, or something equivalent, to tell us who we
are, that we are ultimately descended from the Supreme Being,
and therefore have dignity and value. It has also served to set the
in-group apart from the out-group. In reaction, it has been deliberately employed by some individuals—Jesus and Gandhi come
immediately to mind—to reject the division of their societies into
castes and classes of relative honor.

Gandhi called those whom others regarded as "untouchable"
Harijan, children of Hari, God who has stolen our hearts. This
was not the first time such a teaching had been presented to the
Indian people, for the Buddha had broken definitively with the
caste system some twenty-five centuries earlier. That the same
point had to be made again so much later only shows how
reluctant we are to give up classifying and comparing ourselves
with one another and preferring some classes to others.

Jesus, too, had said plainly that no one was to be given a
privileged title of honor, because "You are all brothers," and he
had taken pains to point out the authoritarian style of the Gentiles and to warn his companions not to imitate it.[2] Nevertheless,
the institutions we have erected ostensibly in his honor are
structured hierarchically and ruled by distinct classes of persons
distinguished by their respective titles, costumes, and powers
over those beneath them. That all people are equal because
equally children of God is not a popular doctrine when it comes
to practice. It is one of those hard sayings—who can bear to
hear it?

What does it really mean, and how can it open to us a new
method for understanding ourselves and relating to our world?
Suppose we put ourselves in Jesus' place and try to imagine the

experience he had in connection with his baptism. We may assume that his meditations on the meaning of life—his own and that of Israel—had been leading up to this moment. What, after all, are human beings? What—who—is any one of us, we who are intense points of personal awareness in the midst of a world of meaningless suffering, where God is mostly silent? Who am I?, we constantly cry into the Void. Let me purify myself, we say, let me wash away all that is not my truest self, let me dissolve all that is not the inmost core of my existence. Let me be baptized in this renunciation that I may see my central reality and know my true name.

Thus Jesus comes to John and is baptized by him. And as he came up out of the water, it seemed to him that the heavens opened to him and the Spirit of God descended upon him as if it were a dove; and he heard a voice say to him, "You are my beloved son in whom I am well pleased."[3]

Jesus did not receive this word that he was a child of God as a cliché, but as the stunning revelation it was meant to be. Overwhelmed by this realization, he was driven by the Spirit into the wilderness, where he remained fasting and praying for forty days. "If you are the child of God, then . . .?" How many answers to this question did Jesus try? We know at least that he immediately rejected a number of possibilities. Being a child of God does not mean that you are to use magic to fulfill your material desires. It does not mean that you are to defy the laws of nature and expect miracles to sustain you. It does not mean that you are to dominate the rest of the world.

But he also evidently came to some positive conclusions which show in his later preaching and behavior. Being a child of God does mean that you are to regard all as equal, to be as impartial as God, who sends sun and rain on just and unjust alike. It does mean that you are to love your enemies as well as your friends. You are to deepen your purity beyond ritual observance. You are to rejoice and consider yourself blessed even in circumstances that the judgment of the world accounts as misfortune.

And so, in this view, those whom our caste-consciousness has deemed last come out first—first in the sense that everyone is first, for all are rewarded alike by the divine generosity. The comparative measures that we have been accustomed to use have been discarded. All are equally worthy, and equally unworthy, for worthiness is not the issue. To be a child of God means that your real life is maintained by God and is not measured by your manipulation of the environment. It means that you forgive and heal your sisters and brothers endlessly, as God endlessly forgives and heals you, continuing to pour life into you from moment to moment. It means that you live your true life in each other person, as each of them lives in you. It means that you give your life to be the nourishment of all and hold nothing back for yourself alone. It means that you are a sacrifice for the people, and that the more you give yourself up in this way, the more you will rise to newness of life and ascend into divine union.

This is a tremendous answer. In many ways it is familiar, but it is also unexplored or unassimilated: for we still do not practice it. Why? Part of the reason may be that we retain a metaphysical view that contradicts it. The vision of reality that Jesus has outlined is incompatible with our routine assumption that we are all separate, isolated, but comparable units.

In order to practise the politics of the children of God, we need to understand, and be converted to, the metaphysics that underlies these moral propositions. And this is where our united heritage from East and West begins to be functional. For, affirming both the nondualism that has been the central insight of the East and the personal freedom that has been the chief value of the West, we can gain an overall picture of our reality, a picture that would constitute a new method of ordering and appreciating our experience.

Before proceeding further, let me be clear: I take the image "children of God" literally—that is, children truly inherit the nature of the parent. If God is represented as having a certain character, God's parenthood implies that the children also have it. Thus, if God is holy, the children are to be seen as holy. If God is indefinable, that is our clue that each human person is also indefinable.

What does it mean to be children of God in the light of a metaphysics of global spirituality? In summary, I would say that it means to be incomparable, to be love, to be perichoresis, and to be incarnate as creative process.

2

"To whom will you compare me?" Isa. 46:5
"When they measure themselves by one another, and compare themselves with one another, they are without understanding." 2 Cor. 10:12

Here is the basic notion of this metaphysics, without which the rest of the system will not work. The real person is incomparable, incommensurable, indefinable, indescribable, not to be known or valued by reference to or relation to something else. In this sense the children of God can be said to be absolute and transcendent like their Parent. There is fear of this doctrine in some quarters on the grounds that it threatens the transcendence of God, as though in order for God to be properly transcendent there must be other beings from whom God can be distinguished and to whom God is utterly superior. But transcendence really means that the transcendent being is simply free of any necessary reference to whatever it transcends. It is precisely its *not* being compared with those beings which makes it transcend them.

A sense for our own absolute, or non-relative, being is the key to the freedom that will enable us to see ourselves in a new way, as if from outer space, and to form a deeply unique community for the whole Earth. There first has to come a moment of what looks like complete withdrawal of each being from each other, because each is said to be independent of any comparison with others. Ordinarily, we recognize our physical, intellectual, and emotional dependence on one another and believe that recognition and affirmation of our interdependence is the foundation of the ideal community. But interdependence, a sharing and dovetailing of lacks, is not the ideal. Perhaps we might call the ideal community "inter-independent"; for it must be a more intimate sharing of life than can be achieved by merely filling up each other's deficiencies. We are looking for a unity based not on deficiency but on superabundance.

Let us consider what happens when we define ourselves by dependence, relation, and comparison. Don't we superficially answer the great baptismal question—"What name shall we give?" "Who are you?"—by citing our occupation, our relation to spouse or parent or child, our nationality, our religion, our race, our wealth, our fame, our achievements, or perhaps some special feature that looms large in our social life such as sexual orientation, or some physical or mental handicap, or a drug dependency, or a prison record? And don't many of us build our lives around this particular descriptive answer? This is often how we think of ourselves and of other people. Our self-esteem and sense of having a satisfactory life are framed in these terms. We struggle and strain to be able to say to ourselves and others, my description is valued in my society. Or, if we cannot do that, we try to get our description valued as highly as one we have been denied: we declare that being the way *we* are is just as good and beautiful as the way *they* are. But we still think that we *are* this description. And our life consists of trying to get the description valued, or trying to get the valued description. It doesn't occur to us that our value doesn't lie in the description at all.

Notice that when we define ourselves by descriptions and comparisons and relations the value comes from scarcity. As long as I have the only Lincoln Continental on my block, I'm an important person. As soon as every garage on the street has a Continental in it, mine doesn't count any more. The comparison, the contrast, insured the value and gave me a sense of who I am. Much the same is true of our sense of achievement. If everyone can run the four-minute mile, I have no sense of accomplishment in doing it. This seems so right to us that we even say, "Where all are honored, no one is honored."

Our notion of value seems to be that in order for anything to be valuable, it has to be scarce. Because some people—most people—*don't* have it, we believe it's good. Deprivation, non-being, is the foundation of this sense of value.

Our feeling good about ourselves thus depends on other people's feeling bad. They must wish that they could have what we have, or do what we do, in order for our possession or our achievement to be important. If no one else wanted to have it or do it, then even if I were the only one in the world to have it or do it, my Lincoln would be worthless. Comparison, contrast— someone up, someone down—that is the way our judgment of life goes.

Even in a casual encounter some shadow of this standard governs our interchange. Can my personality dominate the other? Can I succeed in getting my opinion accepted, my choice deferred to? Can I get my way? Can I have the last word? Even in subtle ways this criterion operates: Didn't I handle that situation better than he did? Wasn't I more virtuous, more charitable, more humble? Whatever it is that we value, we convince ourselves that we have it by comparing ourselves with our neighbors.

What happens when we are not top dog? When we are deprived, poor, oppressed, rejected, despised, ridiculed, ignored? We are hurt, not only in our physical poverty or cultural deprivation, but in our sense of ourselves. My "Who I Am" is injured, and this injury seeks compensation. Because the sense of value is a contrast sense, this injury can be compensated *either* by attaining the value of which we were deprived, *or* by putting some others down, so that in comparison with them we now are on top. Then those underdogs will in turn have to do the same thing in compensation for their injury, and a chain of sin will be forged, and the hurts of one generation of interacting persons or races or classes or nations are passed on to manacle succeeding generations.

All this doesn't come about simply because people are evil or greedy or weak or proud. It comes about because of the way we have structured our sense of value, making it depend on comparison, deprivation, frustration, injury. And this in turn is related to our assumption that we *are* our descriptions, our relations to persons and institutions, our possession of a set of definable attributes.

It is important to understand this if we want to serve peace and justice, to lift up the poor and free the oppressed. We can then understand that fighting, defeating, depriving, and oppressing are *systematic necessities of our present mentality.* We have to have the contrast in order to have the sense of value, in order to have the sense of Who We Are.

Our present structures are full of injustice but we cannot accomplish our purpose simply by placing the currently oppressed class over those who now have goods and power. The contrast would break out again somewhere else. What we need to change is the deeply ingrained mentality that requires contrast in order to feel real and feel good. This can be done—if we understand how our real self transcends our descriptions.

The quest for the real self has perhaps more preoccupied the East than the West. Sage after sage has meditated on human suffering and asked, "Who am I?" And again and again the answer has come back: Suffering is involved in everything about our lives as we presently live them. It is caused by our craving for the valued description. But there is a way out, because in fact we are not that description. We do not have to have a valued description in order to be real and to be happy. All those descriptions are mere combinations of appearances in our experience. They change constantly, falling into now this pattern, now that, like fragments of color in a kaleidoscope. *That's* not what we mean by a *real self.* The real self is what is back of all those descriptions, quite independent of them. Nor is it the possessor of the descriptions. It itself has no description. There is nothing you can say to define it. You cannot refer it to some other being and say it bears this relation to that being, and that tells what it is. You cannot compare it with another being and say it is better or worse or bigger or smaller. As long as we remain accustomed to thinking that reality is whatever can be defined or described— whatever has attributes and can be related and compared to other beings—this Real Self looks to us like nothing at all: it is emptiness, a void, a No-Self, a big zero.

Indeed, the sages say, all we can say of it, in terms of our descriptive experience, is that it is Neti, Neti, not this, not that; it is Nirguna, without attributes, not composed of strands woven together as all descriptive beings are. Not being a descriptive or defined being, it has no need or desire to enhance its description; it has no fire of craving for more and better attributes. That fire has been blown out: Nirvana. The Western saint, too, who proceeds by the Via Negativa, who enters the cloud of unknowing, who strips the soul of all descriptive goods and qualities, knows that one comes in contact with Deep Reality only when one reaches this central Nothing, this Nada.

But this sense of nothing, of emptiness, is only the last of the appearances in the world of contrast perception. It is in comparison with descriptive being that the real self appears to be empty and to be nothing. As a descriptive being, a being defined and known by its attributes and its essence, it is truly a nothing, and nothing can be said of it. But it *is* experienced, and vividly experienced, as the true reality, as fullness of being, as activity of existence. We cannot look at it from outside, for from there we can see only descriptions. It must be experienced from the inside, by actually *being* it. It is sheer I AM, without adding "I am this," or "I am that." No, only "I am who I am." The children of God bear the Name of the Parent, and if they would be true, they must take care not to take that Name in vain.

Thinking of ourselves in this way enables us to experience ourselves as existence, as act, instead of looking at ourselves as essence, as substance. It suggests that we experience ourselves as verbs rather than as nouns, as interflowing processes of living rather than as bounded and separated entities. If our sense of being, of being real, and being good, is not a sense of *what* we are but *that* we are, a sense of existing and acting that is independent of the descriptions through which our particular actions take place, then we begin to get a new picture of reality. Now contrast is not needed to give value, because the value lies in the act of existing itself, and it is *this act which we are,* a far greater thing than any description in which we might be clothed. "Why," asked Jesus, "are you worried about how you will be clothed? Life is far greater than clothing."

But this is only the beginning. The realization of the true self as transcendent of all descriptions, as free of the need to identify or value itself by contrast, as being the act of existing, as inheriting the name of God I AM, is only the first step in working out the metaphysics of the children of God.

3

"Let us love one another, for love is of God, and whoever loves is born of God . . . for God is love." I John 4:7–8

In order to explain this idea of love properly, we must go more deeply into the psychology of the true self. The central point is that to experience the true self, we must coincide consciously with the act of existing and not be thinking *about* ourselves. The self that we think about is a particular entity possessed of various attributes, and it is these attributes that we actually think about when we consider that self. Furthermore, thinking about ourselves makes us treat ourselves as objects of knowledge and turns us into split beings: subjects who know and objects that are known. This is the basic form of dualism that all spiritual traditions urge us to avoid. "Let your eye be single," they recommend; "then your whole being will be illuminated."

Padma Sambhava, who brought Buddhism to Tibet in the eighth century, said:

> There are not two such things as sought and seeker. . . ; when fully comprehended, the sought is found to be one with the seeker. If the seeker . . . when sought, cannot be found, thereupon is attained the goal of the seeking and also the end of the search itself.[4]

It is that which the eye cannot see when it looks for itself. An eye attempting to see itself is an eye trying to double itself. When the eye realizes that it *is* the eye, *is* the seer, then the eye is single, and that is Illumination, that is Enlightenment.

Wei Wu Wei, who draws on Vedanta, as well as Taoism and Zen, puts it this way:

> Although [Original Consciousness] is all that [people] are—and despite the fact that in it, therefore, they have nothing to attain, grasp or possess—[nevertheless] in order that they may "live" it, [as distinguished from] having objective understanding of what it is, . . . they must *de-phenomenalise themselves,* dis-objectify

themselves, dis-identify their Subjectivity from its projected phenomenal selfhood. . . . This displacement of subjectivity is from
apparent object to ultimate subject in which it inheres, . . . from
supposed individual to universal absolute.[5]

Therefore, we should try to coincide with ourselves as the act
of existing which we are, with that fountain of living energy that
springs up in the midst of us and actually *is* eternal life.[6] This
sense of sheer existence, before the attention is directed to some
object, has no form and hence no limitation. It is in this sense
that we may call it infinite. It is existence, not essence; it is
formless, not formed; it transcends time and space; and it is
experienced by coinciding with it noetically, not by thinking
about it or knowing it as an object.

This formless existence-self is active, not passive. It is experienced as coincidence, or confluence, with the fountain of eternal
life in our heart. We are this springing up, this flowing out. It is
our own act of living. And when we consciously unite with it, it is
also our will. This is the fundamental meaning of uniting one's
will to the will of God. We feel it as an act in which we are
engaged. It is process; it is motion; it is flow; it is radiation.

Notice that whenever our attention is engaged passively, as
distinguished from this sense of sheer active existence, what we
are doing is reacting, re-sponding. The action has begun outside
us, somewhere in the environment. Something has presented
itself to be noticed, to be known, to be valued, to be acted upon.
We may attend or not attend; we may award positive or negative
value—that is, like or dislike; we may elect to act or not act, to
act in this way or that way. But all these alternatives have been
presented by the environment and offered to our attention and
our will for *choice*. The environment has also put pressure on us
in one way or another to claim our attention and our choice. The
situation is characterized by *passive attention* because we are
passive to the actions of the environment on us. And it is characterized by *choice freedom*. We are free to make choices among
the alternatives offered us by the environment. When we make
these choices and engage our will in these responses, we do so
because of the qualities in the situation presented by the environ-

ment and the relation that these qualities bear to certain qualities in our attribute-self. For instance, we love people who please us, do us good, are friendly to us.

In order to be able to love people who do not please us, do not do us good, are not friendly to us, we must take some other stance. We may say to ourselves that after all they are human beings too and on that ground deserving of our love, regardless of how they behave toward us. Or we may say that our religious leader has claimed identity with them and asked us to love them, and for the sake of that obligation, we will strive to do so. But in these cases we are still giving reasons for the love. Something outside ourselves stimulates and calls forth the love. We are still passive.

In order to love without regard whether the beloved is worthy or unworthy, without any motive arising from the environment, in order to love as an original and authoritative act, we must situate ourselves at a still deeper source of freedom. Beyond choice freedom there is *creative freedom,* which is grounded in *active attention,* the sense of simply coinciding with existing as a unitary outflowing act.

Choice freedom is a response to a stimulus from the environment; creative freedom acts from itself alone, not as a response, not as a re-action, but as an original act, proceeding only from itself as a first cause. It is called "creative" because it creates as it acts. The passive, or responsive, lover first finds an object worthy of love and then loves. The active, or creative, lover first loves and then there is a beloved.[7]

The self that can do this is the existential formless self. The self composed of descriptions can only engage in motivated love in terms of relations between itself and those loved. This is why we find it so difficult to love all our neighbors. Our emotions respond only to people and situations which please and benefit us. As Jesus said, anybody can do that. If we want to live the divine life, as befits children of God, we must learn to love the way God loves—creatively, originally, not because those loved deserve it, or are attractive, pleasing, or beneficial. And not because they *fail* to have these characteristics, and we can be grandly virtuous by loving our enemies. Divine love doesn't have *any* "because." It is itself the original act and is not referred elsewhere for an account of itself. Long before there is a "because" in the world, God loves. The act of being God *is* the act of loving—and this loving creates the world.

If we are really children of God, we are capable of entering into *this* kind of love. In fact, we must fundamentally and centrally *be* this kind of love, if it is true that we are children of God. Just as we must each be a pure I AM, transcendent of all descriptive predicates, so this very I AM must be a great outpouring *Fiat*, MAY YOU BE, a radiating love-energy. Our attitude toward all other beings will be the will that they may be, and may be fully, abundantly.[8]

A disciple of the Buddha came to him one day and said, "It seems to me that love and friendliness are a great part of the illuminated life." "You are wrong," said the Buddha. "Love and friendliness are *all* of the illuminated life."

In this way another chain reaction is set up, which is just the opposite of the sin chain, in which each injured party hurt another in an attempt to regain the sense of superiority that was equated with well-being. In the love chain, the lover is free from any need to establish self-esteem, and so has abundant energy to expend on others. This affirming energy, entering into the beloved, will—if accepted—so liberate the beloved from the need to maintain contrast relationships in order to feel good, that the beloved will also be free to devote excess energy to loving still others. As the Buddha said, "Hatred does not cease by hatred at any time: hatred ceases by love."[9]

This is what happens when the Enlightened One acts as a Bodhisattva, when the Baptized One acts as a Savior. This is how we can discover community based not on interdependence, the sharing of lacks, but on superabundance. We have great reserves of personal energy, but they are presently employed in ego-defence. Once this energy is liberated, we will have enormous amounts of personal love-energy to share with all. There is no necessary scarcity of love.

Notice that the lover, acting out of the formless existential self, does not say (as a descriptive self would), "I am I insofar as I am different from you, insofar as I am not you," but "I am I precisely insofar as I give myself to you, live in you, unite with you." We see, then, that love does two things simultaneously: it both differentiates and unites. There is differentiation because what love *is* is the outgoing energy from one to another. But what does this outgoing act do? It unites with that other. And the more a lover goes out in love to unite with the other, the more the lover is established *as* a lover. The more I give myself away in love, the more I become myself, because that's what I *am,* a lover.

Their having a different collection of attributes does not distinguish lover and beloved. The act of creative loving itself establishes their existential differentiation—for the beloved will also be a lover in turn—and establishes this differentiation at the same time that it establishes union.

This is how we begin to develop our new method of organizing and appreciating our experience. Crucial to it is a new way of differentiating or distinguishing ourselves. We had been doing it by comparison; now we can glimpse how it can be done out of a sense of an existential formless selfhood which acts with creative freedom to love all.

4

"In that day you will know what I am in my Father, and you in me, and I in you." John 14:20

"I pray . . . that they may all be one . . . even as . . . we are one." John 17:22

Perichoresis, the traditional Greek word for the activity of the Trinity, refers primarily to the way the Persons live in one another. It is particularly strong in the traditions of the Orthodox Church. According to James and Myfanwy Moran, "Orthodoxy believes that . . . in the Holy Trinity the divine life is conferred on and shared by the three persons only because they give it one to another out of love: divine life is a personal offering between them, given and received freely."[10] This is a great clue and helps us to resolve what has been perceived as the problem of non-dualism.

The Eastern traditions, for the most part, insist that when one is fully enlightened, there is no longer a distinction between "me" and "my environment." The basic dualism of subject and object has been transcended and therefore all the other perceptions, conceptions, and values according to contrast and preference have also been overcome. (One can, of course, still see a black cow standing in a snowfield and understand how a circle differs from a square.) When consciousness is *limited* to the passive mode of receiving what is presented to it by the environment, there must be a distinction between it and the environment and distinctions among the various items in the environment. But when the consciousness, by concentrating its attention in the *active* mode, coincides with its own act of existing, the fragmentation of the world as experienced stops, and one is aware of unity with the whole.[11]

The West treasures individual personality, and worries that the individual personality might be lost in such a nondual experience. Our insight into the nature of love should enable us to resolve this difficulty. First, we should distinguish between "personality" and "person." Personality refers to the phenomenal observation we make of one another according to descriptions of attributes: Somebody has a particular temperament or disposition or constellation of behaviors. This, clearly, belongs to the fragmented world in which contrast and preference rule.

Person, on the other hand, refers to the living one who transcends those descriptions and is simply the act of existing as a flowing fountain of consciousness. This person is able to love with creative freedom, to love all equally without preference or privilege, above contrast and conflict. When we realize ourselves as persons, we do not cling to our personalities—although we still have them—and do not insist that the success, superiority and satisfaction of our personalities determine the value of our life. Because we are not judging everything by reference to our self-esteem, we are free to love, to will the being and well-being of others.

This act of love, we said, simultaneously establishes union and differentiation. The person who loves cannot be lost in some vague sea of generalized being, because the context is no longer essence but existence. Fear of absorption into the Whole is secretly based on a metaphysical view that sees all reality as composed of different substances distinguished from one another by their respective attributes. Since the possession of mutually negating attributes is considered in that view to be all that keeps these substances distinct from one another, if the attributes are taken away, the beings will all collapse into an undifferentiated mush.

But if the person is defined as the activity of existing, and one is oneself through acts of creative freedom projecting love-energies toward other persons, there is no possibility that anyone will be lost in some general fusion of All. There cannot be such a fusion into any simplistic unity because the lovers are distinct by their acts of loving. *This distinctness is original,* just as the act of creative loving is original and does not depend on the worthiness of the beloved. One starts with the distinctness in the existence itself, a distinctness not dependent on the possession of attributes that are different from those of others: The person *is* a lover; a lover *is* the act of loving; the act of loving establishes differentiation simultaneously with union.

Nevertheless, this union is total. That is the perichoresis. Each loving person is thoroughly "in" each other loving person. There is nothing to prevent it. The two persons are not different from one another because they possess mutually exclusive attributes: they are distinct because they are their own acts of existing. But what does love desire and intend? It wants to give itself completely to the beloved and so to unite with the other as to live in the other's own life. The lover is not satisfied with knowing about the beloved from afar. The lover wants to know the beloved, to understand the beloved, to feel with the beloved.

Let me put this in terms of our language. When we talk *about* someone, someone who is not present, we say "her" or "him." There is a definite sense of absence and separation in the I-it, I-her, I-him, we-them relation. But when the person spoken about comes into our presence, our whole consciousness changes. We say "you" *to* the person, and everything feels very different. We somehow enter into that other person, and we let the other enter into us. We engage one another. Something of what is myself becomes involved with what is yourself.

But this I-Thou relation is still not the ultimate union. This face-to-face encounter is not fully satisfying to love. Love wants to share in everything of the beloved's life and wants to give its entire life to the beloved. It wants to experience what the beloved experiences, from the beloved's own point of view, and to permit the beloved to share the lover's life with the same fullness. What love really wants is to enter into the beloved and coincide with the beloved's own subjectivity. This ultimate relation of love we may therefore call the "I-I" relation.

It is not a face-to-face encounter. It is a coincidence of two subjects, both facing the same way. One does not know or love the other as a subject knows or loves an object. One unites with the other to the extent of coinciding with that person from the inside, experiencing what it is to be that person from the subject side. This is the union properly called "mystical." William Shannon, commenting on Thomas Merton's experience and writings, puts it concisely: "In contemplation . . . the subjectivity of the contemplative becomes one with the subjectivity of God."[12] Each subject thus sees through the other's eyes, feels with the other's heart, wills in conjunction with the other's will, and flows together with the other's action.

There is now no sense of outsideness at all, no sense of separation. Each one dwells "in" the other. But each continues to feel clearly "I am I," for the subjective act of existing *is* what each subject is.

An image may help. Consider two spotlights playing on a stage floor. You see two pools of light at the ends of the two beams. Then the two spots move toward one another, partly overlap, overlap more, and finally coincide; there is now only one circle of light on the floor. But each of the two beams is playing into the one circle. With respect to that circle of light, each of the two beams can correctly say, "It is I."

In this relation, the subjective sense of being one's true self is not lost or blurred, but actually strengthened, for one feels fulfilled in one's inmost nature as an unlimited, undefined person who is a self-giving lover.

This is ec-stasy, passing out of oneself to enter into the other, there to be as the other. This means en-stasy, passing into the other's own self-realization. But what is the other's enstasy, the other's self-realization? Why, it is again that the other is also an undefined person and a creative lover, also passing out in ecstasy to unite with the enstatic self-realization of still a third person. Thus our first lover, in uniting with the second, unites with what is the very heart of that person's being and action, namely that person's outgoing love for the third, and so on. In this experience, both models of spiritual life, that which culminates in ecstasy and that which culminates in enstasy, can be verified.

This subject-subject coinherence—this I-I relation—achieves the perfection of personal integrity at the same time that it overcomes duality. It offers us a model of nondualism that is also perichoresis, uniting a basic insight of the East with a fundamental value of the West. If perichoresis—the way the Divine Persons are conceived as giving themselves totally to one another and thereby constituting their unity—is a valid view of God and we take the assertion that we are children of God, we arrive at a powerful image of what human community could be.

We too can each of us be a unique whole person whose existential reality flows out in ecstatic and creative love to other persons and so deeply bonds with them that in our confluent activity we are one living being. The image of the unitary living body has often been applied to the human race, and stories of the dismembered divinity have offered mythic explanations of our fragmentation relative to our original and true nature. The perichoresis image preserves a vivid sense of individual personal subjective existence without weakening the unity that is not only our political aspiration but what mystics of all cultures affirm as our ultimate reality.

Here we find that inter-independence based on superabundance which can replace even the best inter-dependence based on scarcity and deprivation. Note that this attitude, this personal orientation, does not mean that the Earth will not run short of oil or clean water; it does, however, imply that we can deal with such problems more freely and creatively than is possible given our present mentality. Inter-independence understands sharing not as a need imposed by scarcity but as a value in itself.

When there is a felt sense of one's life being in all equally, there is firm motivation to develop, to garner, to distribute, and to conserve for the benefit of the Whole, for each of us says, "I am the Whole." We do not have to struggle to balance our several greeds and hold our national self-interests in some equilibrium of power; we can live in a genuine community. Only because we lack a spontaneous perception of ourselves as a living Whole do we continue with our current destructive struggles.

To try to reach politically negotiated arrangements, or even to preach morally inspired sharing is not enough because our basic perception would still be one of scarcity, of loss, of sacrifice. We need a new sense of self-being as full of abundant life; we need the capacity to share that life as a free and joyous natural act.

This can come about only by first realizing ourselves as transcendent and then by identifying ourselves with the Whole. But we must not lose the sense of the unique personal integrity of each subject. The model of perichoresis offers a way to have a sense of ourselves both as subjective centers of living reality, and as totally united with all by our own free and natural act.

5

"The Word became flesh and dwelt among us, full of grace and truth." John 1:14

"My word . . . that goes forth from my mouth . . . shall not return to me empty, but it shall . . . prosper in the thing for which I sent it." Isaiah 46:11

All that has been said so far has stressed the transcendent character of what has been called our true self. This had to be clearly understood and established first so that the incarnate aspect of this global spirituality for the future could be properly presented as a creative process. Once we experience ourselves in terms of existence rather than essence, as active rather than passive, as undefined and incomparable, full and free and in loving union with all, we are able to appreciate our incarnate expression as beauty and art rather than as limitation and restriction.

Let us use the imagery of Trinitarian theology once more, this time from another point of view. The root of reality is called the Source or Parent of all, and it is conceived as expressing itself breathing forth a meaning, a word. The Word is, so to speak, the form that the Holy Breath takes as it issues from the Source. The Word is further seen as taking on flesh in the human world: the self-expression of Infinite Being takes a finite form. It does not lose its infinitude by so doing. That full reality, the incarnate Deity, is both infinite and finite, both formless and possessed of form.

This is also the message of Hindu and Buddhist teaching. Brahman, the Ultimate Reality, is both Nirguna, without finite form, not composed, and also Saguna, with finite composed forms. And the enlightened Buddhist realizes that Nirvana, the state of transcendence, is actually not different from Samsara, the world of process and particularity. One's reality belongs to both simultaneously. Both traditions alert us to the important fact that spiritual life does not end with the mystic experience of union with the Absolute. Rather, that is where it begins. Once we have properly grasped our transcendent and incomparable reality, we are ready to live a creative life, as children of a creative God should do.

Our incarnate life in the world is a process: it flows, it improvises like a skillful musician, it creates a work of art. When our consciousness enters completely into the realization of ourselves as free to love all equally and to unite with the Whole, we experience the artistic development of the human process, and the world process, as fulfilling the divine creative act. This will include all types and levels of our human activity, our economic and ecological arrangements, our social relations, our scientific and technical exploration and invention, our artistic expressions.

Perichoresis suggests a new model for organization in these enterprises, one that preserves differentiation by existential act while entering into a profound and thorough union with all. There are other images being developed now that do a similar thing. Their constellation indicates that already our consciousness is turning in this direction. David Bohm has proposed the implicate order as foundation for the various explicate systems that appear to our observation. Karl Pribram has popularized the hologram as a metaphor for the way the least particle of the whole nevertheless contains the Whole. Fritjof Capra has taken up the nondualistic philosophies of the East and shown their compatibility with contemporary physics. All these schemes have in common the abandonment of the separate-entity concept of individual being. In some way each of them suggests that what is from one point of view a *part,* is from another point of view, the *Whole.* This is the sort of spontaneous perception of our being that we need in order to create our united world of the future.

These thinkers have made useful suggestions because they have dared to try something completely different. They have studied the basic assumptions of the old systems and asked, "What if we made some other assumption?" All creation has to be courageous enough to do just this. We have to understand that loyalty goes first to life itself and not to our received ideas about life. The Angel of the Resurrection reminds us not to seek The Living One among the dead.

Thus, although vigorous protest against old structures that limit or violate the dignity of the human person is certainly in order, what is even better is simply to turn away from these structures wherever possible and set about creating and demonstrating new ones. This is the call of the future: "Let us go where we have never been before!" If we are truly children of God, this is surely a most appropriate thing for us to do as our inheritance from the God who says, "Behold, I make all things new!"

And so, after withdrawing from our sense of limited identity with a restricted self, after realization of our transcendence and freedom and our nature as ecstatic lovers who enter into the profound union of the nondual perichoresis, we turn our faces outward again in the creative process of incarnation. Let us note, as a final image of this life of ours, that after the death of the old perceptions, and after the Sabbath rest in the realization of transcendence, we come into the Resurrection, which takes place on the First Day of a new working week.

Notes

1. Hoyle mentioned his prediction again in a speech to the Apollo 11 Lunar Science Conference, Jan. 6, 1970, in Houston. Cited in Donald D. Clayton, *The Dark Night Sky* (New York: Quadrangle/N.Y. Times Book Co., 1975), p. 127.

2. Matt. 23:8–9; 20:25–26.

3. Mark 1:11.

4. Cited in Ken Wilber, *The Spectrum of Consciousness* (Wheaton, IL: The Theosophical Publishing House, 1977), p. 334.

5. *Ibid.*, pp. 331–32.

6. Cf. John 4:14.

7. Cf. John 4:19.

8. Cf. Gen. 1:3; John 10:10.

9. The Dhammapada. See, e.g., E. Easwaran, *God Makes the Rivers to Flow* (Petaluma, Ca: Nilgiri Press, 1982), p. 32.

10. *Parabola*, Vol. 7, no. 4, p. 53.

11. Wilber, pp. 314–15.

12. William H. Shannon, *Thomas Merton's Dark Path: The Inner Experience of a Contemplative* (New York: Penguin, 1982), p. 223.

MADONNA KOLBENSCHLAG

The American Economy, Religious Values, and a New Moral Imperative

Madonna Kolbenschlag, a Sister of the Humility of Mary and author of Kiss Sleeping Beauty Good-Bye, *has worked as a Congressional aide and has more recently been associated with the Woodstock Theological Center in Washington, D.C. Her essay addresses the contribution that the replacement of individualistic with communitarian values can make to improving the quality of life both in the workplace and in the American economic system as a whole. Kolbenschlag examines the effects of capital-intensive technology on workers' power and autonomy, of the market economy on human relationships, and of corporatism and bureaucratization on the accountability of power. She describes participatory arrangements in the workplace that, however tentative and modest, counter the accelerating trend toward impersonal atomization and finds possible models of even bolder experiments in the new ecclesial forms emerging in the Christian base communities of Latin America and such communities as Sojourners, Koinonia, and the "personal parishes" of the North.*

It is perhaps one of the peculiarities of social and economic crisis that hard times often generate an elaborate architecture of "legitimation" for the particular response that has gained implicit acceptance. Depressions and recessions have sometimes resulted in a crucial shift in the perceived locus of power, accelerated by the emergence of a "moral imperative" or myth of legitimation which often hypnotizes those who exercise little or no control over the phenomenon.

There are two periods of economic crisis in the history of the United States that reveal dramatic shifts in the concentration of power. The first occurred in the late nineteenth century when a monetary crisis and severe economic fluctuations coincided with the growth of monopolies and concentrations of industrial power—and, inevitably, of private fortunes. The moral imperative generated by this situation emphasized the personal morality of the entrepreneur as the answer to the problem of "trusts" and surplus wealth in the hands of a few. It was essentially an individualistic response, based on a privatized notion of social responsibility.

One of the most articulate artisans of the new moral imperative, and of the structural foundations of corporate industry was the self-made millionaire, Andrew Carnegie. A convinced believer in the "natural" laws of competition and the survival of the fittest, this economic Darwinist attributed his success to his adherence to Christian values and the workings of a higher providence. In his view the man of wealth was "chosen," and special responsibilities accompanied that selection: "The survival of the fittest means that the exceptional . . . are the fructifying forces which leaven the whole."[1] Once he had made his fortune, the man of wealth acquired a responsibility for "trusteeship." Carnegie promulgated this doctrine, which still pervades American philanthropy, in his famous essay on "The Gospel of Wealth": "The millionaire will be a trustee for the poor, intrusted for a season with a great part of the increased wealth of the community, but administering it for the community, far better than it could or would have done for itself."[2] Carnegie's curious amalgam of social Darwinism and the stewardship of the elite, which had national as well as international ramifications, provided the most significant articulation of the individualistic and elitist moral imperative.

This understanding of trusteeship keeps power in the hands of the wealthy, those who already have a monopoly access to every kind of resource. The new myth of legitimation saw wealth as passing through the hands of a few who were gifted to administer it wisely and generously for the common good. Preachers echoed this naive faith, which all but canonized the voluntaristic, individualistic ethic. Russell Conwell's famous "Acres of Diamonds" speech popularized this position to an absurd degree: "To make money honestly is to preach the gospel. . . . Ninety-eight out of one hundred of the rich men of America are honest. That is why they are rich."[3]

The same moral imperative offered a characteristically privatized response to social problems. More often than not, the response to poverty and deprivation was a "social gospel" based on compassion and assistance for the impoverished individual, and provided by high-minded individuals—rather than any significant effort directed toward social reconstruction. The settlement house and the Salvation Army were emblematic of this social ethic.

By the 1920's, however, prophetic voices were challenging this simplistic understanding of the social gospel. What had been dimly perceived in the late nineteenth century now emerged with greater clarity and urgency. Walter Rauschenbusch announced that the old individualistic approach did not provide an adequate understanding of "stewardship": "The most fundamental evils in past history and present conditions are due to converting stewardship to ownership." Such an approach "calls for no fundamental change in economic distribution, but simply encourages faithful disbursement of funds. That is not enough for our modern needs."[4]

Nevertheless, as Rauschenbusch groped his way toward a new "cooperative principle in economic life," he still placed the responsibility for change in the hands of the powerful: "Men of wealth have greater responsibilities. . . . If this new type of religious character multiplies . . . they will change the world when they come to hold the controlling positions of society."[5]

With the Crash of 1929, the individualistic privatized response to economic crisis collapsed and the locus of perceived power shifted again. The people looked beyond themselves for a solution to the catastrophe; this time, the trusteeship of the common good was taken over by the government. The philosophy of the New Deal provided a new moral imperative and a new *corporate* ethic for dealing with the inadequacies and injustices of the economic and social order. Structurally, it first took the form of an unprecedented amount of legislation, regulation, and government control, most of which was embodied in the National Industrial Recovery Act. The role of government was upgraded from referee to agent as it assumed the 'guardianship' of the social well-being of its citizens. Individualism gave way to entitlements; and the welfare system, rather than the millionaire's charity, became the trustee for the poor. The social gospel was translated into programs run by the Federal government rather than private voluntary organizations.

Roosevelt's fireside chats and dramatic regulatory innovations epitomized the new paternalism and familial cooperativeness inspired by the New Deal. As one commentator has observed, however, "It would be a mistake to envision the New Deal years as being marked simply by a spirit of community. Americans generally united into interest groups. While they realized that cooperative ventures could be more effective than rugged individualism, most citizens acted cooperatively to protect as much of the content of individualism as possible."[6] In other words, the locus of power brokerage shifted somewhat (at least in terms of expectations) toward government, and inevitably, toward bureaucracy. But this did not entail any significant change in the perception of the individual in the social order nor the displacement of old myths; the response which the New Deal institutionalized cannot properly be described as *communitarian*.

Since World War II, although there is greater awareness that economic rights are as important as political rights, our confidence in the power of government to stabilize and compensate for economic disequilibrium has eroded. The growth of government programs has not inspired a truly communal social consciousness. The corporate-bureaucratic response has often proved inadequate not only because of the changing characteristics of a global economy but because of some of the inherent paradoxes in the effects of government intervention. In the U.S.,

the Federal government has come to play a complex and contradictory role in respect to the economy: on the one hand, imple-
menting policies that support and subsidize capital, and on the
other hand, carrying out social programs that support people
who are dislocated or disadvantaged by economic shifts beyond
their control, or who have been rejected by the labor market.

1

Neither the individualistic (no matter how pietistic) nor the
corporate imperative seems adequate today to motivate economic behavior that promotes the common good. All too often
the socio-economic order seems driven by self-interest at the
expense of the social contract, and increasingly, the system
seems impelled by a mindless momentum of its own. Citizens
perceive their situation as one of disempowerment—of having no
control over one's personal or collective economic fate. How
then shall we define an authentic self-interest that promotes the
common good, and where is the locus of authentic power that
can effect change?

The first of these questions is perhaps easier to answer than
the second. We know that self-interest can be compromised and
distorted by artificially induced motivations, that "people's
wants may themselves be a product of a system which works
against their interests."[7] Thus the values that Americans believe
in, and the values that drive their existence, can be and often are
contradictory. Americans believe in "life, liberty and equal opportunity for everyone," but often it is competitiveness, ac-
quisitiveness, security, consumerism, and elitism that motivate
their behavior.

Whence come these spurious values that often undermine the
common good? Today, increasingly, they are instilled by a process of economic socialization. Our economic system transmits
and reinforces the value of consumption, for example, through
control of the social imagination by advertising and the media,
through the demands of the commodity market and corporate
competition (phenomena as disparate as computers and "cab-

bage patch" dolls exhibit the same dynamic). The system conveys and sells not only products but a consciousness and a definition of reality, inducing "fears, fantasies, titillations and discontents that express themselves through the fabricated necessities of compulsive production, joyless consumption, and economic and psychological scarcity." In effect, consumption is no longer a means to life, but becomes the meaning of life.

Thus it would appear that our economic system—which imprints social and psychological repertoires while it moves goods and services—is a key factor in defining the individual's perception of self-interest, and in predefining the field of choice within which one must define one's interests. It would not be an exaggeration to say that the economic system has become the primary carrier of values in our society. For example, it has the power to motivate people to make choices—within a range of options defined by the system—that violate their long-term interests in order to satisfy their more immediate ones. Moreover, it has the power to displace a preferred value system with pseudo-preferences and the illusion of choice.

Our understanding of self-interest and the common good is complicated in another way by the economic system. Economic logic leads us to presume that for every question there is a "right" answer, for every problem, a "right" solution. Programs and policies, therefore, ought to work, or to be replaceable by those that do. In reality, however, every social situation involves conflicting interests and often irreconcilable priorities. One person's solution can be another's problem. Hence the common good cannot be easily reduced to political trade-offs, much less to programs of sweeping social reconstruction. Neither the energy of the social atom (the individualistic solution), nor the external manipulation of the molecule (the corporate solution) is enough.

The second question, which requires us to identify a new locus of authentic power that can effect change, points us in the direction of a *communitarian* consciousness and a moral imperative which would support and legitimate relational structures that would facilitate a just social order. I believe this is the third option, an alternative to what we have seen thus far in U.S.

culture, and perhaps the only viable response to the changing character of the economic system in our times. Moreover, the present situation represents an unprecedented challenge for the Church, as an alternative carrier of values, to incarnate its own communitarian ethic in the social order.

A communitarian social ethos would of necessity imply a consciousness of self as situated and incorporated in a social organism. It would imply a way of life that is inherently cooperative and a social ethic that motivates individuals to act for the common good. In sociological terms, this may require what Harry Boyte has described as a "metamorphosis at the grassroots," a transformation of a passive, individualistic, atomized citizenry into active, mediating, engaged actors in the socioeconomic scene. Politically, this would mean, among other things, a constituency that sees government neither as the enemy nor as the solution, but rather as "the instrument of the people themselves, of living communities joined together." Boyte notes that the idea is as old in U.S. history as the Plymouth Plantation and the Iroquois Confederacy: the sensibility of the "commonwealth."[8]

A communitarian consciousness would look first to the common good as the fundamental criterion for the fulfillment of its genuine, long-term, legitimate self-interest. Economic behavior and public policy would be evaluated in terms of certain characteristics which seem essential to the notion of the common good in a democratic, pluralistic environment. Obviously, identifying and agreeing on such characteristics is a complex exercise. Moreover, the notion of the common good cannot be understood as a static philosophical or political concept—it is necessarily specific to a time and place. A contemporary, culturally specific understanding of the common good relative to citizens of the United States might include four principal values:

(1) a quality of life that enhances and improves the social relations between individuals and groups, and that promotes tolerance, communication, cooperation, bonding. Pockets of "engaged" citizenry, motivated only by ideology or a special-interest agenda, would hardly be an advance over general apathy.

(2) a quality of life that broadens, rather than constricts, the

boundaries of human choice. This means working to free the individual from debilitating conditions and social cul de sacs, encouraging freedom of opportunity and moral agency, within the boundaries of an authentic standard of fairness to all.

(3) a quality of life that provides an adequate standard of living, and holds out the possibility of improving the material conditions of life. This implies the acceptance of a concept of ownership and use as a relative right in the light of others' necessities.

(4) a quality of life that promotes the individual's access to the resources of power, and an appropriate degree of input into and control over the systems that affect her life—and a corresponding responsibility and accountability for the use of these resources.

Public policies as well as individual behavior are often justified by appealing to the consonance between a policy or action and some accepted myths or shibboleths that are part of the dominant belief system. Today, more than ever, appeals to abstract "democratic" myths as justifications for policy must be scrutinized carefully. Even if the essential value of the structure is defensible (e.g., the "free market" or private property), the effective value may be relatively indefensible in the light of the common good. An evaluation of the quality of life within a given system necessarily places greater emphasis on the criteria of effects and consequences than on the intrinsic value or motive of specific structures or policies. No one would deny, for example, the intrinsic, essential value of unionization and its coherence with democratic process and the rights of the individual person. But, in practice, particularly the larger unions seem over a period of time to have been co-opted into a kind of "forced collusive interest" with capital that has brought a net loss in real wages, diminished worker control over work conditions and corporate development, and resulted in a fractioning rather than consolidation of class-interests.

Thus, economic phenomena and structures cannot be adequately assessed by examining their intentional aspect only. An analysis of effects based on an accepted notion of the common good would provide a more ethical norm for evaluation of the economic system. For example, in assessing the criteria of access to power, certain facts about the contemporary situation will be evident. In a monetized economy, market and credit functions become increasingly abstract and remote from the ordinary citizen. The transnational character of capital as well as the sheer velocity of money transactions is plunging the global economy into a turmoil of easily destabilized values. What one analyst has called "the financial hall of mirrors" renders the individual not only powerless but illiterate in a system where computer technology now allows the same amount of money to simultaneously support five-to-ten times as many transactions as previously, or where "creative accounting," manipulation of money supply and bank reserve requirements, monetizing of loans, proliferation of credit cards and speculation in commodity futures distort real values.

The individual is further disempowered, distanced from the resources of power, by technology itself. As technology grows increasingly more capital-intensive, the worker becomes more of a commodity: more susceptible to unemployment, obsolescence, marginalization. Within the workplace itself, at the micro-level, recent studies indicate that the introduction of automated systems (e.g., word-processing equipment) has the effect of "deskilling" workers, converting varied, challenging processes into routine, repetitive tasks. The introduction of such equipment often results in a major shift in the locus of power: workers have less control over their situation and work patterns, bosses have more. As one researcher notes,

> For those who design, manufacture, sell and administer the new technology, automation does mean more control over labor costs, faster and more complete information, higher levels of expertise, responsibility, and salary. But for clericals, automation means something completely different—more routinized jobs, more standarized work, greater pressure and less sociability.[9]

Another study suggests that automated offices are an attempt to replace looser patriarchal forms of control (typical of secretary-manager relationships) by more direct capitalistic, impersonal forms; such workplaces are inherently oppressive because they result in a more real subordination and disempowerment of workers.[10]

The impact of technology is only one aspect of the larger question of how the present configuration of the American economy structures human relationships. Braverman's classic description provides a kind of paradigm:

> The industrialization of food and other elementary home provisions is only the first step in a process which eventually leads to the dependence of all social life, and indeed of all the interrelatedness of humankind, upon the marketplace. . . . The population no longer relies upon social organization in the form of family, friends, neighbors, community elders, children, but with few exceptions must go to market and only to market, not only for food, clothing, and shelter, but also for recreation, amusement, security, for the care of the young, the old, the sick, the handicapped. In time not only the material and service needs, but even the emotional patterns of life are channelled through the market.[11]

The development of market relations as a substitute for individual and community relations has an increasingly atomizing effect. It results in the overwhelming paradox of contemporary social relations: increasing fragmentation in the midst of increasing interdependence. Even as our social life becomes a dense and close network of interlocked activities in which people are more and more interdependent, we are becoming increasingly atomized, and our contacts with one another separate us instead of bringing us closer together.

This atomization is directly related to one of the most crucial phenomena affecting the relationship of capital and labor in the United States: namely, the segmentation of the work force and the fractioning of class interests that has accompanied it. More than in any other developed nation this phenomenon has exacerbated the negative impact of the economic system on social relations and has inhibited cooperative solutions to problems generated by the system.

As a result of the "social structure of accumulation" which the economy imposes, three distinct segments have developed

within the work force, characterized by increasing differentiation
and divisiveness in interests and priorities. Gordon, Edwards and
Reich have described a primary sector including jobs involving
relatively independent work and those involving "subordinate"
work (often semi-skilled white-collar or blue-collar jobs); and, a
secondary sector, or pool of casual workers with little or no
attachment to the industry and very minimal employment rights
and benefits. Social analysis of this segmentation reveals that it
explains the divisions within the American working class on the
basis of several factors: (1) workers in each segment experience
very different relations with their employers, their co-workers,
their unions and advocates. These differences produce divergent
political views and work against solidarity; (2) this segmentation
has played a major role in transmitting the effects of past and
present race and sex discrimination. Employers have manipulated ethnic, racial and gender differences in order to maintain
advantage and control—a "divide and conquer" strategy; (3)
differences that have emerged in the structures of family, school
and community institutions since World War II have increasingly
come to mirror many of the qualitative differences among the
labor segments.[12]

Another category of effects which impinge on the common
good is connected with the phenomenon of corporatism and
bureaucratization. The historic transformation of capitalism in
the United States has led to larger and larger corporations and
the concentration of wealth and resources in the hands of fewer
and fewer people. The bureaucratization of the economic process
has systematically transferred power from individuals to non-
intentional entities, prompting observations like Theodore
Lowi's: "The crucial question is not '*Who* governs?' but '*What*
governs?'" For the most part, power is exercised within these
corporate cultures according to processes that are authoritarian,
oligarchic and devoid of any democratic procedures or controls.
In this kind of economic system, power is delocalized, nonaccountability is diffused through the system, and the most significant product of the system is waste.[13]

It is clear, therefore, that many effects of the current economic
system in the United States negate the values of the common

good, which would insure a desirable quality of life for the majority of American citizens. The atomizing and fractioning of social relations, the objectification of persons and processes, and the perpetuation and reinforcement of dominance/dependency structures and relations are compounded by the narrowing of the individual's and the community's field of choice and access to the resources of power, and the enormous cost in human as well as monetary terms. The situation becomes positively pernicious when it is enhanced and exacerbated by public policies which seem to divide the "have's" from the "have-not's" even more ruthlessly. Two recent studies have confirmed that in the last five years the distribution of income in the United States has become more unequal, and that the middle class has shrunk as many families have sunk into poverty or near poverty.

Levy and Michel of the Urban Institute note that average disposable income among the poorest one-fifth of families has declined by almost 10%.[14] In the last five years tax burdens have increased disproportionately for the poorest fifth of the nation. Stephen Rose's recent study of social stratification in the U.S. revealed that three out of four people who move out of the middle class today move downward into accelerating economic jeopardy.[15] The Census Bureau reported that the nation's poverty rate, which was 11.4 in 1978, reached 15 per cent in 1982, the highest in 17 years. A recent study at the University of Michigan reveals that one in four Americans experienced several years of poverty in the 1970's.[16] The phenomenon is aggravated by other sociological trends: the rising number of single-parent households and the growth of service and high-tech industries which create two levels of income distribution—high and low—in contrast to the smokestack industries like machine tools which provided a large number of middle-income jobs. It is estimated that 70 percent of new jobs generated in the 1970's can be classified as "women's work"—low-status, dead-end jobs. As Lester Thurow has commented recently, "A bipolar income distribution composed of rich and poor is replacing the wide expanse of the middle class."[17]

Another paradoxical effect of our economic system is the way in which it actually undermines and subverts the family structure that it is supposed to support (family wage system, etc.). The feminization of poverty, which has been exacerbated by current economic and social developments, is a case in point. Approximately 80 percent of all Americans living below the poverty line are women and children. By the year 2000, they may constitute the entire poverty population. Elderly women and single working mothers are the two fastest growing segments of this population.

At the same time one of the most dramatic trends among males age 25–40 is the emergence of an upwardly mobile, independent and single group of high earners who, as Barbara Ehrenreich puts it, "live for themselves, and consume for themselves." It is these "Yuppies" that market researchers are targeting. One multinational marketing manager told her, "The only problem with the family is, they can all share *one* refrigerator, *one* stereo, *one* microwave, etc. But when they get divorced, you double everything."[18]

In ethical terms, the prevailing effects of the economic system are increasingly unjust for greater numbers of people. In theological terms, this can be interpreted as a condition of "social sin." Paul Tillich went so far as to describe modern capitalism as a manifestation of the "demonic," of radical evil, because it is "the war of all against all, accepted as a principle":

> The peculiarly demonic element in the situation of *capitalist* society is this, that the conflict is not the expression of individual arbitrariness or of chaotic anarchy but is necessarily bound up with the maintenance of the *capitalist economic* system and is the result of that system itself.[19]

Gregory Baum offers a less extreme interpretation of the demonic element when he says that institutions operate out of a logic built into them at the start, and which persists even when the human needs they were designed to fulfill are no longer being met. Thus, social structures which are initially and essentially good can in time become oppressive because of the conditions that they produce or foster. Baum suggests that this dialectical view of social developments allows us to speak of social sin without having to claim that personal sin is at the root of every social injustice.[20]

The question inevitably arises: can an impersonal system be said to be "evil" or "demonic"? If the old "sacred/secular" dichotomy is involved, the economic system would be absolved of culpability because as a system it follows laws of its own, and only individuals can use it for immoral ends. But if this dichotomy is erased and the whole of reality is perceived as actively engaged in the redemptive process, then everything becomes transpersonal and moral in an ultimate sense. In such a framework sin can transcend the individual, and indeed this helps give meaning to the idea of "original sin." As Suchocki comments, "In a process world, the past can be understood as the conveyer of original sin and the demonic. . . . The demonic consumes the past and denies any future but its own perpetuation, under the illusion that the future must be only more of the same. . . . Demonic power is a call for repetition."[21]

To the extent, then, that the American economic system tends to perpetuate itself and resists adaptation to the requirements of the common good, it can be said to be radically sinful. It is the fundamental inertia of the system, not its intentional components, that makes this a reality. Two primary characteristics of corporate, bureaucratized systems contribute to this inertia: (1) immobility or resistance to change, (2) nonaccountability or the diffusion of responsibility. In this sense, sin might be defined as "replication"; conversion becomes an act of creative change. Baum echoes this point: "What we experience in modern industrial society is the death of human creativity."[22]

2

Conversion, if it is only an individual proposition, will not be a sufficient response or adequate moral imperative for the modern crisis. Reform capitalism also proves inadequate because it usually invokes the same privatistic and/or corporate (socialistic) imperatives which have already proved to be insufficient in the historical context. Mere appeals to "corporate responsibility," personal entrepreneurial ethics, or government regulation cannot meet the challenge of a radically sinful system.

Michael Sandel has discussed the need for a new communitarian ethic in terms of political philosophy. He notes the inadequacy of the utilitarian and the liberal rights-based social ethic to address the broader demands and dilemmas of contemporary human polity. The unencumbered, autonomous self must recognize the imperatives of the situated self: we are citizens, members of human families and social organisms as well as independent selves. Our personal goals are not the end of liberty. In his view, the communitarian ethic represents a conversion from the politics of rights to the politics of the common good. This would cut across traditional party lines and may thus produce a more creative politics.[23]

Sandel's theoretical concept of the need for a new political economy is translated into one set of concrete proposals by Alperovitz and Faux in their recent book, *Rebuilding America*. They describe the present socioeconomic situation as that of a "broker state," a haphazard arrangement in which spending programs are awarded to those groups that develop sufficient political clout to get a favored space at the spigot, "a free-for-all between a growing number of organized constituencies and shifting interest groups."[24]

On the practical level a step toward the development of an authentic *communitarian* response to the contemporary challenge of the economic system would be a new understanding of *power*. Power should not be looked at as something that emanates from or rests in the person of a leader, but as something that results from the structured interrelationships of people. Power necessarily flows from great numbers of persons whose empowering responses—acquiescence and cooperation—are elicited through various processes of socialization, education, propaganda, reward and coercion. Power is something given to *some* by many others. Nevertheless the power that the elite few possess, the control they exert over the material and symbolic resources of power, often obscures and impedes the proper exercise of power by the many. As Parenti suggests, "To ask whether the people have power is like asking whether Saudi Arabia has oil, for the populace are the very stuff of power, yet it is most often the oligarchic few who extract and refine these resources for purposes of their own."[25] Likewise, even in more democratic surroundings, elections are more of a surrender than an assertion of popular power, "a gathering up of empowering responses by the elites who have the resources for such periodic harvestings, an institutionalized mechanism providing for the regulated flow of power from the many to the few in order to legitimate the rule of the few in the name of the many."[26]

The "many" must come to a realization and active awareness, individually and collectively, of their complicity in this transference of power. They must, individually and collectively, reclaim their power. Some examples might be cited: (1) the unionized worker must be converted from a consciousness hypnotized by security, protections and guarantees to one of participation, responsibility and control. The worker's dependence on seniority must be converted to an active concern about expanding skill capacity; (2) citizens must begin to see themselves as producers of power rather than merely as consumers. In one California county, for example, an increasing number of citizens are beginning to generate their own electric power with small gas turbines. In several other regions public takeovers of electric utilities are a very real possibility in the next few years; (3) citizens also have to gain more access to the resources of financial power; this means direct access through control over credit sources, pension investments and interest rates; as well as indirect access through the exercise of input into corporate investment policies that affect the local community.

The relationship between empowerment and a communitarian ethic has been concretized in an extraordinary way in the city of Mondragon, Spain. The control that the community exerts over the credit resources of the local area and the reinvestment of profits is the heart of this unique experiment in cooperative ownership.[27] Another experiment worthy of note is the COPS (Communities Organized for Public Service) group of San Antonio, Texas—described by some as "the most effective community group in the country, the voice of 150,000 families." A report from the National Commission on Neighborhoods describes the hundreds of millions of dollars' worth of improvements in streets, public facilities and other projects that COPS has accomplished for poorer neighborhoods in San Antonio, and concludes: "There has been a major shift in power from wealthy 'blue blooded' Anglos to poor and working Mexican-American families of San Antonio. COPS has been at the center of this shift."[28] Catholic social teaching has been a significant influence in the evolution of both of these experiments.

The latter experiments are also evidence of a second ingredient which is absolutely necessary for the development of a communitarian moral imperative. Not only must the individual experience a new consciousness of his/her power in the context of a community, but, as John Raines argues, the relationship between the community and capital, the resources of power, demands a new covenant, a conscious and mutually agreed upon relationship between those who make significant economic decisions and those who must live with the consequences of those decisions. In defining the terms of the new covenant, not only must capital's investment in the community be recognized (producing jobs, income, environment), but the community's investment in capital must also be recognized—workers must actualize that power in real terms. The aforementioned criteria for assessing the common good would constitute a minimal baseline for that covenant. As Raines comments, "The pursuit of private profit may succeed for a while, but if undisciplined to the common good, will ultimately destroy its own foundation."[29]

What would be the terms of such a covenant? There is no one answer to that question, but a communitarian consciousness might produce different proposals at the bargaining table. The covenant might include agreements concerning capital reinvestment and profit-sharing between workers and management. It might include provisions for education and re-training, as well as "conversion" strategies. In the most crucial area of all, workers and managment might agree to a 3:1 ratio as the maximum differential between the salaries of workers and executives. Moreover, the social cost of corporate involvement in the community must be assessed and equity established.

Such a covenant is extremely unlikely, however, in the absence of a change of consciousness that transcends class divisions and self-interest. How can such a change be brought about? What might be the most effective change agents in this transformation? In effect, a new communitarian socialization must displace the economic socialization that presently prevails. Government and organized religion can, at the very least, act as catalysts in this process. Religion, especially, will have an important role in the creation of a new moral imperative, a new legitimating myth for the new consciousness. Furthermore, government and church can exercise their power most effectively by promoting empowerment in those institutions which most effectively socialize for change.

Up until recently the prevailing views of social analysis have assumed that the most effective agents involved in modifying social behavior have been the family and the neighborhood, in conjunction with such factors as education and religious belief. Today there is an emerging body of research which suggests that we may have underestimated the capacity of the workplace itself as a powerful change agent for social behavior in general.

Several recent studies indicate that participative experiments in the workplace have the potential to enhance adults' functioning in three primary life sectors: the workplace itself, family life, and the local community. The studies show that the new activities require that the individual learn new skills as well as attitudes, sometimes under considerable stress in the initial stages. Gradually the individual internalizes these new skills and attitudes and then extends them to other settings in his or her life, particularly the community and the family.

One study found that employees in the innovative Topeka General Foods plant, a work setting with a highly participative management system, were unusually active in civic affairs.[30] Another study reported that in the shipping industry in Norway increased participation in the workplace seemed to spill over into participation in other organizations.[31] A study of the Swedish work force revealed a correlation between participative work activity and political and leisure activity.[32] Crouter's studies of the Jamestown and Sperry Rand experiments[33] indicate that the participatory changes introduced (a labor management planning committee, on the one hand, and a worker-owned cooperative, on the other) have fostered a collective sense of efficacy within both communities and a new consciousness that will enable them to meet their next shared crisis with an efficient community mobilization strategy, as well as with a sense of optimism and control.

One observable spillover may have even more long-range implications than the immediate benefit to the civic community, and that is the effect on childrearing and domestic life. The qualitative aspect becomes primary. One woman observed: "Working here takes more time away from my personal life and family life, but it has helped in terms of dealing with my family. I'm more willing to get their opinions. We hold 'team meetings' at home to make decisions."[34] Another young assembly worker noticed changes in himself: "Working here has given me a chance to learn some responsibility by going to team advisor meetings and facilitating our team meetings. Sometimes I'm withdrawn, but you have to talk. It teaches you how to effectively communicate." Another worker described his experience: "I began to be more open at home talking about my feelings and things like that. . . . My wife would look at me like I was crazy."[35]

There are already signs that the introduction of participatory arrangements in factories, businesses and government agencies across the United States is precipitating a radical shift of perceptions of power and responsibility in the workplace itself. More than a thousand firms have introduced participatory management structures over the past few years, and the results indicate that the overall effects are positive: a shift from adversarial to cooperative relations between management and labor; improved morale; climbing productivity. More than 5000 firms have greatly expanded employee ownership of common stock, and some have elected employees to their boards of directors. The evidence of these tentative and modest experiments suggests that more collaborative styles and structures are in the process of evolution.[36]

The formation of a communitarian consciousness is fundamental to shaping and sustaining a viable socio-economic covenant for the future, and I believe the evidence suggests that this consciousness may find its most fertile soil in the process of behavior modification in the workplace. Neither the family, the schools, nor the churches appear to have the same track record or potential when it comes to the developmental impact on our *adult* population.

3

What role can the Catholic Church play in this process? Since Vatican II it has exercised its magisterial and prophetic role most visibly in respect to social justice. Its official presence has been primarily made known through acts of proclamation and denunciation, not without salutary effects on the body politic as well as the faithful. Now it would seem that we are arrived at a new moment, when equal priority must be placed on the church's mission as a "gatherer of peoples," a covenanting and reconciling force that brings unity out of diversity of interest, and even out of diversity in belief structure. Hannah Arendt voiced the desperate need for such a gathering force in the world today: "What makes mass society so difficult to bear is not the number of people involved, or at least not primarily, but the fact that the world between them has lost its power to gather them together, to relate and to separate them."[37] The Church, as a universal mediating structure, is in a unique position to facilitate the development of a new consciousness and participate in the new communitarian socialization in a number of ways, primarily (1) through its own resources of conscientization (it will have an important role to play in the creation of a new moral imperative or legitimating myth), (2) by promoting a solidarity that empowers, and (3) by modeling alternative relations and structures.

This last will perhaps present the most critical challenge for contemporary Catholicism. We have come to a "watershed" with the arrival of the post-industrial era: the Church cannot continue to legitimate the structures of patriarchal, hierarchical and caste dominance which have become so alienating in the wider arena of the socio-economic order. Nor can it merely manipulate symbols and language to proclaim the message of the Gospel: it must bring forth new structures of just relations from its own internalization of Gospel justice. Fidelity to this mission will unquestionably result in cognitive and experiential dissonance, the painful process of learning new ways of thinking and behaving, of struggle—what Choan-Seng Song has called a "theology of the womb."[38]

Where are the prototypes? They are not likely to originate with the hierarchy, although the legitimation it eventually supplies will add momentum to the process. New forms are emerging among ordinary Christians in crucial areas: the Christian base communities of Latin America; communities like Sojourners, the Church of the Savior, New Jerusalem, Koinonia, the ARC community in North America; new ecclesial communities of women, and even in the conservative bastions of Roman Catholicism, the "personal parish." There are common threads in the spirituality that is emerging in these small paradigm-covenants of communitarian consciousness: simplicity of life; a concern for the poor and the powerless, social analysis and political participation; an "Exodus" theology that breaks with the past and engages in the struggle for personal and social conversion, a creativity that confronts the demonic replication of the past; above all, self-disclosure and sharing of goods and resources.

In different degrees and in different ways these ecclesial experiments in discipleship are providing an alternative to the solutions implied in some of the most pertinent church teachings. For example, in "Pacem in Terris," Pope John recognizes the "insufficiency of modern states to insure the common good." There is a hint of the "corporate" solution in his call for "public authorities (supra-national authority) that are in a position to act on a world-wide basis."[39] What the covenant prototypes and the peace movement are perhaps demonstrating is that the solution to shaping a just socio-economic order may begin at the bottom of the pyramid instead of at the top.

The communitarian spirituality that is emerging from these covenant-prototypes is a spirituality that addresses the economic situation as a fundamental religious and moral problem. It rejects the old "sacred/secular" dichotomies and erases comfortable dualisms. This point is emphatically articulated in the document produced by the Sao Paulo Congress of Theology on the "Ecclesiology of the Popular Christian Communities": in describing the "spirituality of liberation," the document says it is a spirituality that implies "overcoming dualisms alien to biblical spirituality: faith and life, prayer and action, commitment and daily work, contemplation and political struggle, creation and salvation. Spirituality is not merely a distinct moment in the process of the liberation of the poor. It is the mystery of the experience of God *within* this process."[40] This spirituality inevitably produces a new politics.

This essay has not presumed to offer precise solutions; it has merely tried to describe the topography of our current situation and the need for a new spirituality and politics to address it. The crisis of the socioeconomic order is an inherently religious challenge, and for the Church a crisis of generativity and creativity as well. The dualisms which functioned so efficiently to create the present crisis are in the process of disintegration. The emerging integrative consciousness suggests that power and responsibility for the socio-economic order will increasingly be viewed in a communitarian context that transcends the merely individualistic and corporate responses to the imperative of the common good.

Notes

1. Andrew Carnegie, quoted in *Anthology,* arr. by Margaret Barclay Wilson (New York, 1915), p. 172. Among others, Richard Hofstader recognizes Carnegie as a key figure in the legitimation of "Social Darwinism," see Hofstadter's *Social Darwinism in American Thought* (Boston: Beacon Press, 1955), pp. 45 ff.

2. Andrew Carnegie, *The Gospel of Wealth,* p. 18.

3. Russell Conwell, *Acres of Diamonds,* ed. William Webb (Hallmark edition, 1968).

4. Walter Rauschenbusch, *The Kingdom of God and the Social Gospel* in *A Rauschenbusch Reader,* by Benson Landis (New York: Harper & Bros., 1957), pp. 45 ff.

5. Ibid., p. 43.

6. Lawrence Chenoweth, *The American Dream of Success* (Boston: Duxbury Press, 1974), p. 78.

7. Michael Parenti, *Power and the Powerless* (New York: St. Martin's Press, 1978), pp. 16, 150.

8. Harry C. Boyte, *Community Is Possible, Repairing America's Roots* (New York: Harper & Row, 1984), and "Rebuilding the American Commonwealth," in *Beyond Reagan: Alternatives for the 80's*, ed. Gartner, Greer, Riesman (New York: Harper & Row), pp. 316–333.

9. Anne Machung, "Word Processing: Forward for Business, Backward for Women," Business and Professional Women's Foundation, 1983, p. 12. An edited version of this essay appears in Brodkin, Sacks and Remy (eds.), *My Troubles Are Going To Have Trouble With Me* (New Brunswick, N.J.: Rutgers Univ. Press, 1984), pp. 124–139.

10. Jane Barker and Hazel Downing, "Word Processing and the Transformation of Patriarchal Relations of Control in the Office," in *Capital and Class,* 10 (Summer, 1980), pp. 64–97.

11. Harry Braverman, *Labor and Monopoly Capital* (New York: Monthly Review Press, 1974), p. 276.

12. David Gordon, Richard Edwards and Michael Reich, *Segmented Work, Divided Workers* (New York: Cambridge University Press, 1982), p. 213.

13. Samuel Bowles, David Gordon and Thomas Weisskopf, *Beyond the Waste Land* (New York: Doubleday & Co., 1983).

14. Frank Levy and Richard Michel, "The Way We'll Be in 1984: Recent Changes in the Level and Distribution of Disposable Income," monograph for the Changing Domestic Priorities Project (Washington, D.C.: Urban Institute, 1983). The divisive effect of many of the Reagan Administration's policies has been described in political as well as economic terms in Frances Fox Piven and Richard Cloward's *The New Class War* (New York: Pantheon Books, 1982).

15. Stephen J. Rose, *Social Stratification in the United States* (Baltimore: Social Graphics Co., 1983).

16. Greg Duncan, Mary Corcoran, Patricia and Gerald Gurin, *Years of Poverty, Years of Plenty* (University of Michigan Institute for Social Research, 1984).

17. Lester Thurow, "The Disappearance of the Middle Class," *New York Times,* February 5, 1984.

18. Barbara Ehrenreich, "Hearts of Men and the Wallets of Women," lecture at George Washington University, May 7, 1984.

19. Paul Tillich, *The Religious Situation* (New York: Meridian Books, 1956), p. 109.

20. Gregory Baum, *The Priority of Labor* (New York: Paulist Press, 1982), p. 58.

21. Marjorie Hewitt Suchocki, *God, Christ, Church* (New York: Crossroad, 1982), pp. 25, 26.

22. Baum, p. 59.

23. Michael J. Sandel, "Morality and the Liberal Ideal," *New Republic,* May 7, 1984, p. 17.

24. Gar Alperovitz, Jeff Faux, *Rebuilding America* (New York: Pantheon Books, 1984), p. 16.

25. Parenti, p. 197.

26. Parenti, p. 201.

27. Thomas Henk, Chris Logan, *Mondragon: An Economic Analysis* (Boston: George Allen & Unwin, 1982).

28. G. R. Fowler, *People Building Neighborhoods,* National Commission on Neighborhoods Report, vol. I, case study appendix, 1979, 474.

29. John C. Raines, "Capital, Community, and the Meaning of Work," *Christianity and Crisis,* October 17, 1983, pp. 378–379.

30. R. Walton, "Alienation and Innovation in the Workplace," in J. O'Toole (ed.), *Work and the Quality of Life: Resource Papers for Work in America* (Cambridge, Mass.: MIT Press, 1974), p. 239.

31. L. Klein, *New Forms of Work Organization* (London: Cambridge University Press, 1976), p. 72. Quoted in Ann Crouter, "Participative Work as an Influence on Human Development," unpublished manuscript, October, 1982.

32. R. Karasek, *Job Socialization: A Longitudinal Study of Work, Political and Leisure Activity.* Revised Working Paper No. 59 (Stockholm: Institute for Social Research, 1978), i. Quoted in Crouter.

33. Ann Crouter and James Garabino, "Corporate Self-reliance and the Sustainable Society," Woodlands Conference on Growth Policy, November, 1982. See also C. Meek and W. F. Whyte, *The Jamestown Model of Cooperative Problem-solving,* unpublished manuscript, Cornell University, 1980, and D. Zwerdling, *Democracy at Work* (Washington, D.C.: Association for Self-management, 1978).

34. Urie Bronfenbrenner and Ann Crouter, "Work and Family Through Time and Space," in S. Kamerman and C. Hayes (eds.), *Families That Work: Children in a Changing World* (Washington, D.C.: National Academy of Sciences, 1982).

35. Zwerdling, 1978, p. 25, quoted in Crouter, "Participative Work," 1982.

36. John Simmons and William Mares, *Working Together* (New York: Alfred Knopf, Inc., 1983).

37. Hannah Arendt, quoted in Sandel, p. 17.

38. Choan-Seng Song, *Third-Eye Theology* (New York: Orbis Books, 1979), p. 137.

39. John XXIII, "Pacem in Terris," 136–137, quoted in *The Gospel of Justice and Peace* by Joseph Gremillion (New York: Orbis Books, 1976), pp. 229–230.

40. "Final Document," International Ecumenical Congress of Theology, February 20–March 2, 1980, Sao Paulo, Brazil, quoted in *The Challenge of Basic Christian Communities* ed. Sergio Torres and John Eagleson (New York: Orbis Books, 1981), p. 241.

GEORGES KHODR

Violence and the Gospel

Georges Khodr is the Orthodox bishop of Mount Lebanon. The violence in his country—daily, random, mindless—is perpetrated, more often than not, in the name of God. Christians, Khodr suggests, must search and judge their Scriptures and the conflicting attitudes they contain. Khodr's own judgment is unequivocal: ". . . there is no possible path from the warrior-God of Exodus and Joshua to the God of Jesus Christ. That monstrous image cannot be made acceptable." He then examines the primitive Christian refusal to justify war and finds in it a way that breaks the spiral of violence through which "a country crumbles completely and people feel like animals, tracked night and day," astonished that they remain alive. At the very least, Khodr demands convergence not between Christians and others, but between Christians and the heart of their own tradition.

This essay is not an analysis of violence but a hymn to that evangelical virtue which is especially attractive to those who have had too long a familiarity with death. Such an experience is fruitful only if it is understood in the light of the Gospel. Otherwise, repeated daily atrocities can bring people to the edge of nothingness, to a despair inspired by the total collapse of society. Faced with the sense of non-being that such experiences induce, only a vision of light can disclose signs of a christic time.

241

1

In the middle of a storm the only question is how to be saved from it. In such a situation it is normal for people to be tempted by the immediacy of a drab ultra-pragmatism. When it seems to extend indefinitely to total despair, my only question is how to save myself from death. But when death becomes the only fact of everyday life, because it is no longer an exceptional event, it becomes banal. It is just another object, like a stone, and only acquires meaning if it is huge or occurs in large numbers.

In the abyss of the annihilation, both of things and of people—starting with those wreaking the destruction—the true sin is insensibility. Confronted with violence, we can join in the deathly dance, and conceive of an heroic rescue because we have the hands of a strangler and can no longer find an expert who will establish the distinction—if it ever existed in God's eyes—between the combatant and the murderer. Meanwhile we defend values we never practiced, which are ambiguous or disturbing because we defend them on a level other than their own, and have become perverted by hatred or mutilated by being cut off from a cohesive context of values. We will never sufficiently realize that murder springs from the heart, that no evil is external, and that violence is simply the forthright expression of pride and of the vanity of tribes which cannot recognize God's face in the Other. There can be no genuine discourse about sin because sin is the irrational. When the soul is perverted by sin, it is no longer structured by the Logos, the source of its peace and order. Repetition of sin gives birth to passion, which is moral folly in the pure state, the death of the Logos, and then simply death.

When the apostle says that death is the penalty for sin, he is not talking about a punishment meted out to the sinner from outside by a divine verdict: God is not an executioner. It is simply that death is inherent in every evil that our mind presents to us; every sin contains the germ of death. It is, first, the destroyer of inner being, and potentially of every being. Doesn't the adulteration of relationships between people derive from an initial message that has woven false links between them, suffocating the truth? Physical violence is only an eloquent expression of self-hatred, due to fear of the truth that we no longer transmit because we don't want to live it. To victimize oneself out of hatred of God and then to falsely reestablish oneself in life by inflicting death on others represents the implacable logic of those who have deliberately cut their ties with the source of life. In God's very name they have confirmed themselves in promethean folly, offering the challenge of a kind of freedom, denying the Word of God who alone rules over us and in whom our freedom is based.

The hieratic society that empties the name of God of all content practices a horrible paganism. "God" becomes just a word used to express the will to power and the religious symbol becomes a sign of terror. In this way God can ultimately be transformed first into a concept, and then into an idol, instrument of a history that one no longer receives from him but forges for oneself and then attributes to him. Holiness gives place to heroism: only the warrior is holy.

In this situation each faction makes its own interpretation of divine thought since God alone conducts war. Our faith in God is based on this foundation, for it is he who scatters death among our enemies and in the control over these deaths God becomes authentic. Is not man called his vicar, as the Koran affirms? Naturally, each group assigns this role of vicar to itself. And if we believe we are divinely invested with this function here on earth, it follows that we have power over life and death. All war is metaphysical; one can only go to war religiously. In the state of peace we can easily believe ourselves secularized. Regardless of what words are used, wartime encourages us to be mystical. If we didn't believe that the transfer from the will of God to the human will was being carried out legitimately, we would begin to question ourselves as interpreters of human destiny. This doubt would lead to reconciliation and hence to the rationality that consists in situating the Logos as superior and anterior to our personal option, a rationality that includes the Other.

What we need from the outset, therefore, is the non-existence of others. They may seem to exist, since we are fighting them, but that is only a minor detail since the mystique of war is more important than the war.

The others have no historical reference point; if they had, they would be part of a discourse of unity. In a certain kind of war it is not a question of conquering, since we are victorious from the start because of how we think about God. Victory is a sort of platonic idea, whatever its empirical expression. If the latter is not commensurate with the eternal model, it is the empirical reality that has to change. By identifying ourselves with the whole, we issue an anathema. So much the worse for the facts if we do not numerically constitute the whole. There's always a sacred alliance that God can support. Otherwise, God wouldn't have a permanent vicar. The historical event that we repeat is simply a sign of the metahistorical truth with which we are providentially entrusted. It is this mission which founds the present and guarantees the future. Defeats only encourage the myth that we have cultivated, which already proclaims the final end of others. When the soul is invaded by the thirst for blood, faith gives way to ideology. The religious vocabulary is maintained but the words change their content. They become symbols of empirical reality or of the meaning we think we find in the concrete situation.

The mythological reading of the past becomes the framework of interpretation: that is why others are eliminated from the physical or moral world. If they do not have the right to live today, their existence in the past must have been an error. Although we cannot train them to renounce their identity, and it is too costly to eliminate them from the land of the living, we can suppress them from the abode of the dead by making a travesty of history. They must not be allowed to become part of the historical memory of their people. Their expulsion from time is more important than the present anathema against them. If it is more convenient to tolerate them in space, the first rule is that they accept the status of aliens in history.

But a victim who does not revolt is not destroyed completely. The combat is carried out to the end only if the minority does not renounce its reading of history. The necessity of ideology forces the minority to renounce its identity, or at least to adopt a mask what will perhaps veil its personality for a long time. Ideology recognizes a special time during which foundations were laid.

Such a period does not simply refer to a period of history but to a rhythm, a sort of Bergsonian *durée,* which will liberate you, if you are its accomplice—whether out of fear or self-interest—from your specific identity in order to hurl you into what has been chosen for your salvation because it constitutes the truth.

2

What I have described is a subtle, frightening violence, but which, strictly speaking, can dispense with the use of force. Ultimately, the physical weapon is present only as symbol of the anathema.

For there is no question but that it is the gods who make war. Earth only reflects the impiety of heaven. Death, the last enemy, is so foreign to our nature that it has to be submitted to divine reason. Repressed by men and women as an eternal thorn in their history, it can be grounded only in God who has the right to choose his lieutenants according to his good pleasure. That is why a doctrine of death does not really have its place in a religion of *fatum,* in which gods and goddesses endure human passions; a doctrine of the death of others is conceivable only in mono-theism, in which God does not know this love-passion that leads him to death. If God does not choose death as his lot, and his resurrection, as well as that of others, which emerges from it, he would inevitably vow those who are not his own to destruction. The God who does not recognize the dialogue interior to himself will give even less recognition to the dialogue with pagans or infidels. To the hebraic sensibility, the questions of Job receive a final answer in the rewards that he obtains after his test. For those who recognize the incommensurable, however, it is only in later monotheism, in which one finds revealed the Lamb which has been sacrificed before all ages, that a response is given to Job.

I will pass quickly over the history of Christian peoples in their justification of violence. "Holy wars" were led against "infidels" by various Christian sovereigns, especially in Spain. If the Crusades did not borrow all the elements of Jihad from Islam, it is nonetheless true that the rights of God, of western pilgrims, or of the Byzantine empire, were defended by mystics. Addressing the English, St. Bernard of Clairvaux declares that "The earth trembles because the Lord of heaven is losing the very land where he appeared among men. . . And now, because of our sins, the enemy of the Cross has commenced to raise his sacrilegious head and to lay waste the promised land." For St. Bernard the crusade represents a sign of salvation, the pardon of sins, and eternal glory. This master of Christian spirituality is, on every count, in agreement with Islam, which practices conquest in the name of God and sees itself in the role of conqueror. But Islam is not tied to a place but to the Word and justifies holy war out of a desire to propagate God's word in conquered territory. In countries united to the house of Islam the Moslem religion is imposed on polytheists if they agree to live by it, but hardly ever on Jews and Christians.

In addition, Moslem holy war requires the combatant to prepare himself spiritually by struggling against his passions. St. Bernard, without knowing it, is a disciple of Islam in that the crusader, like the Moslem, is to achieve salvation through combat on behalf of God. Here the position of the Church of the East is clear. St. John Chrysostom pronounces anathema against anyone who teaches that we are allowed to kill heretics. Moreover, the Church of Cappadocia with St. Basil, as well as the Church of Byzantium, have categorically refused to canonize soldiers killed in battle as martyrs.

It is not my intention to discuss the idea of just war in St. Augustine and St. Thomas Aquinas. I don't believe that Christian reflection on this theme has ever been as perverted as in Byzantium, where each morning every Orthodox church in the world sings: "God save our people and bless our heritage. Give our pious emperor victory over the barbarians." It is true that the Byzantines only accepted the idea of defensive war, and that for them the *oecumene* included all the Christian nations of the empire. In their eyes the failure to halt the barbarian invasion would have meant the oppression of the Church and the rule of the uncivilized. I can also understand their fierce desire to save Constantinople, dear to God and to his Mother, before its fall in the 15th century. How many holy monks, illustrious prelates, and venerable witnesses of the most beautiful liturgy in the world were able to sing in the Acathiste that the Theotokos was the rampart of the Empire? How could the Church, which in a completely biblical coherence, produced the only equilibrium I know of between a theology of the cross and a theology of glory, how could it for so many centuries, in the purest places of meditation, confuse the cause of Christ with that of the Empire, and later of all the Orthodox kingdoms? How could it affirm in its liturgy that the cross is the power of the emperor? This was the atmosphere familiar to the Prophet of Islam, which the Koran will consecrate and surpass. At the time of the Cistercian reform people knew little about Byzantium and understood it badly, but the Western intelligentsia was fascinated by Islam which they read in its sources.

3

Nevertheless, this question cannot be properly clarified as long as violence is not exorcised and its biblical foundations overthrown. If Orthodox Christians really admit that the God of the Old Testament led Israel from victory to victory and submitted all nations to it, they have no reason to question the theology of defensive war of the Byzantines or the Crusades. Keep in mind that it was with the purest intentions that the tribunal of the Inquisition erected its stakes. It was with the ideal of the perfect man that the Nazi warrior carried on his belt the inscription from Isaiah: "Gott mit uns." What does the Bible say on this subject?

"When Israel saw the mighty deed that Yahweh had performed against the Egyptians, the people revered Yahweh." (Ex 14:31)

"I shall go through Egypt and strike down the first-born in Egypt, man and beast alike" (Ex 12:12). Yahweh fights for them and brings them into the land of the Canaanites. During the occupation of the land, the Eternal One "will expel the Canaanites, the Hittites" (Josh 3:10) and the other peoples. He delivers Jericho and its king and pronounces this curse to its captain:

"Accursed before Yahweh be the man who raises up
and rebuilds this city [Jericho]!
On his first-born will he lay its foundations,
on his youngest son set up its gates!" (6:26)

At the conquest of Ai Joshua will say: "When you have captured the town, set fire to it, in obedience to Yahweh's command." (8:8) In this conquest led by God himself we have, ahead of time, the policy of scorched earth and genocide. And the Psalms praise these great deeds. Of the enemies of the people, David says:

"As fire devours a forest,
as a flame sets mountains ablaze,
so drive them away with your tempest,
by your whirlwind fill them with terror." (Ps 83:15–16)

The God Sabaoth, in the service of Israel and its hegemony over the land of Canaan, only reflects the thirst for conquest of a confederation of semitic tribes, a spirit that is totally foreign to the unfailingly loving nature of the One who is the God of nations and rules history in all its developments. God, whose name, presence, truth and unicity are love, cannot lend himself to the massacres perpetrated by Joshua son of Nun.

There is a related issue in the way St. Paul deals with the concubinage of Abraham. The perfect chastity which he advocates in his Epistles is not invoked as a judgment on the patriarch. Nevertheless, when the apostle employs allegory to explain Abraham's two wives as figures of the two alliances, he does not necessarily eliminate the historical meaning of the text. The author of the Epistle to the Hebrews seems scarcely to criticize the prostitution of Rahab, which becomes part of the history of salvation: "It was through faith that the walls of Jericho fell down" (Heb 11:30) and by faith the Hebrews "conquered kingdoms" (Heb 11:32).

In opposition to this bloody deity there is the image of the gentle God whose voice is heard in the great prophets, especially Jeremiah and Hosea, and in the Song of Songs. In the betrothal of Yahweh and his people, just as in the Servant songs, we recognize the accents of the Gospel. Confronted with the irreducible opposition between these two faces of the Lord, Marcion, in the middle of the 2nd century, thought that the wars, judgments and punishments described in Scripture could not be attributed to the good God, father of Jesus Christ, but to an inferior deity, the just God of the Jews. It was obvious that the Church, in order to preserve the unity of Scripture, had to reject Marcionite dualism. Byzantine iconography is so impregnated with the identity between Yahweh and Christ that it always writes on the nimbus that surrounds Christ's head o ων, the Septuagint translation of Yahweh in the epiphany of the Burning Bush. The patristic exegesis of the Old Testament is basically typological. Clement of Rome, who tells the story of Rahab and the spies in detail, says that the scarlet cord that the prostitute attaches to the window is a type of the blood shed by Christ. The raising of Moses's arms above the battle between Israel and Amalek will be interpreted by the tradition as a type of the cross, an exegesis reflected in Byzantine hymns and vigil readings.

The problem concerns the *how* of revelation, the real meaning of inspiration. If it is right to affirm that, in a certain manner, the Old Testament is an icon of the New, the latter is also type or prototype of the Old, in the way that Saint Basil calls the bread and wine of the Eucharist before the epiclesis antetypes of the Body and Blood of the Lord. Thus I would rather apply the term type to the realities of the New Testament, with the Gospel already inaugurating the eschaton. Nevertheless, the typological exegesis of the Fathers adopted by the liturgy can veil the historical meaning. That is why I would like to propose, in a complementary sense, what could be called a kenotic reading of the Scriptures, I borrow the term from the Epistle to the Philippians where it is a question of the humiliations of Christ, from the form of God to the form of man, from the form of man to the form of a slave, from the form of slave to death on the cross. In the kenosis the divinity of nature does not disappear but it is not made manifest. In this mystery divine knowledge becomes operational only through human growth. The synergy of the two natures also runs through Scripture, which is the body of Christ. Because of divine condescension the Word is sometimes profoundly hidden beneath words, underneath the fleshly covering of Scripture. This is what the West calls the personality or subjectivity of the sacred author. In fact, all divine writing shapes itself in human terms and everything human bears in itself the divine model. In the light of this explanation I refuse to attribute the wars waged by Israel to the divine will. Otherwise we get trapped in the morality of means, making death an instrument of life, and the destruction of various tribes becomes a condition of faith, and part of God's plan for the exaltation and prosperity of a particular people.

Yahweh cannot be pardoned for his mighty deeds of war by peoples who were crushed because of the weight of history and the unreadiness of Israel through the ages. In any case, the notion of progressive revelation can be understood only in terms of spiritual maturity, a purification even within divine beauty. For there is no possible path from the warrior-God of Exodus and Joshua to the God of Jesus Christ. That monstrous image cannot be made acceptable. The progress of revelation seems to me to depend on Hegelian dialectic and there is no trace of this awareness of evolution in Hebraic thought. I do not believe that the Bible is truly a history of salvation: God reveals himself in time, but history is not the matrix of divine thought. It is the locus of revelations, and later, of the incarnation of the Word. Hence it is the area of faith's intelligibility, but it can in no way be its formative principle. If history is all human, it receives the divine without any confusion. That is why Scripture is not the unfolding of the divine in time but the identity of divine epiphanies across time; the only difference between the epiphanies is that they are not clothed with the same splendor, because of the divine pedagogy, or the economy that God uses, out of love, veiling himself to different degrees.

But if everything was consummated on the cross, the ultimate truth about God is a truth of love. If Christ is the revealer and the locus of divine discourse, he presents himself, in his life and death, as the only exegete of Scripture and its sole reference point. On this basis God was not the author of the sufferings of Canaan and of conquered peoples. When Joshua commanded armies, He who will later bear the same name was already, in his precedence to Abraham, on the side of the victim, just as he was on Isaac's side when the God of Abraham commanded him to offer his son as sacrifice. Yahweh was not revealed by his raised arms and his powerful hand but in the very weakness of those whom the armies of God Sabaoth were overwhelming. That God was a simplistic reading that Israel made of its own power. Israel was the people of God but not the body of Yahweh. This reality of God's body was not able to be revealed prior to the intra-trinitarian kenosis and the nothingness of love brought about by Jesus. It was necessary for the Lord, by his suffering, to attain the perfection of his humanity so that the very perfection of God would be known.

It is only by beginning with this feebleness of God that we can understand Jesus' teaching and the unanimous tradition before Augustine about not resisting evil.

The great tempter, face to face with the apparent power-lessness of Jesus on the cross, demands that he come down from it. The supreme temptation is to believe that we can change the world without God, or that one can, one ought, to impose human instruments on God. At the moment when the Lord of the universe seems to have abandoned the world and to have therefore proclaimed his own death, humanity lays hold of this emptiness in order to make justice reign. The revolution and the counter-revolution, which are of Promethean scope, have as their point of departure the absence of God as Savior. Berdyaev was right to maintain that every revolution is degraded because it starts out with the illusion that one can establish justice by getting rid of people, and putting itself in their place, establish other principles of government.

A new combination of forces, representing other social back-grounds, will have to intervene, bringing a new social dynamic, so that a creative breath can animate the poor, who have pre-viously been left out of consideration. Violence is presented as the only adequate response to the invisible violence exercised on "the victims of oppression." There are, of course, dehumanizing situations, structures that represent "established" violence. A large percentage of humanity is reduced to such despair that violence seems to be their only recourse. Those who cannot exercise their right to participate in power or exercise a public function because of their color, religion, or ideological neutrality, those who are deprived of their right to vote, and cannot get an education, adequate food and medical care, are undergoing an injustice which is the worst of violences. Civil war or war on behalf of others, which produces further complications and reproduces itself indefinitely in a vicious cycle that ends only with general famine, shows the absurdity of violence. At that level of intensity and extension to protest against violence is meaningless. The institutionalization of war makes it impossible to bring up St. Thomas's question about revolt against the tyrant. There is obviously what Dom Helder Camara calls a "spiral of violence," whose dialectic is injustice/revolt/repression. One is beyond the simple right or duty to change the government when all governments are reduced to powerlessness in an uncontrollable situation that has reached the ultimate in irrationality. Under these conditions violence is no longer even a means. When hatred, fear, suspicion, corruption, fanaticism and oppression have reached their climax, the question of the option between one and another political solution becomes superfluous. Every political attitude is a calculation and hence something less than complete testimony, for at this level of the disintegration of society, as defined by parallel existences, every policy is political.

A genuine politics is conceivable only when it grows out of an interior debate. Since such discourse includes the other, one already places oneself beyond the question of means. I have to liberate myself from the narrow notion of the group and my identity in the group in order to welcome another face, in the light of which I can perceive my own, and enter the world of the person. In the perspective of a purpose that foreshadows a communion of love, society is not just an empirical reality concerned with law and economic development. From the point of view of effectiveness, it is a matter of trying humbly to put order into a society according to appropriate and provisory formulas. Perhaps we can't aim at anything else, especially in the Third World where everything is so fragile. Politics can't be redeemed in its inner being. If humanity has a purpose, a society of men and women is not a number but a communion of people, which is ultimately conceivable only if they are all deified together by the

Eucharist. Both citizenship and the state are consummated only in the eschatological community that will put an end to tribal status, nations, and separate languages. I am only presenting a testimony; I make no claims as to the political merits of such an evangelical commitment. It would be political suicide if politics is considered an autonomous domain. In a spiritual vision, however, the frontiers between human communities tend to disappear, and it would be absurd to have one behavior completely governed by *realpolitik* and another dictated by a search for the Kingdom. If the Kingdom of God is seen in filigree in the empire of Caesar, that is because there is no such thing as civil society in the pure state. The latter is ordained to the society of communion that englobes it or gives life to it. As Origen said, "The Church is the cosmos of the cosmos"—it is itself the spiritual universe which contains the historical universe.

The unanimous tradition of the primitive Church against war clearly shows that it was a doctrinal position. One might have thought that loyalty to the Empire and Paul's adhesion to the *pax romana* would have meant acceptance of the military order. But apart from the centurion Cornelius and the jailer baptized by Paul at Philippi, we don't find any mention of a Christian soldier before 170. The non-participation of Christians in the defense of Jerusalem in the year 70 and their flight to Pella shows that they were hardly interested in the destiny of Jerusalem. The pagan Celsus, about 178, exhorts Christians to aid the Emperor with all their strength in order to support justice, to fight for him and serve as soldiers because if the Emperor were left alone and abandoned, the *res publica* would fall into the hands of the lawless and the barbarians.[1] We know from the writings of Tertullian that there were a large number of soldiers in the Roman armies, and nevertheless, in his Catholic period, Tertullian writes that the Lord, by disarming Peter, has challenged every soldier. No uniform is legitimate among Christians, he asserts, if it is linked to an illegitimate duty.[2] Those who desire baptism in the Lord must abstain from military service and every public function.

Origen, drawing on Tertullian's interpretation of Jesus' arrest, when he forbids Peter to kill the soldier, says that Christians cannot defend themselves against their enemies, that they cannot destroy anyone, that they are no longer to take up the sword against a nation, no longer to learn war. He responds to Celsus's argument by saying that if the barbarians are evangelized they will submit to the law and become gentle, and only Christians will rule, since, in that case, the Word would have taken possession of all souls.

Among the apologists we find the same attitude. Athenagoras, after speaking of massacres, the devastation of cities, the burning of homes along with their inhabitants, and the destruction of entire populations, affirms that no suffering in his life can make reparation for such sins. As for Christians, he says that they cannot allow anyone to be put to death, even for a just cause. For Clement of Alexandria those who practice war no longer fear God.

My point in citing these texts is to show that the earliest Christians not only had a horror of war and refused to justify it, but believed they could overcome it by faith, prayer, and the power of God. Whether or not this attitude is utopian, it ought to be preserved since it establishes a testimony that introduces the fire of the Spirit in a death situation that can grow to such proportions that every option becomes meaningless, and the only thinkable "solution" consists in killing the largest possible number of one's opponents. Although this means a political triumph, it will soon bring about the resumption of hostilities. When no one has the means to carry out such a policy, ideology is not only overcome but shown to be false, foreign to its initial, natural purpose, which is the maintenance of existence. When the will to death becomes a pleasure and the princes of the city are armed children, one can't even bring up the theory of non-violence because it will be judged on the basis of effectiveness and preached as a political theory. But the sweetness of the Gospel imposes itself apart from any concern for effectiveness, out of a search for salvation, as a sign of the Kingdom that is to come. When a country crumbles completely and people feel like animals, tracked night and day, and are constantly astonished they remain alive, the Lord becomes their only resting place.

In such a situation faith is no longer only the evidence of what

one does not see. It is something that welcomes you when you
have just escaped from a sniper. It is even that which welcomes
the sniper when he recognizes that he is assailed night and day
by his victims, whose faces he recognizes. Listen to this statement of Maxim the Confessor:

> If possession of the indestructible Kingdom is given to the humble
> and gentle, who would be so without love and desire for divine
> goods as not to make a supreme movement toward humility and
> gentleness in order to become, as far as it is possible for human
> beings, the imprint of the Kingdom of God by bearing within them
> by grace the exact configuration in Spirit to Christ, the great
> King?. . . . The soul, in which the majesty of the divine image has
> been naturally infused, is transformed by free will to the likeness
> of God . . . it becomes the all-splendid habitation of the Holy
> Spirit . . . Christ always dies voluntarily and mysteriously, be-
> coming incarnate in those who are saved, creating the soul to
> which a virgin mother gives birth.

Because of its close, everyday contact with those who weep,
the Gospel represents, above all, compassion, simplicity of heart,
a gentler glance, the baptism of tears. The patience of the saints
allows us to understand that a considerable number of men and
women no longer have any grounds for imagining a future, either
immediate or long-term, but God reveals himself to them in his
splendor in the very midst of their humiliation. This Kingdom,
which is within us, becomes the portion of those who no longer
judge. For those who have lived through the experience of a
nameless abyss, there is nothing but sacrificial death and martyrdom. The new creation is within you. You know this, quite apart
from every reference to history, or any human realization.

This position does not challenge the Christian's political commitment in other situations. But it has even greater understanding for becoming disengaged, with a view to the Kingdom. Such
a disengagement is serious only in an awareness of political
reality; it means a complete purity in the face of every manipulation of public opinion and adhesion to the national cause with an
independence of mind, an openness to the foreigner, and a
knowledge of all the elements of transfiguration in the historical

event. Those who are apolitical are not free men and women, but have fallen into an absence, a human regression. It is out of an interior strength that one can renounce the use of force and every form of domination. That is the liberating knowledge to which the meek of heart bear witness, in imitation of the One of whom it is written: "He will not brawl or cry out, his voice is not heard in the streets, he will not break the crushed reed, or snuff the faltering wick." (Mt 12:19–20; see Isaiah 42:3–4)

Jesus' "way," already described in the first Servant Song of Isaiah, reflects the very behavior of Yahweh when he appears to Elias at Horeb. There, unlike at Carmel, the encounter with God is not accompanied by the massacre of prophets:

> Then he [the prophet] was told, 'Go out and stand on the mountain before Yahweh.' For at that moment Yahweh was going by. A mighty hurricane split the mountains and shattered the rocks before Yahweh. But Yahweh was not in the hurricane. And after the hurricane, an earthquake. But Yahweh was not in the earthquake. And after the earthquake, fire. But Yahweh was not in the fire. And after the fire, a light murmuring sound. And when Elijah heard this, he covered his face with his cloak and went out and stood at the entrance to the cave. (1 Kings 19:11–13)

This gentle murmur was the locus of divine revelation, the ultimate revelation.

It is not by chance that of all the virtues with which the sacred humanity of the Lord was clothed, he retained only one to propose to his disciples: "Shoulder my yoke and learn from me, for I am gentle and humble of heart" (Mt 11:29). This virtue, among others, will be the fruit of the Spirit (Gal 5:22–23).

A Christian people, whose heart has been converted to the Holy Face and which lives the kenosis of the face of God, may in fidelity to the absolute never produce anything spectacular, but simply transmit the words that have been said to it, the forms that contain its prayer. Carrying the cross of Jesus in obedience to the commandment of love, it will bear witness, in the darkness of history, to the eternal passover.

Translated by Joseph Cunneen

Notes

1. Origen, *Against Celsus*, VIII, 68.
2. *De Idolatreia*, 19.

VINCENT HARDING

Toward a Darkly Radiant Vision of America's Truth

Vincent Harding, author of There Is a River: The Black Struggle for Freedom in America, *is professor of Religion and Social Transformation at Iliff School of Theology in Colorado. His open letter to Robert Bellah and his co-authors of* Habits of the Heart *is more important for the vision it describes than for its criticism of a widely praised book. (In a reply to Harding, Bellah says, "The authors . . . are at work on another book, tentatively titled* The Good Society, *that will have much more to say about the rest of the world and about those kinds of Americans who do not appear prominently in* Habits" *[Cross Currents, Winter 1987–8].) Harding's vision recalls Walt Whitman's "Song of Myself," an ideal self "Of every hue and trade and rank, of every caste and religion, / Not merely of the New World but of Africa Europe or Asia. . . . a wandering savage. . . ." For Harding, America's possibilities will become reality to the extent that its people "dream the new world in richer, deeper hues (and wilder moods) than [they] ever knew before," to the extent that they claim as ancestors "both Jefferson and David Walker, Lincoln and Frederick Douglass, Whitman and Frances Ellen Watkins Harper."*

To the authors of *Habits of the Heart*
   A Letter of Concern,
   An Invitation to Re-Creation

Your country? How came it yours? Before the Pilgrims landed we were here. . . . Actively we have woven ourselves

258

with the very warp and woof of this nation. . . . [a]nd gener-
ation after generation have pleaded with a headstrong,
careless people to despise not Justice, Mercy, and
Truth. . . . (DuBois, 1961:189–190).

D ear Friends,

    Near the end of *Habits of the Heart* you issued a gener-
ous invitation to all of your readers. You said that your work was
intended "to open a larger conversation with our fellow citizens,
to contribute to the common dialogue." Thus, you encouraged a
person like myself to "test what we say against his or her own
experience," to "argue with us when what we say does not
fit . . ." (307). I have chosen to respond, to enter the conversation with you and to engage in the larger dialogue. Appreciating the spirit of your invitation, I have decided to address you
directly in the form of this letter.

    In light of my own encounters with the history and present
experience of this nation, I must argue with you. I find *Habits* a
work that is clearly informed by the best of intentions, but a
work that is fundamentally and sadly flawed. It is because I am
so fully committed to your quest for "a new social science" that
will help us to deal with "new realities" in our nation and world;
because I also resonate with your sense of urgency about our
need to create a "public philosophy" that will free us to move
toward humane understandings of the "common good" in America—because I stand firmly with you in all this, it has been
painful for me to recognize and be jarred by the critical disjuncture I sense between your intentions and your creation. But
the disjuncture is real, and I want to share my sense of its nature
and sources, as well as some thoughts concerning its possibility
for correction.

    At the very beginning of *Habits,* you provide what I believe to
be the key to understanding the open wound that runs
throughout its pages. There, citing the restraints of "a small
research team and a limited budget," you say "we decided to
concentrate our research on white, middle-class Americans"
(viii). You then make an arguable, but cogent case for your

emphasis on the middle class as central to American life; however, you make no case at all—except for budget and staff—for
the decision to exclude middle-class people who were not white.
From your perspective, it appears that the only real problem
created by such a decision was that "we were not able to illustrate much of the racial diversity that is so important a part of our
national life" (viii).

I want to suggest that the problem you have created is far more
profound. Illustration of racial diversity is not the primary loss.
What you have missed is a major portion of the painful reality, the
ambiguous richness and the anguished integrity of this nation's
past and present—as well as a full sense of the magnificent
possibilities of its future. In other words, I believe that your
choice of a white middle-class focus has distorted the picture of
America you have seen and projected, thereby defeating some of
your own best hopes. I have chosen four elements of *Habits* to
illustrate and elaborate my concern.

1

Let me begin with the problems which were created by your
methodology. For me, there is something fundamentally appealing about a book that promises to be "based on conversations
with ourselves, our ancestors, and several hundred of our fellow-
citizens." In spite of what I know about your unquestionable
integrity and intentionality, the appeal literally paled (the pun is
only slightly intended) when I realized with whom and to whom
you are really talking. For instance, the conversations "among
ourselves," refer essentially to four white, middle-class men and
one white, middle-class woman. There is no way to avoid the
problem that this presents. You claimed to be researching and
writing a book whose "primary focus" you say is "cultural,"
whose fundamental questions have to do with what it means to
be an "American." Carrying out that task in the midst of one of
the most fascinating and frustrating multi-cultural and multi-
racial nations in the world, you are severely limited and confined
by your chosen base of white middle-class, Euro-Americans.
Carefully reading your text, I can see no other conclusion.

This is no judgment on you, friends; but it may well be a judgment on your judgment, on your decision concerning how best to study America and Americans in the 1970s and 1980s. For instance, had your own research team included one or two similarly sensitive, skilled and concerned non-white social scientists, do you think they could have possibly made a decision to look at the questions of "Who are we as Americans? . . . What is our character?" without including a significant body of Americans of color in their quest for answers?

While it is true that your group's basic composition almost forces you to miss the richness of our nation's multi-vocality, I think more is at stake. As I shall continue to say in a number of ways, this is far more than a matter of diversity. In a society still suffering from major residues of white supremacist thought and action—a terrifying blindness in a largely non-white world—it is imperative for our nation to break out of its prison of whiteness. *Habits* honors Martin Luther King, Jr., for his leadership in this work, but your own grouping, in its self-constitution, failed to follow that leadership. Thus your concern for the "common good" was severely compromised by your failure to expand yourselves, to enrich your own primary community. As a result, you missed one of the major lessons of our history: middle-class white America has never been able to heal itself without a major rediscovery of its interdependence with the rest of this nation. (Isn't it only natural that the search for the common good should be a common enterprise?)

In light of your self-definition, your "conversations with our ancestors" are similarly flawed. Indeed, I found the woundedness of this aspect of the work very painful. As I read your book, there could be no doubt that the "ancestors" of the white, middle-class Americans carrying out this important inquiry were also white and middle class. Do you understand the pain? What does it mean for this American, and others like me, to come upon a roster of "exemplary Americans" from the past and find only Benjamin Franklin, Thomas Jefferson, John Winthrop, Abraham Lincoln, Walt Whitman? Surely these are all honorable men in their way (although I say that with some ambivalence). But what does it mean for our children to be told by scholars of your caliber and reputation that these are the "exemplars" of America? The later introduction of Martin King does little to erase the impression that "exemplary Americans" are, by example, *white men*. Friends, this is not simply an absence of diversity, this is a distortion of truth.

Let us take one ancestral case in point, Thomas Jefferson. In discussing America's biblical and republican traditions, you touch very lightly on the reality of American slavery as the major antebellum contradiction to those worthy traditions. And when you refer to slavery, you tell us that Jefferson, one of your exemplars, "vigorously opposed slavery in principle" (30). You then cite his marvelous words concerning the first requirement of a democratic government: "Equal and exact justice to all men, of whatever state or persuasion, religious or political" (31). Wouldn't your work have been far richer and more fruitful to the difficult truth of America had you found some way to discuss and illumine the continuing presence of that clamorous contradiction in Jefferson's own life and in the lives of most of your white, male, democratic exemplars?

Even better, in your search for representatives of the biblical and republican strands in pre-20th century American life, how much more American your work would have been had we been introduced to Frederick Douglass, Sojourner Truth, David Walker, Harriet Tubman or Henry Highland Garnet. Here were exemplary Americans who lived the biblical and republican traditions. Steeped in those traditions, these were the ancestors who opposed slavery not only "in principle" but in full practice, often at great jeopardy to their lives. These were women and men (along with many nonconformist white sisters and brothers who did not manage to become your exemplars either) who lived out the great American ideals while carrying on a faithful struggle against the most powerful threat to democratic community and biblical faith in the America of their time. In the process, they transformed the faith and tradition, becoming creators and bearers of the seed which eventually produced Martin Luther King, Jr., and his companions in the freedom movement. These are *my* exemplary Americans. I trust them and their freedom-obsessed white allies much more than a group of white men who too often managed to carry biblical and republican traditions in one hand and acceptance of slavery in the other. For reasons that

I will later explain, I consider *all* of them my ancestors, but, for the transformation of America, I choose my models (exemplars) from among those women and men who were moved by their religious and democratic faith to become active participants in the long and risky struggle against slavery.

One last word on ancestors may be appropriate, friends. I think there is a revealing irony in the fact that your preeminent "ancestor" was not an American, but the brilliant French lawyer, social critic and author of *Democracy in America,* Alexis de Tocqueville. You claim him as "the predecessor who has influenced us most profoundly in thinking about life in America." But what did you do with Tocqueville's harsh and powerful commentary on the destructive relationships which existed between white Americans and their black and Indian co-inhabitants of this land? That aspect of his work seems totally absent from your treatment of the American past.

On the basis of what he had seen, heard and felt in the United States, Tocqueville wrote, ". . . the European is to the other races of mankind what man is to the lower animals . . . he makes them subservient to his use; and when he cannot subdue he destroys them" (1855:362, v. I). Perhaps even more directly related to our conversation is Tocqueville's subtle sensitivity to the contradictions at work among the white lovers of democracy and freedom. At one point, as you probably recall, he compares the Spanish settlers and the North Americans in their deadly approach to the natives of the hemisphere. His conclusion was:

> The Spaniards were unable to exterminate the Indian race by those unparalleled atrocities which brand them with indelible shame, nor did they even succeed in wholly depriving it of its rights; but the Americans of the United States have accomplished this two-fold purpose with singular felicity; tranquilly, legally, philanthropically, without shedding blood [surely an overstatement—even before the "winning of the west"] and without violating a single great principle of morality in the eyes of the world. It is impossible to destroy men with more respect for the laws of humanity (1855:385–386, v. I).

I find it sad and problematic that in your fascination with Tocqueville and your exemplary Americans you have nothing to say about this visitor's trenchant criticism of the oppression of the children of Africa and the despoiling and destruction of the natives of the land which were being carried out by—or at least under the aegis of—a number of your heroes. Even the American constitution, which you admire for creating "a machinery of national government consciously adapted to the social reality of expanding capitalism and the attendant culture of philosophical liberalism," requires re-visioning. For at the heart of its "expanding capitalism" was the business of speculation in the lands of the Indians and speculation in the bodies of the Africans. And the philosophic liberalism of that time, as in our own moment of history, was usually adjusted to accommodate and justify such profitable "social reality."

If one takes Tocqueville seriously—just as when one listens to Douglass, Walker and Truth—it seems to me that the argument can be made that the contradiction between your exemplars' purported love of freedom on the one hand, and the real destruction of the lives and freedom of non-white men and women on the other, has been at least as much a major theme in American history as the conflict between individualism and community. (Of course, when somewhat more fully interpreted, white supremacy can be seen as a form of racial individualism, clinging to the prerogatives of whiteness, denying the larger community of the peoples of creation. Do you see the pernicious dangers of a continuing focus on the white middle class in the light of such a history as ours?) Ironically enough, your failure to pay any serious attention to this *other* American tension may be connected to the same problem Tocqueville faced when he was unable to see black-white relations in America as a crucial manifestation of his own majority-minority theme. That is, neither you nor he included black people in your definition of the American community. Friends, I do not mean to be harsh, and I am not ignoring the contrary commitments of your personal lives. But if I move solely in the context of your book (which is all the evidence most readers will have) then, in spite of its important references to Martin Luther King, Jr., I can come to no other conclusion.

Unfortunately, the essential method of exclusion also continued into the heart of your "conversations with our fellow citizens," thereby shaping—and limiting—the definitions you would give to "matters of common interest." Somehow, as I reflected on your decision to omit black people and so many others from the class of "fellow citizens," my mind went to Richard Wright's *12 Million Black Voices*, a work now almost half a century old. Both asking and declaring his question, the powerful black artist wrote:

> If we had been allowed to participate in the vital process of America's national growth, what would have been the texture of our lives, the pattern of our traditions, the routine of our customs, the state of our arts, the code of our laws, the function of our government!

Immediately he provided a response: "Whatever others may say, we black folk say that America would have been stronger and greater!" (Wright, 1941:145)

What struck me was the fact that, in the forty-five years between Wright's book and yours, social scientists who are concerned with a new "public philosophy" must surely have learned that black people have participated deeply "in the vital processes" of this nation's post-World War II development, and have affected its traditions, its culture and its law. And yet, at this point in history, you could still decide that you could explore fundamental questions about the nature of Americans and their character without including black citizens in your essential conversations. Beyond the pain evoked in me by your choice, I can only join with Wright and the nameless others who must say of your work as he said of America, it "would have been stronger and greater," had you understood the necessity of engaging black fellow citizens in your conversations. Indeed, whether you know it or not, many of the questions you were raising about the American "character," are questions that have been consistently forced into the public arena by the freedom-seeking, community-creating activities of your black fellow Americans. To reverse Wright's question, can you imagine what post-1945 (to say nothing of post-1776) America would have been like without the insistent challenge we blacks mounted to the republican and biblical traditions of this nation? Was it primarily a failure of budget and staff, or a failure of imagination which excluded us?

I am convinced that the very questions you posed to your contemporary white fellow citizens would have found a richer and more complex set of responses had you also raised them in the presence of the non-white middle-class people in America. Among them are surely keepers of a profound set of tensions. Many of them have been reared (to use an old fashioned word) in communities where the extended family, the clan, or the tribe continues to make powerful claims on the person and does much to shape that individual life. What would they say about individualism and community, about the need to leave family and grounding? What would the resilient and fascinating phenomenon of black family reunions contribute to the discussion?

Within the black community, there are many persons who are deeply ambivalent about the American middle-class mainstream in which they now move. They still have lively, painful, beautiful ties of blood and commitment to that vast, burdened body of non-middle-class Americans who are totally absent from your work. Indeed, each of the non-white middle-class groups bears its own set of ambivalent feelings about movement into the American mainstream and what it does to structures of family, community and memory. What is the therapy they are experiencing for their divided hearts? Their stories are a crucial element in the continually developing narrative of America. Can you afford to ignore them in your work?

So, too, when you tried to explore the lives of those men and women who are participating in "newer forms of political activism that have grown out of the political movements of the sixties . . . ," could you imagine the richness that might have been available to you? For instance, what is happening with the black Americans whose freedom movement did so much to shape the new realities of post-World War II America? How do middle-class black activists now relate to the "system" that had traditionally been the source of such ambivalent responses? Are we in it? And if so, what difference does it seem to make? Are we black folk bearers of a new vision of the public good or simply more stylish copiers of all the old, flawed and dangerous flotsam that drifts in the mainstream? Do we have a second (or first?) language that is more adequate than others to probe our experience? Has not the language of faith, emotion and community been one of our strengths in the past? Where does it stand now? Wouldn't it have been fascinating to listen, to compare? Indeed, wherever you turn, whether to love and marriage or to religion, the experiences of peoples of color (even in their middle-class manifestation) are surely necessary to provide a true sense of what America is now and what it is yet to be. How could you have come to another conclusion—especially in the light of your concern for the "riches" of culture, for the largeness of method? I am really puzzled.

That, friends, is at the heart of much of the pain I experienced as I read your book. First, methodologically, I felt that when you decided to go white you had separated yourselves from some of the most vibrant, complex and truly "American" middle-class experiences in this country. Of even more importance, though, was my sense that you were cutting off yourselves (and, perhaps, many of your readers) from authentic encounter with the future of this nation. For while some persons do not know it, I assumed you knew that we are not now and never had been a white, middle-class nation. And in our own perilous times it seems absolutely essential that all of us who write for the public about the definition of America must make it powerfully clear that our *only* humane future as a nation is located in a multi-cultural, multi-vocal, multi-racial territory. Indeed, to ask in the 1980s what is an American, and even to begin to try to answer the question on exclusively white grounds is, in my view, both backward and dangerous. It is to deny a truly "public philosophy."

Surely our fellow citizens need to receive a much more useful vision from some of their most compassionate scholars. As it now stands *Habits* is too great a temptation to all the old white fantasies which gave Euro-Americans the sole right to define the past, present and future of the nation. In today's world this is a dangerous, perhaps suicidal misperception. On this matter, I think it is worth quoting Martin Luther King, Jr., at length, partly because he is your one black exemplar, and because his wisdom is very much to the point on the matter of the dangers of extending and encouraging the white fantasy. Shortly before he was assassinated, King was involved in the preparation of an article for *Playboy* magazine that did not appear until months after his death. In it he reminded Americans that "Integration is meaningless without the sharing of power." (Is the publication of such a book as *Habits* an act of power?) Then he extended his concern, saying:

> The implications of true racial integration are more than just national in scope. I don't believe we can have world peace until America has an 'integrated' foreign policy. Our disastrous experiences in Vietnam and the Dominican Republic have been, in one sense, a result of racist decision-making. Men of the white West, whether or not they like it, have grown up in a racist culture, and their thinking is colored by that fact. They have been fed on a false mythology and tradition that blinds them to the aspirations and talents of other men. They don't really respect anyone who is not white. But we simply cannot have peace in the world without mutual respect (Washington, 1986:317–318).

Such is the ultimate danger of all-white perceptions of America and Americans.

I am sure you had no intention of encouraging the image of an essentially white America, of a nation that can be defined primarily in terms of its European-derived middle class; but I am afraid that is one of the images cast into the public mind by your work. (I cringed to read such statements as "America was colonized by those who had come loose from the older European structures, and so from the beginning we had a headstart in the process of modernization" (276). And I wondered where in this generalization were *we* who were *cut* loose by the modernizers from the even older African structures; where were *we* who were dispossessed by the modernizers from the even older native American structures?) As a result, in my eyes, it is not hard to see you standing in Joe Gorman's shoes, filled with what you called "a fundamental generosity" of character, but also setting forward "a mythical past" of white "representative" men, and white, racially insensitive (and/or supremacist) social movements. In the process, we are given a sanitized study, which, as you described Gorman's beliefs, "provides little help in contemporary problems and almost no framework for thinking about . . . the larger society" (13), a society erupting all around us in many colors and conditions—most of them neither white nor middle class.

2

In addition to the methodological dilemma created by the narrowly white middle-class focus, your decision to limit the sources of your history and your ancestry leads to other serious difficulties as well. In your important and commendable search for "new visions of the public good" which might help us resolve some of the problems created by destructive individualism, you look to the nation's post-Civil War history for possible guideposts. In the process, you identify "six distinct visions of the public good" which have emerged in the United States over the last century, suggesting that they developed as "responses to the need for citizens of a society grown increasingly interdependent to picture to themselves what sort of a people they are and where they should be heading" (257). Placing the visions in pairs, you see "each pair emerging in a period of institutional breakdown and subsequent reintegration of the national economic order." Then you begin with what you identify as the "alternative visions . . . of the Establishment versus Populism" (257), and engage in what can only be called misinformed nostalgia when you characterize Populism as "the great democratizer, insisting on the incompleteness of a republic that excluded any of its members from full citizenship" (259). I find this very strange and very sad—for several reasons.

First of all, friends, it seems to me that if there is a logical, historical beginning point for exploring institutional breakdown and the rise of alternative visions, it is surely at the supreme national crisis of the Civil War. Out of that war came two clearly opposing visions for the post-slavery, post-war American nation. One was the vision of the overwhelming majority of the nation (the Establishment?) which called for the continuation of white supremacy and domination; the other—carried primarily by black Americans (and such non-exemplary whites as Wendell Phillips)—of shared power in a democracy of black and white "fellow citizens." While it was not the only major choice after the war, the option for the creation of a just and multi-racial democracy was central. Indeed, those critical alternatives and our various American responses to them provide a powerful motif of continuing tension in the nation's life, a tension which you seem to miss or to ignore. Thus you do not include in your understanding of visions of the public good such a succinct and magnificent statement as the one by Frances Ellen Watkins Harper, the exemplary black American poet, activist and stirring freedom lecturer. She set the critical question before the nation in 1875 when she said:

> The great problem to be solved by the American people, if I understand it, is this: Whether or not there is strength enough in democracy, virtue enough in our civilization, and power enough in our religion to have mercy and deal justly with four millions of people but lately translated from the old oligarchy of slavery to the new commonwealth of freedom; and upon the right solution of this question depends in large measure the future strength, progress and durability of our nation (Foner, 1972:431).

Harper's vision was typical of much that can be found in any serious examination of nineteenth century black social, political, economic and religious thought. It preceded the Populist vision and was far more faithful to the democratic vocation of America. In your confinement to white exemplars, you miss this source of so much of the nation's best democratic and anti-individualistic history. For instance, you seem not to know the voice of W. E. B. DuBois who proclaimed at the beginning of this century that:

> The problem of the twentieth century is the problem of the color-line, the question of how far differences of race . . . will hereafter be made the basis to denying over half the world the right of sharing to their utmost ability the opportunities and privileges of modern civilization (Meier, 1971:56).

Had you claimed the voices of such ancestors, then you would have recognized how deeply flawed were your three favored historical carriers of the vision of the Public Good—Populism, Welfare Liberalism and Economic Democracy. For, beginning with the Populists, each of the movements and participants roughly grouped under these headings displayed a fundamental refusal to choose a multi-racial democracy over a white su-premacist vision of America.

Thus, only from the most narrow and racially insensitive (or historically uninformed?) position could you possibly declare that the Populists and progressives "wanted a national com-munity that would be genuinely democratic and inclusive." Both groupings, and others like them lead naturally to Martin Luther King, Jr., your own most favored hero of the recent struggles for a new America. You cannot get to King in any organic way if you totally neglect the matrix of the black struggle for freedom, if you ignore the Afro-American biblical and republican traditions—or if you present an entire chapter on Religion in America and keep it stunningly white. Of course, this is not to say that other American—and non-American—traditions did not contribute to the flowering of King and the modern black movement for a new Public Good. But it is to say that there is nothing in *Habits of the Heart* which helps us to trace the essential Afro-American Chris-tian democratic roots of the man and the movement. In other words, your choice of focus ironically cuts you off from the heartland of your/our major 20th century exemplar.

3

Indeed, my friends, I think it is unavoidably clear that your important search for the way to "create a new social science for new realities" is seriously hindered by your own narrow defini-tions of both the old and the new American realities. As I have tried to indicate in this missive, America has always been much richer, more multi-vocal, more colorful—and far more painful—than you have pictured it in your dealings with history or with contemporary society. And, even more important, America is now and must become far more varied in its visions and traditions (even when we confine our view to middle-class manifestations) than you have suggested. Essentially, moving from past toward future, I am inviting you to expand, radically expand, your vision of ancestors, friends and fellow-citizens. For if you, among the best and the brightest in academe (and I say that without tongue in cheek), cannot discover and reflect such powerful lively realities in your work, how can we hope for a new social science, at least, and a new nation at best? Wasn't it this new reality that Martin King was trying to encompass in his last years—breaking beyond the middle classes, calling men, women and children of all colors and conditions? Building on the many American traditions of democratic struggle, he was helping to shape a new public philosophy, moving toward a new society, inviting *all* of his fellow-citizens to become exemplars in the perilous, beautiful quest for a new community in America. (By the way, friends, it seems to me that King was also raising serious questions about certain matters of community and chaos that you touch lightly, if at all. For instance, by the end of his life he was engaged in an unrelenting critique of American racism, materialism and militarism, as well as their companion, "paranoid anti-communism," making it clear that he saw all these leading to our government's policy of attacks against revolutionary movements of the poor all over the world. Indeed, his serious search in his last days for a way toward non-violent revolution of the poor and their allies both encompassed and transcended the best in the American biblical and republican traditions. He was opening a door that you do not explore at all.)

I am calling upon you to open your hearts, to develop new habits of vision, connection and hope. Without such an enlarging process, your work carries a series of tragic ironies from the past into the present, threatening our future possibilities, leading you to become the objects of your own harshest critiques. For instance, in your helpful appreciation of the role of authentic community as a source of true individuality and interdependence, you raised a valid warning about disabling communities. You noted that in the United States there are authoritarian groups who differ from "genuine communities [in] the shallowness of and distortion of their memory and the narrowness of what they hope for" (162). Is this a social and intellectual trap toward which you too have unintentionally moved? Because of the unfortunate selectivity in your choice of ancestors, friends and fellow-citizens, is there not an inauthentic sense of "American" community at work among you, one which tends toward shallowness and distortion in your view of the past and narrowness in your hope for the future?

And when you criticize Ted Oster and other modern American individualists, do you sense the possibilities of the critique being turned on your work? You say,

> When thinking of the imperative to 'love thy neighbor,' many metropolitan Americans like Ted . . . consider that responsibility fulfilled when they love those compatible neighbors they have surrounded themselves with, fellow members of their own life-style enclave, while letting the rest of the world go its chaotic, mysterious way (179).

May I ask this: who are *your* neighbors of past, present and future? Is that gathering of *relatively* compatible middle-class white people who form the core of your partners in dialogue really true to the fundamental meaning and mystery of our chaotic, multiracial nation and our largely non-white and non-middle-class world? Or are they part of an "individualism" of race and class?

As it stands now, friends, it may be that Mike Conley of Suffolk (181–185) is closer to you than you have dreamed. He opposes an influx of non-white people into his community and does not excuse himself; but says, "I don't want them living near me, causing trouble for me." In a sense, Mike seems to reflect the reality (rather than the good intentions) of your work. To deal with human subjects—past and present—who are not white and middle class would have simply caused too much "trouble" for your research design, the make-up of your team and your budget constraints. So we have a book in which the choices made by your team and the decisions made by Mike actually lead to the same outcome: there are no non-whites (except for a deracinated Martin Luther King) in the world of *Habits,* no troublesome presence. As a result, the verdict you pronounce on "people such as Mike" becomes a verdict for you to ponder: "There is no rationale here for developing public institutions that would tolerate the diversity of a large, hetereogeneous society and nurture common standards of justice and civility among its members" (185). Could this not be said of *Habits*? Do my non-white students mistake the work when they say, "I just don't see myself here"? In spite of your best intentions, I think the problem is real.

4

But I cannot leave you here, just as you must not leave my students outside the ambit of your questions and explorations concerning who *we* Americans really are. Personally, I deny that you can even begin to forge an answer to those questions while we are locked out of the arena of your research and your memory (to say nothing of the debilitating absence of all the other Americans who are not now and never have been middle-class white people). As I trust you have gathered by now, I am seriously asking you to re-vision your work, to change your habits and to enlarge your hearts.

Obviously, this is no simple task, but neither is the re-definition of American and Americans. In our generation, people like King and Fannie Lou Hamer, Clarence Jordan and Viola Liuzzo, Malcolm X and Diane Nash, Bob Moses and Cesar Chavez, Paul Robeson, Micky Schwerner and Roy Sano—to name only a relatively familiar few—have taken up the un-simple task which has obsessed freedom-loving Americans since the nation began: to re-create, again and again, a vision of America and Americans worthy of the terrible grandeur and the heart-rending agonies of our unique and common pilgrimages. In that tradition, Langston Hughes called us to "make America again." In a sense, it is a call, is it not, to re-create our habits, our institutions and our hearts.

I would suggest that one possible beginning point for those of us who are committed to re-creation is a new recognition of who *our* ancestors really are. To claim Tubman, Truth, Walker and Douglass, to recognize such beautiful ones as Lame Deer and Ida B. Wells-Barnett as our forebears is crucial to the development of a truly "public social science," as well as the establishment of a sound basis for a wide-ranging and profound vision of "the public good."

And it is also absolutely necessary to redefine and give public manifestation to our understanding of our "fellow citizens." So, let the conversation that established your important and deeply flawed book continue. But now it shall include others whose truth must inform and re-shape the heart of American life. We widen our circle (and I use possessive pronouns now because the re-building, healing, re-creative task belongs to us all), not in a quest for modish "diversity," but out of a deep hunger for authenticity. In that spirit, I would suggest at least four groups whose voices must enliven the conversation and re-invent the book . . .

Speak to your black fellow citizens. We may well be the American middle-class community that has made the single most powerful contribution to the creation of a new, justice-seeking public philosophy since World War II. Speak to them and discover the organic setting out of which King came. Recognize through them the necessity of the struggle for a redefinition of the American biblical and republican traditions. Work with what it means to claim both Jefferson *and* David Walker, Lincoln *and* Frederick Douglass, Whitman *and* Frances Ellen Watkins Harper. Allow Sojourner, Harriet and Ida B. Wells-Barnett to open us up to a host of sister ancestors—like Angelina Grimke, Prudence Crandall and Susan B. Anthony—who have not even appeared on your list of exemplary white Americans. Speak to black citizens, recognize how many of this middle class live on the edges of all the earlier, harder, more brutal times. Understand the pain that often seeps through the newly constructed, flimsy walls of class among us. Touch the sensitivities, often dulled, but sometimes filled with razor-sharp memories of poverty, joblessness, protest and despair, qualities of life so dearly missing from the rather bland America you have drawn for us. Listen to them and discover again that there is no "character" to American life without the anguish, the blues and the harrowing, democratizing victories of its strangely radiant communities of blackness.

Speak to Asian-Americans. (How could you, based primarily in California, have ignored them in your plans? What would it have been like for you to have worked with a Japanese-American social historian like Ronald Takaki?) Especially be certain to move among those hundreds of thousands who have been thrown up on our shores in the wake of our nation's latest imperialist ventures in Southeast Asia. Literally taste the differences in the ways they identify themselves as Americans; recognize the fascinating variety and depth of their cultural, religious and political experiences as they become part of the continuing transformative drama, recreating the American "self," deepening the American story. Who are we becoming as we absorb not only their foods, but experience their family life-styles, explore their spiritualities? Who are we Americans, as these Asian ancestors become ours, as the lotus lines are crossed? Was it not you who said "if we are ever to enter that new world that so far has been powerless to be born, it will be through reversing modernity's tendency to obliterate all previous culture?" Did you not declare: "We need to learn again from the cultural riches of the human species and to reappropriate and revitalize those riches so that they can speak to our conditions today?" The new world is already upon us, friends. Our wealth in human resources is beyond every past dream. Enter, listen, teach and learn. Let there be new dreams, worthy of our new realities.

Of course, the new world that has been borning among us demands that we speak and hear Spanish. Speak to those who are part of the steadily surging millions of our Hispanic fellow-citizens. They are totally absent from your first visions—again an amazing omission by scholars who have lived in what was once Old Mexico. Listen to those who have crossed the rivers—reawakening memories of North Stars which once filled the skies and hearts of *our* exemplary ancestors. Surely they raise more than philosophical questions about the nature of our "second language." Indeed, as so many of these children of the hemisphere move into our common body politic from such places as

Central and South America, they bring us the gift of new ways to ask the question: "Who are we, as Americans?" They insist on reminding us that the only singular geographic entity that is justly called "America" is the hemisphere itself. They force us toward our riches and our shame, opening the possibility that the peculiar agony now wrenching the poverty-crushed, historically disdained Central nations of this America is one that our ancestors, our fellow citizens and we ourselves cannot ignore. For the pain is in our heartland, and it does not have to continue. Speak to those who come from there. Ask them about the past and future meanings of America. And listen.

Then, my brothers and sisters, as you dream the new world in richer, deeper hues (and wilder moods) than you ever knew before, if you never speak another word, if you never hear another song, listen to the Natives of this land. (Were there any songs among your fellow-citizens, your ancestors, yourselves? Can Americans ever be known without the songs we sing in our hearts?) Hear the chants and whispers, listen to the dyings and the rising again, let the drums sound, enter the lodge, welcome the sun, dance, be still, join the eternal birthing that does not require a second language of logical words, that emerges from the deep places of our Grandmother and sings wordlessly in the center of our expanding heart. Do such things. First as acts of respect, as lessons in humility. For how dare we think that we can define the meaning of America, of American-ness, without entering the world of those who were here before the land was named, before our other, European, ancestors had even awakened? ("*Modernity's tendency to obliterate all previous culture . . .*"!) Listen and beware.

Listen as well to learn. For was it not you who wisely dreamed, "if we are to enter that new world that so far has been powerless to be born . . ."? Do you, do we, really want to find the power to be born? Again? Listen to the natives of this land. For though they themselves speak with many voices from many places of great pain, they surely open to us deep, powerful wisdom as well, especially concerning our search for the relationships between individuality and community. For who has suffered the ravages of America's individualism more fully than they? And who among us has experimented for more millenia to develop creative expressions of the common wealth? Listen to Lakotas and Ojibwas, to Hopis and Navahos; listen to Black Elk, Chief Joseph and Seattle. Listen to the echoes and the shouts. Listen to the mourning in the wind. There is power in the blood.

Listen. For survival and transcendence. I must assume that you know there can be no twenty-first century definition of the public good that does not find some way to include the reality of our interdependent relationships with the life forms around us—whose health and well-being we need at least as much as they need ours. Our ancestors, the Chinooks, our ancestors, the Creeks, our ancestors, the Kiowas—all our Indian ancestors knew this. (Just as our African ancestors knew it.) To ignore their cries and their love calls, to live and interview and write as if they did not exist is madness. Extend the dialogue. Deepen the definitions—for the sake of our sanity. Let your new insight become: "A social science concerned with the whole of society would . . . have to be historical and environmental, multi-vocal, as well as philosophical."

Then listen to Chief Seattle, an exemplary American, and receive the most profound levels of his gift and his promise, beyond the words, as he says,

> . . . when the last Red man shall have become a myth among the White man . . . when your children's children think themselves alone in the field . . . or in the silence of the pathless woods, they will not be alone . . . your lands will throng with the returning hosts that once filled them and still love this beautiful land. The White man will never be alone. Let him be just and deal kindly with my people, for the dead are not powerless. Dead—I say? There is no death. Only a change of worlds (Brown, 1982:68).

Here is American religion, American wisdom, American hope. Listen and receive it. (There is power in the blood.)

Let it enter your circles as an invitation and a challenge, sisters, brothers, fellow citizens, friends. For it calls you away from the dangerously constricted arena of your methodology, your history and your hope. It announces that white Americans, whatever their class (or professions), are not alone, cannot be alone, cannot survive or overcome alone (cannot be trusted alone?). The word from Chief Seattle announces that you are surrounded, undergirded, covered, and pierced through, by the hands and hearts of all those ancestors of every kind who also love this land and who have experienced "a change of worlds." You are surrounded by life, my friends, and you are challenged by the children of these life-givers, children who now invite you out of your racial individualism into the darkly radiant, expanding community of all those Americans who are changing, recreating this world, your world, our world, for the common good.

To receive such a word is to be given some guidance for our largely uncharted journey together toward the meaning and mystery of this chaotic and magnificent nation we share. Perhaps now you will understand why I wanted you to hear the chastening words my exemplar, DuBois, offered to your unlistening ancestors—our ancestors—almost a century ago when he wrote:

> Your Country? How came it yours? Before the Pilgrims landed we were here. Here we have brought our three gifts and mingled them with yours: a gift of story and song—soft, stirring melody in an ill-harmonized and unmelodious land; the gift of sweat and brawn to beat back the wilderness, conquer the soil, and lay the foundations of this vast economic empire two hundred years earlier than your weak hands could have done it; the third a gift of the Spirit. [And I would add a fourth: the gift of an insistent determination to wrest the realities of freedom and justice from the promises of this land.—vh] Around us the history of the land was centered for thrice a hundred years; out of the nation's heart we have called all that was best to throttle and subdue all that was worst; fire and blood, prayer and sacrifice, have billowed over this people, and they have found peace only in the altars of the God of Right. Nor has our gift of the Spirit been merely passive. Actively we have woven ourselves with the very warp and woof of this nation . . . Our song, our toil, our cheer, and warning, [our love of freedom] have been given to this nation in blood-brotherhood [and blood-sisterhood] . . . Would America have been America without her Negro people (DuBois, 1961:185)?

Without her Hispanic people? Without her Natives of the bloody land? Without her new and old Asian re-creators? Your country?

Let the questions break open the circle, re-define our common task. And let them end this missive, for I am sure that I have never written and you have never received so long a letter before. But that is surely part of the danger and the promise of open invitations and open hearts. With gratitude for your initiative, I now offer my openness to you.

In search of our new nation,

Vincent Harding

References

Brown, James E.
    1982   *The Spiritual Legacy of the American Indian.* New York: Crossroad.

DuBois, W. E. B.
    1961   *Souls of Black Folk.* (1903) Greenwich, Conn.: Fawcett.

Foner, Philip E. (ed.)
    1972   *The Voice of Black America.* New York: Simon and Schuster.

Meier, August, Elliott Rudwick, and Francis Broderick (eds.).
    1971   *Black Protest Thought in the Twentieth Century.* Second edition. Indianapolis: Bobbs-Merrill.

Tocqueville, Alexis de
    1855   *Democracy in America.* Volume I (Two volumes in one). New York: A. S. Barnes.

Washington, James (ed.)
    1986   *Testament of Hope.* San Francisco: Harper & Row.

Wright, Richard
    1941   *12 Million Black Voices.* New York: Viking Press.

EUGENE FONTINELL

Faith and Metaphysics Revisited

Eugene Fontinell, long an editor of Cross Currents, *teaches at Queens College (City University of New York) and is author of* Toward a Reconstruction of Religion *and* Self, God, and Immortality. *He maintains in this essay that only a radically changing faith is possible in our time. He finds no guarantee that the faith with which one began will survive the critical scrutiny and transformation for which he calls. It is no longer enough to show that something has been believed or prohibited at earlier moments in the life of the faith community. In relation to his own Roman Catholic faith, he says that there has not been nor can there be any once-for-all determination of just what is authentic rather than apparent revelation. On the other hand, the believer is not set adrift. Belief itself is necessary both religiously and philosophically. Evolving faith allows for significant continuity as the new "grows out of the old and while it is in no simple sense identical with the old, neither is it . . . totally different from it." More important, it makes possible in a radically new world continued encounter with the divine.*

I make no pretense of conducting a disinterested exploration of an abstract problem labelled the relation between "faith and metaphysics." "Reason" may not be, as Hume maintained, "the slave of the passions," but surely there is no reason, or at least no human reason, which exists and operates in isolation from the passions. "Pretend what we may," James stated, "the whole man

281

within us is at work when we form our philosophical opinions. Intellect, will, taste, and passion co-operate just as they do in practical affairs, and lucky it is if the passion be not something as petty as love of personal conquest over the philosopher across the way."[1] Elsewhere, he suggested that "rationality has at least four dimensions: intellectual, esthetical, moral, and practical; and to find a world rational to the maximal degree *in all these respects simultaneously* is no easy matter."[2] But if this multidimensional character is present in every rational or philosophical undertaking, it is preeminently so when what is under consideration is "faith or "belief," particularly religious faith or belief.

The task confronting us when we endeavor to inquire into religious faith is immeasurably complicated by the irreducible and non-subsumable reality of the individual person within whom such faith is concretized and incarnated. The effort to ground this faith by means of rational argument and objective criteria—whether in a religious tradition or in the dominant philosophical and scientific tradition of Western culture—has come on hard times in our century. Michael Polanyi put it well: "Innocently, we had trusted that we could be relieved of all personal responsibility for our beliefs by objective criteria of validity—and our own critical powers have shattered this hope."[3]

Not only James, but Kierkegaard, Nietzsche, and the diverse existentialists who flourished earlier in this century, vividly exposed any rationalistic pretensions to account adequately and exhaustively for the individual person in conceptual categories, however subtle, sophisticated, and complex. At the same time, none of these thinkers would be satisfied with a view of the person as atomistic, so hermetically sealed that anything said by one person would lack meaning for or application to any other person. Luther is reported to have said, "Everyone must do his own believing, as he must do his own dying, but that does not prevent us from shouting encouragement to one another." I would suggest that when we engage in a dialogical investigation of faith, the least and perhaps the most we can do is "shout encouragement to one another." Of course, we may also occasionally shout insults; but insult, properly expressed and humbly received, is among the richest forms of encouragement.

1

The irreducibly personal character of all faith and belief puts me under the philosophic obligation of describing where, fideistically, I'm coming from: I am a "born Catholic" as well as a "once a Catholic always a Catholic." While the first appellation is beyond dispute, there are many who might question the second. Bracketing the authenticity of my Catholicism, I wish to stress that for as long as I can remember, I took for granted both the truth and the reasonableness of Roman Catholicism. I was willing to grant that my Protestant friends were basically decent people and I never subscribed to any notion of "no salvation outside the Church" that automatically consigned non-Catholics to hell. Still, I was deeply puzzled as to how people who seemed otherwise quite intelligent could fail to see that the Scriptures proved Peter was the first Pope and Jesus instituted the doctrine of transubstantiation at the Last Supper.

The rationality of Roman Catholicism was reinforced at my Jesuit college where my philosophy and theology courses firmly established something like the following: reason could *prove* the existence of God; accepting the Scriptures was *reasonable* because they were the Word of God; accepting the Church—i.e., the hierarchy, dogmas, laws, and specific practices—was *reasonable* because in the Scriptures it could be *reasonably* shown that Jesus, who was *reasonably* shown to be the Son of God, had instituted the Roman Catholic Church. I have oversimplified, to be sure, but not, I believe, grossly distorted Roman Catholicism not only in the earlier part of this century but to some extent even today. But neither then nor now was this emphasis on the rationality of Roman Catholicism the whole story. I would note that from my catechetical days there had been combined with— or, better, juxtaposed to—the rationality of the "one, true, faith," its mystery. Faith was, after all, a gift and why some received it was as great a mystery as why some did not. As will become evident, I still adhere to the view that the only worthwhile and justifiable faith is one characterized by *both* rationality *and* mystery.

During and immediately after my graduate studies in philosophy at Fordham it slowly, oh so slowly, dawned on me that there was trouble in my religious-philosophical paradise. Without burdening readers with details—most of which I don't remember anyway—suffice it to say that I eventually found myself convinced that the dominant Roman Catholic view was too rationalistic and the Protestant view too irrationalistic. I saw, or believed I saw, in American pragmatism possibilities for remaining faithful to the insistence upon the fundamental harmony between faith and reason which had been the dominant feature of Roman Catholicism since Clement of Alexandria, while also acknowledging the non-rational, if not irrational, dimension of Christian faith sounded initially by Tertullian and reprised in more sophisticated modes by Kierkegaardian existentialism and Barthian neo-orthodoxy.

I believe that Aquinas' contention that there can be *apparent* but no *real* conflict between faith and reason remains sound. Sound as it is, however, it is, as we all know, not too helpful when concrete instances of conflict confront us. Indeed, depending on where one has located one's priorities, whether in faith or in reason, there will be a tendency to destroy or diminish the other. For example, when faith was the dominant cultural value, the temptation and tendency was to cut reason to fit the ongoing version of faith. As reason in the mode of modern science gradually achieved cultural ascendancy, faith was either formulated to conform to real or alleged scientific knowledge or else emptied of any real signification. Current efforts at harmonization, including my own, remain prey to this second temptation.

In attempting to delineate a viable relationship between faith and reason, we can quickly exclude simplistic extremes. I am confident that none of us would wish to argue for or defend a blind, purely emotive, totally unreflective faith. (Which is not to say, of course, that such a view of something quite close to it has not reemerged with a vengeance in our time.) The most succinct Christian version of this mode of faith has been expressed as follows: "God said it, Jesus did it, I believe it, that ends it." I am equally sure, on the other hand, that none of us would attempt to argue for a faculty of pure reason untouched by personal, historical, and cultural factors. The demanding task, then, is to articulate a mode of faith, real or ideal, which will avoid irrational emotivism and subjectivism, while not making any claims to ground faith in allegedly rationally objective criteria.

The Italian philosopher, Battista Mondin, based a recent article, "Faith and Reason in Roman Catholic Thought," on the following premise: "The famous formula expressing the Roman Catholic position concerning the problem of the relationship between faith and reason is: *fides non destruit sed perficit rationem.*"[4] I would contend that this sentence tells only half the story and is misleading unless combined with its mirror: reason does not destroy but perfects faith. Unless these two claims are held in existential and reflective tension, the tendency will be to affirm one pole of the dialectic at the expense of the other. This is not to deny, however, that existentially and psychologically we are, for the most part, believers before we are knowers. "We philosophize," Whitehead tells us, "because we believe; we do not believe because we philosophize. Philosophy," he continues, "is a criticism of belief—preserving, deepening, and modifying it."[5] Readers will, of course, recognize this as a decidedly contemporary echo of the traditional "faith seeking understanding."

2

The general interrelationship between and inseparability of faith and reason is widely recognized and accepted, however diversely, across a wide spectrum of late 20th century thinkers. Nevertheless, the concrete difficulties of being a reflective Christian believer have not diminished but have immeasurably increased and intensified as this century draws to a close. Even if others did not ask the question, we who choose to view ourselves as reflective Christian believers most assuredly must ask whether we can be Christians and philosophers without falling prey to self-deception or bad faith. Can the radical, critical, open-ended questioning which distinguishes—or ideally ought to distinguish—those who engage in the philosophical undertaking ever be honestly conducted by those who are Christian believers? Will we not tend to attenuate our critical faculties when confronted with scientific and philosophical claims or historical events which threaten our most cherished beliefs? A formal and abstract response to these questions is relatively easy; the living existential response is immeasurably more difficult. Contemporary believers are subject to a variety of modes of self-deception.

We have learned of psychological self-deception from Freud; economic and class self-deception from Marx; cultural self-deception from Nietzsche; linguistic self-deception from Wittgenstein; and more recently and still more controversially, textual self-deception from Derrida and the deconstructionists. The saving grace in all of this, however, is that it is not only Christians or theistic believers who are susceptible to one or another form of self-deception. Every human being in every time, in every culture, at every level of intellectual development, is subject to self-deception. Its universality finds classic expression in George Eliot's *Middlemarch:*

> There may be coarse hypocrites, who consciously affect beliefs and emotions for the sake of gulling the world, but Bulstrode was not one of them. He was simply a man whose desires had been stronger than his theoretic beliefs and who had gradually explained the gratification of his desires into satisfactory agreement with those beliefs. If this is hypocrisy, it is a process which shows itself occasionally in us all, to whatever confession we belong, and whether we believe in the future perfection of our race or in the nearest date fixed for the end of the world; whether we regard the earth as a putrefying nidus for a saved remnant, including ourselves, or have a passionate belief in the solidarity of mankind.[6]

But what does all of this have to do with "faith and metaphysics"? Simply this, what one understands by faith and by reason and by the relation between faith and reason is bound up with and inseparable from metaphysics. Further, that claim as well as every other claim I have made and will make is similarly enmeshed in a "metaphysics." If I quickly add that I am employing the term "metaphysics" in a functional rather than a substantive sense, you will immediately recognize that I am doing so from a particular metaphysical perspective. In any event, I will understand by "metaphysics" an "angle of vision" or perspective permeated by a set of principles or presuppositions from which we view reality or the world, and by means of which we transact with and constitute reality or the world.

In this sense of metaphysics, no human being can escape the metaphysical net, from the most intellectually unsophisticated to those deconstructionists and heideggerians who are currently heralding the "end of metaphysics." The "end of metaphysics," if it is the end, can only be the end of a particular metaphysics which may indeed have a variety of distinct expressions bound together by a number of shared features or family resemblances. Further, if a particular metaphysics does end, it will inevitably be succeeded by another metaphysics, since we can reject one metaphysics only from the perspective of another. Note that I say "reject" and not "refute." As John Herman Randall noted years ago, "No great philosophy has ever been refuted: it has been discarded as irrelevant to another type of experience."[7] If "metaphysics" seems too respectable and auspicious a term for this string of nonsystematic assertions which I will continue to hurl at you, simply understand me to be saying that no one can escape being grounded and enmeshed in a web of metaphysical assumptions—or, if you prefer, a cluster of fundamental or basic assumptions—all of which preclude any absolute proof inasmuch as they must be presupposed by whatever would be considered a valid mode of proving. Thus my rubric of "metaphysical assumption" covers such diverse claims as "there must be a sufficient reason for everything that is," "whatever I clearly and distinctly perceive is true," "all knowledge must be traceable to sense impressions," and "all existential realities are processive or processing." This last is one of my own controlling assumptions. I will take it up later.

First, however, a word about the relation between "faith" and "metaphysics." All too simply stated, my view is that every faith is permeated by a metaphysics and every metaphysics is grounded in some faith. In a letter to Helen Keller, James wrote, "The great world, *the background,* in all of us, is the world of our beliefs."[8] And even Nietzsche, no friend of theistic faith, will not acknowledge any science without presuppositions; "a 'faith,' must be there first of all," he says, "so that science can acquire

from it a direction, a meaning, a limit, a method, a *right* to
exist."9 Now all of this today may seem commonplace to reflective believers, but, if I may allude again to my personal history, it
was far from commonplace thirty-five years ago, at least not for
me and not for most Roman Catholic thinkers. Paradoxically, my
realization of this necessary interpenetration between any faith,
including Roman Catholic faith, and metaphysics suggested a
way out of, or at least a way of living with, what I was increasingly experiencing as an erosion of my faith, what is sometimes described, perhaps a bit grandiloquently, as a "crisis of
faith." Up until that time I held the view that classical metaphysics, or at least those features of it shared by diverse
Thomisms and Augustinianisms, and Roman Catholicism were a
package deal. As the song says about love and marriage, "You
can't have one without the other." At the same time, no one was
willing to simply identify classical metaphysics and Roman
Catholic faith. No one would come right out and say that the
principles of classical metaphysics called for the same degree of
adherence as did the dogmas of Roman Catholicism. But it
seemed evident that those dogmas, particularly those pertaining
to God, were soaked through and through with language, ideas,
and categories derived from classical metaphysics. My dilemma
is obvious: if I could no longer honestly give allegiance to the
fundamental claims of classical metaphysics, was I also obliged
to surrender that faith which had played the most important and
formative role in my life?

It was at this point that American pragmatism, principally as
expressed by James and to a lesser extent by Dewey, appeared to
offer me a way of remaining significantly continuous with my
religious community while rejecting the central features of classical metaphysics. We have to take another nostalgic turn down
memory lane if I am to communicate a sense of the situation—or
at least how I perceived the situation—within which I arrived at
my world-shaking, "road to Damascus" insight. We now know
that the 1950s were the final years of the near-smothering, coun-
ter-reformation/Vatican I attitude which had dominated the leadership of the Roman Catholic community almost from the
inception of the modern world. In the Roman Catholic lexicon,

the "modern" at worst referred to an evil, a threat to the well-being of the church, and at best to novelties that were either misguided or irrelevant to saving one's soul. In the post-World War II period, however, there were beginning to emerge stirrings and rumors, exciting to some, unsettling to others, that in Europe, principally in France, some unusual, if not unorthodox, ideas were beginning to circulate. Those of us secure within the conceptual walls of those protective fortresses called Catholic colleges and universities, began to hear such names as deLubac, Congar, Mounier, and Marcel, and if you were lucky, there might come into your possession a mimeograph copy of the writings of a priest called Teilhard de Chardin, who was apparently suggesting that evolution was not totally the work of the devil. The early issues of *Cross Currents* first brought many of these and other such thinkers to the attention of an American audience. At Fordham, the great teacher, Robert Pollack, was introducing a new generation of students to a variety of stimulating and provocative ideas, including the suggestion that Christian humanism was not an oxymoron. More widely known was John Courtney Murray, who was getting himself into all kinds of trouble with the ecclesiastical authorities for presenting the daring hypothesis that in the event Catholics found themselves a majority within a nation, they would not be absolutely bound to jail all non-Catholics. At this time, it should be noted, even those of us who were struggling to be more sympathetic to non-Catholic modern thinkers and to call attention to important truths in their thought felt compelled to add that of course such truths were already present in the "fullness" of the Roman Catholic tradition. I must also note that we were compelled not primarily because of fear of ecclesiastical authorities, but because we, in some vague but very real way, believed it.

3

Then came John XXIII and the windows were opened and in blew the refreshing and invigorating winds of the modern world and Catholics found themselves in the euphoria surrounding

Vatican II. The magic word suddenly was "change," a word and phenomenon which for several hundred years had been viewed by Catholics as at best suspect and at worst a threat to that which they held most dear. In words written at the time describing this shift I said, "It no longer required daring to speak out publicly in favor of change, development of doctrine, learning from non-Catholic thinkers, even for free speech and freedom of thought within the Church. The 'closed' Church has become the 'open' Church, according to most Catholic spokesmen." These words appeared in an article entitled "Reflections On Faith and Meta-physics,"[10] which grew out of an effort to review for *Cross Currents* several books by Roman Catholic thinkers on God. One of those books was John Courtney Murray's *The Problem of God*,[11] and it was here that it became strikingly evident to me that even the best and most intellectually sophisticated among Roman Catholic thinkers presupposed the inseparability of Roman Catholic faith and the central feature of classical metaphysics, that beneath or behind or beyond the evident reality of change, there exists permanent, immutable reality or realities. Hence, any change in Roman Catholicism that did, is, or could take place would be restricted to the surface, to accidentals: the underlying essentials are immutable, incapable of being touched by change, however widespread and pervasive that change may be in human experience. It seemed to me then as it seems to me now that the metaphysics presupposed by such a view is profoundly opposed to that metaphysics which has been emerging in a variety of modes over the last two-hundred years—a metaphysics which affirms change so radical and pervasive that no existential reality escapes it. Thus I realized that not everyone who says "change, change" will enter the kingdom of process. At the same time, I was wary of romanticizing change: significant change in any aspect of life "ain't no day at the beach."

I have never, then, minimized or denied the significance and strength of that view which insists that however difficult it may be to express, Roman Catholicism must never surrender its claim to be the bearer of and witness to absolutely immutable truths. Neither I nor anyone else is likely in the near future to bring forth a metaphysics and a model of faith derived therefrom which will have the richness, subtlety, and conceptual sophistication which characterize the best versions of the traditional thinking, past and present. Still, I firmly believe that some alternative efforts both of thinking and living are called for and the hope is that the community will be sufficiently secure in its faith to allow those efforts to emerge—they will emerge in any event.

Roman Catholics, even in pre-Vatican II days, bristled at the charge that their community was monolithic, and I think we can safely dismiss such a charge as failing to acknowledge the rich diversity that has characterized their community since its inception. Still, we must question the extent and depth of the pluralism which is officially allowable within the Roman Catholic community. Parenthetically, I would note that pluralism is not merely a problem for Roman Catholics—it is a characteristic of reality and any knowledge that we may achieve. James echoes the Hegelian view when he says that "any partial view whatever of the world tears the part out of its relations, leaves out some truth concerning it, is untrue of it, falsifies it."[12] This leads James to posit a "pluralistic, restless universe, in which no single point of view can ever take in the whole scene."[13]

Much more can and needs to be said about pluralism and faith, but let me focus now on the implications for faith when it is lived and reflected upon within a metaphysics sharply opposed to the metaphysics that has served Catholicism and indeed Christianity for so long and so well. In September 1985, Bishop James Malone, then president of the National Conference of Catholic Bishops, submitted a statement to the secretariat of the synod of Bishops in which he said: "The Church stands in need of a new philosophical and conceptual framework—perhaps, also, a new symbolic and affective system—through which to proclaim the gospel to the modern world. New instruments must be developed for the presentation of authentic Catholic doctrine at all levels and to all groups. In this task creativity and fidelity are equally imperative."[14] This sounds to me like a call for a new metaphysics and my question is whether those who support such a call are aware of the possible consequences of attempting to reconstruct Christian faith in the language and experience of any new metaphysics which would be more than a refining and refur-

bishing of the old metaphysics. I have long believed that, ironically, those called conservative Catholics have more keenly
sensed the risks and dangers involved in such change. From the
outset of my own exploration I have felt "the conservatives see
that you cannot traffic in new ideas without running great risks
and, perhaps more important, that, to the extent new ideas are
really contacted, old ideas will be changed."[15] No thinker, in my
opinion, has grasped more profoundly than John Dewey the risk
involved in serious thinking. "Let us admit the case of the
conservative," he cautions; "if we once start thinking, no one
can guarantee where we shall come out, except that many objects, ends and institutions are surely doomed. Every thinker
puts some portion of an apparently stable world in peril and no
one can wholly predict what will emerge in its place." He goes
on to say that "no one discovers a new world who exacts guarantee in advance for what it shall be, or who puts the act of
discovery under bonds with respect to what the new world shall
do to him when it comes into vision."[16]

The inevitable and quite proper question posed to anyone
advocating change, whether in society at large or within a particular faith community, is, "Where do you draw the line?" In my
view the only honest response to that question on the part of one
presuming to think and live on the basis of the radically processive assumption which I will shortly describe is, "There can
be no line drawn once and for all that forever remains beyond the
possibility of being redrawn or even erased." This is not to deny
that lines are and must be drawn. But they must be defined and
justified on the basis of their efficacy for and enrichment of
human life. They cannot be justified solely on the basis of their
having been drawn by the hierarchy, or by Christians of an
earlier age or even by the Scriptures. Again, this is not to say that
any such lines may not weather the test of time and developing
human experience. Some will, others will not: all remain subject
to reasonable inquiry. Those lines drawn by and within a religious community cannot claim a privilege and protection from
critical scrutiny and evaluation denied lines drawn by other
segments of the human community.

4

Let me now briefly describe my key metaphysical assumptions and within the framework of those assumptions try to sketch a model of faith which is open to radical development while maintaining a significant continuity with the faith experiences of those members who constituted the life of earlier moments of the community. One of my central metaphysical assumptions is that reality is processive through and through. Negatively this perspective excludes any metaphysical or ontological dualism. In a radically processive world there are no absolutely permanent or unchanging realities, since all realities, or at least all existential realities, are processes. Such a world is most succinctly expressed in James's metaphorical phrases, "unfinished universe" and "world in the making." A crucial feature of reality, then, is that it is open to radical novelty. But the world or reality I am presupposing is not only radically processive, it is also radically relational. Negatively, this view excludes all atomistic individuals or unrelated or totally self-sufficient realities. Positively, it maintains that all realities are constituted by their relations. I have taken from James the suggestion that the concreteness of reality is best expressed in the metaphor "field" or "fields". "We must suppose," he tells us, " 'fields' that 'develop' under the categories of continuity with each other. . . . All the fields commonly supposed," he goes on to say, "are incomplete, and point to a complement beyond their own content. The final content," he concludes, "is that of a plurality of fields, more or less ejective to each other but still continuous in various ways."[17] Fields, as I employ the term, are processive-relational complexes, transacting with and consequently constituted by a variety of other fields. Thus the world or reality can be most succinctly described as "fields within fields within fields . . ." Similarly, the individual person or self is an initiating center of activity transacting with and constituted by a variety and diversity of fields both narrower and wider. This field metaphysics renders plausible and allows for a reasonable faith in the reality of a widest field, designated God, with whom human persons can transact and by means of which they are constituted. It has been a particular concern of mine to suggest that if we can believe that we are here and now in part constituted by and in transactional relation with such a God, we can also believe and hope that such a God will maintain and continue this constituting relation even after other relations or fields that now make up our reality have been terminated. My concern here, however, is to suggest a model for a viable mode of faith presupposing the kind of processive-relational world just hinted at.

To begin with, faith must be viewed primarily as a mode of experience rather than as a mode of knowledge. This, needless to say, is a most controversial and problematic claim and without presuming to resolve the formidable difficulties to which it gives rise I would simply like to make a few distinctions which I believe make it a reasonably defensible claim. Within the metaphysics of experience from which I am operating, the primary metaphor or category is experience rather than knowledge and knowledge itself is a mode of experience. In its broadest sense, experience is transaction between diverse fields or centers of activity. So seen, experience or transactional activity constitutes all realities from electrons to God. Focusing on human experience, we can describe it as transaction between a center of activity or organism and its environment, environment being understood as whatever enters into transactional relation with the organism. The living person, then, is the dynamic relational unity which can be described most concretely as a believing-knowing-loving-feeling being. More abstractly, we might describe the human person as constituted by a variety of modes of experience or transactions, variously designated cognitive, esthetic, affective, and religious. While functionally distinct, these different experiences are not separable and, most important, do not relate to different orders of being. This last point excludes by implication any dualism which would assign experience to a subjective order of being and knowledge to an objective order. Subject and object, subjective and objective are derivative categories, functionally distinguished from within a wider field of reality.

Assuming, then, that faith is a mode of experience, the formidable task is to describe its distinctive features. Let me offer a few hints. My first hint follows from the radically processive-relational world I am presupposing. In a static or finished world, faith could play only a passive role of guessing how the world fundamentally and unchangeably is. But in a world in the making, the very kind of world that the world will be depends in part at least upon the faiths and beliefs involved in the making of it. Further, faith and belief are not activities peculiar to a segment of the human community such as those who are members of a formal religion or even those who are believers in a reality called God. Hence, from my perspective, the customary believer-non-believer distinction is not acceptable. All human beings are in some way or ways believers. "The coil is about us," James tells us, "struggle as we may. The only escape from faith is mental nullity."[18] If it is obvious that all humans are believers, it is also obvious that they do not all share the same beliefs. Nor are these beliefs of equal worth in relation to the well-being of the world and human community. The evaluation of these beliefs in terms of their contribution to or diminution of the development, enhancement, and enrichment of the evolving life of the human community is a complex, open-ended, on-going task, whose particulars lie outside this inquiry.

5

Let me now say a few words about how I understand faith in general and then give a brief sketch of what I think is called for in an adequate model of theistic faith. For some years now, I have found it useful to distinguish faith from belief, though they are often and understandably used interchangeably. Belief as I understand it refers to any affair of leading, as a pointing ahead, a going beyond that for which there is evidence at the present moment. Beliefs so understood permeate every moment of our lives, from that of everyday routine to the most sophisticated scientific endeavor. Faith, as I wish to understand it, refers to a complex set of beliefs which bear upon human life in its most comprehensive dimension and effort. Faith plays the role of holding together or attempting to hold together the diverse modes of human experience. It might be described as an integrating experience whereby knowing experience, affective experience, esthetic experience—in short, all modes of experience—are brought into a relatively cohesive whole which is expressed in the life of the person. Faith thereby serves to order, direct, illuminate, and render meaningful human life.[19]

Now beliefs are capable of verification upon which they become knowledge or, better, knowing experiences. For example, at one time we believed that we could land on the moon, we now know that we can. Some humans now believe that there is extraterrestrial intelligent life; if *Close Encounters of the Third Kind* becomes an historical event rather than just a movie, we will know that there is such life. Faith, however, is such that only a lifetime of commitment and lived affirmation is adequate witness to its authenticity, if not necessarily its truth. I do not deny that there may be, even to some extent must be, evidence of authenticity—such as a degree of personal fulfillment or a more humane community—which flows from a particular faith. These, however, can never be definitively compelling; short of an eschaton, a millennium, or a utopia, they can never receive the kind of verification which characterizes knowledge.

In surrendering the strong knowledge claims traditionally made for faith, I am, *a fortiori,* surrendering any claim that absolute certitude belongs to faith. Continuous and inescapable risk and existential doubt are ever-present constitutive dimensions of a reflective faith experience. As Tillich has perceptively noted, "faith embraces itself and the doubt about itself."[20] Further, reflective faith must be lived with the acute awareness that it is radically foundationless. "The difficulty is," as Wittgenstein has observed, "to realize the groundlessness of our believing."[21] Let me repeat that faith here is not restricted to Christian faith or even to theistic faith; rather, it extends to the faith of marxists, humanists, and even atheists.

In denying that faith is primarily and distinctively a mode of knowledge, I am not denying that it will inevitably, inescapably, and properly be bound up with a variety of knowledge claims. Indeed, the model of faith I am proposing recognizes a much greater influence of knowledge and science upon faith than does the traditional viewpoint. Not only does faith necessarily *involve* knowledge but a reflective faith ought to be responsive to the very best and most challenging knowledge available to the human community. What is excluded, of course, is identification of faith experience with any culturally, historically, linguistically, and metaphysically conditioned mode of knowledge. The need, then, is for a model and mode of faith which will be open to radical change, criticism, and transformation yet allowing for significant continuity with the faith of the community at all stages of its development.

It will be most evident in what follows that it is easier to state what is needed than it is to fulfill, even speculatively, that need.

6

Though the model of faith which I am suggesting would be applicable to any faith community, I will restrict my remaining remarks to theistic faith as it relates to the Christian community. Hence, I will understand by theistic faith or faith in God a person-communal-existential orientation and relationship—a dynamic and developing relationship in virtue of which human persons are moved beyond themselves not toward some outward or external object or goal but to a richer life which is at once a fuller realization of themselves and a sharing in the life of that mysterious *Other* whom we have traditionally called "God."[22]

Stated in transactional language, faith in God can be understood as an on-going transaction between the divine and the human, each of which is a distinct field or center of activity. A rather subtle but important point must be made or at least suggested here. The experience which I am calling faith in God, must be sharply distinguished from ordinary experience. I noted earlier that when a belief is verified we no longer speak of it as a belief but a knowledge. A similar point can be made with reference to other experiences. Prior to attending a concert we might believe that we will have a rich esthetic experience; if our belief is confirmed we no longer speak in terms of belief but describe our attendance at the concert as a rich experience. The experience of faith in God is quite different, however, since any alleged experience can neither substitute for nor give confirmation to faith in God. Faith—the groundless, unverifiable faith I have described—would seem to be the necessary condition for any human experience of God. The exception to this might appear to be that moment of experiential union with God to which mystics attest. But even here, as St. John of the Cross seems to suggest, the mystic must have faith that this is an experience of the divine and not the demonic.

In contending that faith in God should be understood as experience rather than objective knowledge, I in no way intend to identify this faith with some individualistic, Cartesian-like experience. Like Luther, we must do our own believing, but we do not really do our believing alone. That a dimension of "aloneness" accompanies in varying degrees all faith, is, I believe, true. But as the dominant traditions of both Judaism and Christianity witness, God encounters a people, a community, a church, not atomistically isolated individuals. Faith is always personal-communal, principally because the individual person as relationally constituted has no reality apart from some community or communities. Further, because the intensity and depth of the faith experience varies among the members of any historical community, we inevitably lean on each other in our believing effort. "Our faith," James states, "is faith in someone else's faith, and in the greatest matters this is most the case."[23] This is preeminently so, of course, for those of us who enter a faith community long after the faith experience or experiences which brought this community into existence. Christianity is a case in point. The original pentecostal experience was, after all, quite brief; only a few of those who over the last 2,000 years were and are believing Christians participated in it. We touch here upon one of the most sensitive and complex questions related to faith: how is the original faith experience to be communicated to and shared by those who were not present as participants in this originary experience? Here, I must be even more sketchy and tentative than I have been throughout this essay.

Recall that I am endeavoring to suggest a model of faith in God in terms of my experiential, processive-relational metaphysics, which I believe enables us to be responsive to the most compelling insights and criticisms emerging from modern and contemporary thought and experience while remaining significantly continuous with the faith of the earlier moments of the Christian community. What is excluded on my terms is any allegedly essential content of faith which remains unchanged throughout all moments of the community's life, though it is expressed in ever-changing words, concepts or symbols. There is no faith experience that is not, as I have previously noted, conditioned through and through—linguistically, culturally, and metaphysically. From my perspective, however, there is no need to apologize for the emergence from the community of sacred scriptures and specific practices, doctrines, and institutions. The notion that there is some kind of pristine religious or faith experience independent of these structures is illusory. At the same time, I wish to reject the notion that any one or any combination of these structures is identical with and absolutely inseparable from the living, developing, transforming divine-human transaction or experience of faith. I would further suggest that where the experiential character of faith diminished, the temptation has been more and more to equate faith with these structures. The obvious reason for this is that it is much easier to delineate a particular biblical interpretation, practice, doctrine, or institution than it is to communicate the mysterious and irreducible character of the personal/communal faith experience.

I have claimed that faith in general involves a complex set of beliefs and that this holds for faith in God. This leads to the most difficult part of my task, perhaps the unsayable part: to describe how this faith experience can be constituted by a set of beliefs subject to those conditions which attend all human beliefs, without that faith experience being identical with and inseparable from those beliefs. This touches upon one of the more complex problems in philosophy, the problem of "identity over time." Applied to a particular historical faith community, the question is, How can we be said to share the same faith with earlier members of the community when the set of beliefs constituting our faith experiences are radically, if not yet totally different?

Having excluded any dualistic account which would select some beliefs as timeless and impermeable to change and transformation, I must look elsewhere. Possibly, and I underline possibly, the ever-developing divine-human encounter is such that it is open to the most radical and unforeseen transformation, assuming that both God and human beings are processive or evolving realities. This, of course, is an extrapolation, an extrapolation which has its own dimension of faith. The grounds for making it, I would maintain, are to be found in the histories of both the human and Christian communities. If we focus on the Christian community, it is quite evident that there is no simple identity among the faiths of a contemporary Christian, of a medieval Christian, and of an apostolic Christian. Many beliefs that were bound up with and considered essential by these earlier Christians have simply not been able to withstand the assault of historical events and philosophical and scientific criticism. As one belief or knowledge claim after another succumbs, Christians are tempted to retreat to an ever-dwindling storehouse of allegedly unchanging beliefs. It may be that some of these may survive indefinitely, but as John Herman Randall observed years ago, "Each new attempt to set up an unassailable preserve for religious truth has had to surrender more territory than its predecessor."[24] An effort, then, however tentative and halting, to construct an alternate model of faith along the processive-relational lines I am suggesting is, I believe, as justifiable as it is needed.

The apparent weakness, decisive for some, of a model of a radically changing faith is that it cannot assure us which among the set of beliefs that here and now constitute our faith will survive and which will succumb to the press of thought and experience. Nor can we now know the particular form which those that do survive will take. Further, there has been and will continue to be wide-ranging variations in the ways in which individuals will respond to events and ideas that appear to conflict with their faith. We can surmise that when history destroyed the early Christians' belief in the imminence of the second coming, some Christians lost their faith. And we know that when evolutionary consciousness made impossible a literal reading of Genesis, many Christians ceased to be Christians. In those situa-

tions and in many similar ones, however, other Christians recon-
structed their beliefs in a manner which allowed them to remain
continuous with their faith community. There is, of course, no
formula for deciding *a priori*, either for the individual or the
community, which beliefs or complex of beliefs can be surrendered while maintaining the integrity of Christian faith. Nor is
there any formula for deciding just which and how many particular beliefs individual Christians can surrender before their
faith is also surrendered. We must not be sentimental or polyan-
nish here. The mode of radically changing faith which I am
advocating carries no guarantee that one's faith will survive the
critical scrutiny and transformation to which it must submit. It is
unsurprising that at the present moment Roman Catholics range
in their views of what can and what cannot be changed without
destroying their Christian faith. At one end are those who are
threatened by the change in or surrender of just about any
doctrine that is or appears to have been promulgated by the
hierarchy. At the other pole are those who are willing to surrender almost any doctrine or doctrinal formulation so long as they
retain or see the possibility of retaining a lived sense of the
presence of God in the world.

7

It may be useful to restate all of this in terms of continuity—a
central category of the processive-relational metaphysics which
I am presupposing. Change implies continuity. The continuous
character of reality, including personal reality, allows for the most
radical change and transformation while incorporating without
simply destroying earlier modes of the reality in question. The
new grows out of the old and while it is in no simple sense
identical with the old, neither is it in any simple sense totally
different from it. The category of continuity, then, allows for a
developing community that retains a significant relation to its
earlier moments without locking the experience and thought and
practice of those members who emerge later into the experiential
modes and conceptual and linguistic formulations of those ear-

lier moments. This does not rule out the possibility of giving a certain privileged status to the initial moments of a historical community's life; nor does it excuse those who emerge later from justifying as fully as possible any changes in practice or doctrinal formulation that they believe called for.

A priori, however, no doctrine, practice, or institution can be held absolutely and permanently protected from reflective scrutiny in the light of the cumulative experience of the human community. This does not necessarily mean that every doctrine or belief will or can be surrendered without jeopardizing the life and character of the community. Indeed, I would argue that without some mode of belief in the reality of God and resurrection, the Christian community forfeits its reason for being. Others would wish to make the same case for other beliefs or practices or institutional forms. My hypothesis rules out none of these claims *a priori;* the point I would insist upon, however, is that no claim can be defended in isolation from the developing thought and experience of *both* the religious *and* the wider human community. It is not enough merely to show that something has been believed or prohibited at earlier moments of the life of the community. Nor will it be sufficient to claim that a doctrine, practice, or institution has been revealed by God and is consequently exempt from that critical evaluation to which all other aspects of human life are and should be subjected. What has been and is being revealed is precisely what is at stake at every moment of the community's life; there has not been nor can there be any once-and-for-all determination of just what is authentic rather than apparent revelation. In the church's faith experience of and with a revealing God, separating authentic from apparent revelation is an open-ended, ceaseless task which the faith community must assume willingly, lovingly, and in fear and trembling. The community's great temptation will be this: to identify with the divine itself its own necessary but necessarily *inadequate* articulation of its mysterious faith encounter with the divine; whoever succumbs to that temptation falls into idolatry.

Any reflection on or discussion of faith in God begins in mystery and needs must end in mystery. Any viable model of faith must safeguard the mystery dimension of faith without transforming mystery into mindless mystification by emptying it of all concreteness through the attempt to free this mystery totally from the ever-changing linguistic, intellectual, and cultural relations by which and through which alone at the present stage of our evolution we humans can encounter the divine.

Some may ask who can possibly live with such a mystery-laden, elusive, tenuous, constantly threatened, ever-changing faith. I must simply respond, "Perhaps only persons of faith."

Notes

1. William James, *The Will to Believe* (Cambridge: Harvard University Press, 1979), p. 77.

2. William James, *A Pluralistic Universe* (Cambridge: Harvard University Press, 1977), p. 55.

3. Michael Polanyi, *Personal Knowledge* (Chicago: University of Chicago Press, 1958), p. 268.

4. Battista Mondin, "Faith and Reason in Roman Catholic Thought from Clement of Alexandria to Vatican II," *Dialogue & Alliance,* vol. 1, no. 1, Spring 1987, p. 18.

5. Alfred North Whitehead, "The Harvard Lectures for the Fall of 1926," cited, Lewis S. Ford, *The Emergence of Whitehead's Metaphysics 1925–1929* (Albany: State University of New York Press, 1984), p. 309.

6. George Eliot, *Middlemarch* (New York: New American Library, 1964), p. 601.

7. John Herman Randall, Jr., *The Career of Philosophy* (New York: Columbia University Press, 1964), vol. I, p. 11.

8. Ralph Barton Perry, *The Thought and Character of William James* (Boston: Little, Brown and Company, 1935), vol. II, p. 455.

9. Friedrich Nietzsche, *On the Genealogy of Morals,* trans. by Walter Kaufmann and R. J. Hollingdale (New York: Vintage Books, 1969), pp. 151–152.

10. Eugene Fontinell, "Reflections on Faith and Metaphysics," *Cross Currents,* Winter 1966, p. 18.

11. John Courtney Murray, S.J. (New Haven: Yale University Press, 1964).

12. James, *A Pluralistic Universe,* p. 45.

13. James, *The Will to Believe,* p. 136.

14. *The New York Times,* September 16, 1985, p. A12.

15. *Cross Currents,* Winter 1966, p. 19.

16. John Dewey, *Experience and Nature* (New York: Dover Publications, 1958), pp. 222, 246.

17. Perry, *The Thought and Character of William James,* II, p. 365.

18. James, *The Will to Believe,* p. 78.

19. Eugene Fontinell, *Toward a Reconstruction of Religion* (New York: Doubleday, 1970, reissued, West Nyack: Cross Currents, 1979), p. 86.

20. Paul Tillich, *Biblical Religion and the Search for Ultimate Reality* (Chicago: University of Chicago Press, Phoenix Edition, 1964), p. 61.

21. Ludwig Wittgenstein, *On Certainty,* trans. by Denis Paul and G. E. M. Anscombe (New York: Harper Torchbooks, 1972), #166, p. 24e.

22. Fontinell, *Toward a Reconstruction of Religion,* pp. 183–184.

23. James, *The Will to Believe,* p. 19.

24. John Herman Randall, Jr., *The Role of Knowledge in Western Religion* (Boston: Starr King Press, 1958), p. 11.

RAIMUNDO PANIKKAR

Chosenness and Universality: Can Christians Claim Both?

Raimundo Panikkar is author of The Unknown Christ of Hinduism, Worship and Secular Man, The Vedic Experience, *and* The Inter-religious Dialogue. *A symposium in his honor, held by the Institute of Religious Studies of the University of California at Santa Barbara in 1977, formed a special issue of* Cross Currents (Summer 1979). *"His theology is simultaneously experiential and speculative," Ewert H. Cousins says in his introduction to the symposium. "It is rooted in religious experience, tapping the wellsprings of Christian spirituality at a point that can make contact with the depths of Oriental philosophy." The present essay explores questions at the center of the convergence process: what does a particular religion's claim to be chosen mean? what does a particular religion's claim to be universal mean? can a particular religion claim simultaneously to be chosen and universal? Panikkar's open-ended exploration leads to a final question: "What is Christian identity today?" And he calls for a second Council of Jerusalem—the first freed Jewish and gentile Christians from the obligations of Jewish law—"in order that humankind as a whole may discern the signs of the times."*

From the outset we should distinguish sharing, participation—*communicatio* which eventually leads to or assumes communion—from information. Our question has nothing to do with the so-called "sciences of information."

The problem, as I understand it, is this:

How far can we communicate with others if we intentionally reserve for ourselves what we take to be our distinctive and most precious feature? Or, as I put the problem in *Worship and Secular Man:* "Unless there is *communicatio in sacris* there is no communication, but only an exchange of goods or words."

The question can be easily answered *if* it is assumed that "we" have a special gift, a particular grace that has not been given to others. Spouses normally do not share the intimacy of wedlock even with their best friends. If there is an exclusive Christian uniqueness it would be a sacrilege to share it with aliens. If Christians are chosen people, they cannot throw their precious pearl to the swine, and the traditional *disciplina arcani* is abundantly justified. Nor is this issue concerning "infidels" a specifically Christian problem: almost every tradition has to confront the 'other'—the *goi, kafir, mleccha,* barbarian, pariah, leper, poor, alien. Our specific problem is not a question of chosenness.

The problem arises with universality. If Christians lay claim to an unrestricted universality, they cannot withhold their treasures from any aspirant. If the conditions for admitting any candidate are tied to a particular culture or religion, the alleged universality is not human-wide, but is linked to the belief that the particular culture and religion represents the acme of humanness. This leads to the well-known opinion that the Christian is the perfect Man and Christianity the objectively superior religion.[1] Universality then means that any and every human being is called upon to become a Christian. The other human and religious traditions are interpreted as *praeparatio evangelica* of an *anima naturaliter* (i.e., *potentialiter*) *christiana.*

This is, granted, a coherent position. If we are the best, we simply invite the others to become this best also—i.e., the same as us. Or, put less crudely, God is calling everybody to become a Christian. The difficulty arises when we concretize the concept of universality, and it becomes insurmountable if Christians accept pluralism and no longer claim that they are the only custodians *de vera religione.* Such an attitude represents a mutation in the Christian self-understanding customary over at least the last millenium. My contention is that the traditional interdict of sharing worship, so common in many religions, is a coherent and justified position under a set of assumptions like caste, pure-impure, chosenness, etc. These assumptions are being challenged or substantially modified today under the general banner of a universal un-hierarchical human dignity.

Let us phrase the question in all its pungency for the Christian case. Ecumenical ecumenism, inter-religious dialogue, authentic tolerance and recognition of the other as an equal are empty, if not hypocritical words, unless we face squarely this mutation in self-understanding. To make a distinction between Christianity as universal religion and particular cultures does not help to soften the acuteness of the problem; first, because most religious traditions would not accept this separation between religion and culture and, secondly, because the moment that the Christian claim is clothed in language it becomes a tributary of the culture of that language. By language we do not understand, say, English or Malayalam, but the language of the Bible, the language of the Councils, the cosmology of Christian thought and the actual words used, such as God, person, grace, redemption, history, nature, etc.

For the sake of clarity, I shall devote the greater part of this essay to an analysis of the notion of chosenness, keeping in mind the issue of universality, and shall end with the question of whether or not they are compatible. I shall begin with an exegetical comment, followed by a theological reflection, to be continued by some philosophical considerations before finishing with certain provisional conclusions.

1

For exegetical comment we take the Acts of the Apostles, chapters 10 and 11. This is one of the longest narratives in Christian scripture and, though the meaning is by no means difficult to grasp, the whole story is repeated in all its details no less than three times. Thus it must surely be regarded as an important subject.

The main message of this passage seems to be clear; we

human beings have no right to make any *a priori* dichotomy between pure and impure, sacred and profane, or, in the mind of Peter in the story, between good and bad. He is told, like one of his predecessors whom he considered the source of his Jewish faith, "Go and kill"—your son in the first instance (Gen. 22:2) and now, in the second, "and eat" all these animals. I would like to lay stress on the parallelism. We have here two momentous episodes. One of the great phyla of humankind is founded on the fidelity of Abraham. Another great tradition is founded on the fidelity of Simon. Abram became Abraham, the father of all believers within what is now called the abrahamic tradition, while Simon became Peter, the rock of all believers within what is until now called the Christian religion. In short, our passage relates a foundational event. Christian history starts here.

The narrative insists not only on making no distinction with regard to creatures, but also with regard to persons. God does not make any distinction of persons (*prosopoleptes,* says the Greek). All our preconceived ideas seem to be shattered. The Holy Spirit is always unpredictable; the least expected thing was that the Holy Spirit should dwell in those uncircumcised Gentiles, and even more, should command Peter to transgress the Torah.

Similar experiences happened to Paul and Barnabas, and the First Council of Jerusalem (Acts 15:1 ff) decided, once and for all, to do away not only with the rule "that a Jew is forbidden by his religion to visit or associate with a man of another race" (Acts 10:28—NEB), but also with the primordial sacrament of the entire Covenant, namely, circumcision. She, the Spirit, said Peter, recounting for the fourth time the same experience, "made no difference between them and us" (Acts 15:9—NEB).

But since the human being cannot live without rites, baptism almost automatically replaced circumcision, and after twenty centuries it is no wonder that Christians have also acquired habits of discrimination between pure and impure, between we and they, between Christians and non-Christians, between baptized and unbaptized. There is a fundamental distinction between discernment of spirits and discrimination of persons. The distinction is, further, revolutionary: only the latter gives "religious" identity; the former demands an ever open spirituality.

Theology used to put the Christian religious issue in more polite ways: there is salvation inside and outside, ordinarily by baptism of water, and extraordinarily by baptism of desire; there is invincible ignorance, clean conscience in good faith, etc. Yet the dream of Peter smashes all these habits and convictions. If the disciple is not expected to fare better than his master, Christians should not pretend that they know better than Peter.

Second, there is a terrific crisis of identity. How can he defend his own stance? Where does he stand? What are the others going to say? There is a great stir in Jerusalem; they have heard that something has happened in Caesarea.

Then there comes a kind of unconditional confidence: "What God has sanctified we should not call impure (*koinou*)" (Acts 11:9). There is more than linguistic irony in the fact that the "impure," here, is the "common," the word being also at the basis of *koinonia,* community, communion.

This apart, the main lesson is that nobody knows beforehand what God wants, thinks, does, or is. If we behave as if we had some criterion regarding the Ultimate Reality which we here call God, we are assigning to ourselves a role which is higher than God's. God then is not free. He has to submit to what we think He is, what we expect Him to do because He has always done it so, or He has promised to do it so: a *deus ex machina.* This, however, is what our text disapproves. We have no criterion whatsoever, when we utter the name of God, by which we may say what this God is, thinks, or wills—how He is going to act, or what He is going to do.

Contemporary mentality finds privilege-minded and hierarchical views on humanity hard to swallow. The restrictions in sharing worship smack of elitism and injustice. The Eucharist was for long centuries considered *de necessitate medii* and not only of precept for salvation (Jn 11:53). And only a few were allowed even to approach the sacrament.

We should not dismiss too quickly the widespread consensus among most traditional religions that only a few reach the goal, are saved and not born again, attain nirvana, and the like. God is absolute Sovereign also over and above our personal conscience and feelings. The case of Abraham is paradigmatic; certainly it was for Peter. God can oblige us to kill our children in spite of the qualms of our private consciences. Humankind at large and certainly centuries of Christianity bear witness to the fact that thinkers of all persuasions have not found it repugnant that only a tiny fraction of people were realized or of Christians saved.

If nowadays, by and large, human conscience revolts against this, we should not forget that the same God who seemed to allow hell for the immense majority of humans now still goes on allowing human hell for most of the people of our times as well. This is the challenge of sacred secularity as a *novum* in our times across religious persuasions. The mutation in self-understanding is not superficial; it entails cosmological and theological quantum-leaps. It defies the old notion of the nature of God as Lord. But that is not our topic now.

What I am submitting here is in fact a commonplace agreed to by almost everyone, intellectuals and common people alike— namely, that a new degree of consciousness, a new epoch is dawning for humanity. We can call it a crisis or a challenge, and we may interpret it however we want, from the personal, depth-psychological, sociological, theological or mystical point of view, as we prefer. I would like to distinguish here only two levels of interpretation, the personal and the ecclesio-theological.

First, the personal. Peter was an individual, and so were Paul and Barnabas. Their deeper beliefs were called in question. We should also face the challenge personally. Are we ready to undergo a similar shattering of all our previous ideas, not once and for all but constantly? Or, are we freezing what this passage seems to say and no longer reading and listening to a living message directed to ourselves? The declaration of Acts 11:18, "God has granted this conversion into life to the Gentiles also," reaches out to the people of the world, to the nations, to each and every race.

Here I would like to stress the dynamic character of this required attitude. It is a *metanoia*, a change of mentality, a transcending of mental habits, that is life-giving because it is a lived conversion, that is, an ongoing process, a constant overcoming of the inertia of the mind.

If Christian exegesis has any value, it cannot be reduced to historical reconstruction, as the founders of modern biblical criticism wanted, but has to extract a living message for the hearer. If Peter recalls four times how he has overcome his prejudices, should we not persevere in overcoming ours? Openness to the Spirit may be frightening—but all fear has to be overcome. "Peace to you" and "Fear not" seem to be the recurring message of the Risen Christ.

The second level is the ecclesio-theological level. We should ask ourselves if we have not too quickly identified Christianity, the Church and Christ: three notions which should be carefully distinguished—although not separated. Have we not in fact monopolized, no doubt with good intentions, the understanding of Christ, on the one hand, and the very reality of Christ, on the other?

I am not arguing that baptism is not the Christian substitute for circumcision or that the New Testament is an ersatz for the Old. I am only saying that from the Christian point of view we cannot deny the call to maintain ourselves in this constitutive openness, the openness Peter showed when he was able to kill, to eat, to have social and convivial relations with those who were not of his race, who were not circumcised. I am reminded of the injunction: "accept the water of life, a free gift to all who desire it" (Rev. 22:17). And I am suggesting that the great ecclesial challenge today arises from what I have called *Christianness* to differentiate it from Christianity, just as this latter is distinguished from Christendom.

I shall not pursue this point further, but shall stick to the main line of our argument.

2

Let us begin with a sketchy reference to what being chosen means in the Old Testament. Significantly enough, the prophet (an individual, or a group), when chosen by God, is generally chosen in order to transgress limits, to break boundaries, and even the law. You are chosen to do something which otherwise you would not do, something contrary to the ordinary way in which things take place. You are chosen in order to go out from your family, to kill your son, or to go into a country which I am going to give you, but which is not yours. You are chosen in order to be a sign of contradiction, to be persecuted and to be deemed a disgrace to your own people. Abraham, Moses, Jeremiah, Ezekiel, John the Baptist—and the list could be multiplied—all are transgressors of the status quo. Jesus is condemned because he broke the law concerning the sabbath. Pharisee, Paul becomes a traitor to the tradition he received at the feet of Gamaliel and elsewhere. Any chosenness seems to imply to be chosen to transgress, to break something. God does not need a prophet, a spokesperson, if it is just to repeat what everybody does or knows.

We are chosen to do something which we don't necessarily like. We know that, viewed from the outside, it is downright transgression, although we tend to justify it from within. *Novus in vetere latet, vetus in novo patet,* said the Christian scholastics referring to the Covenants. Yet the Jews certainly cannot agree. This tension between the prophet and the status quo does not appear in the Old Testament only. Francis of Assisi, Dominic of Guzman, Joan of Arc, Ignatius of Loyola, Teresa of Avila, Don Bosco—to mention only canonized saints in a single tradition— are classical examples of persons who have gone against the status quo of their own days. Nowadays conscientious objectors, peace-marchers, worker-priests, married monks, liberation theologians, and women rebels could be seen as enlightened prophets, deceived victims or both. They are authentic if they take the risk.

Chosenness represents a danger and the possibility of failure. One can understand the reluctance of the prophets and the aversion to any divine call. We are called to exercise our freedom, to enter upon a struggle, not automatically to perform an action in blind obedience, with success guaranteed. It is a call to a guerilla-style action, where the initiative and responsibility are our own. Those who are truly chosen do not execute orders; they follow the dictates of their own free consciences—where the Divine dwells.

This is why the moment that we take chosenness as our self-justification we are no longer chosen. We are chosen to do something that is out of the normal. But to defend or justify ourselves because we are chosen is to disown our chosenness. Jesus did not call on the angels of his kingdom to rescue him from the hands of Pilate (John 10:36). Chosenness is always a call to exercise freedom of conscience and we cannot take refuge in the fact that we are chosen. When we no longer hear this call, which consists in a constant relationship with the Choosing One, we are no longer chosen. There is no need to supply quotations. Let those who think they are justified, beware! (1 Cor 4:4; 10:12, etc.)

This means that if there is one thing that we are not allowed to speculate on or manipulate, it is this idea of being a "chosen people." There is an affinity here with certain other notions which, if we attempt to verbalize or apprehend them consciously, cause us *ipso facto* to betray and accuse ourselves. If you transgress a traffic regulation by ignorance or inadvertently and offer twenty-one reasons to prove that you are in good faith, you certainly make the police suspicious that you are *not* in good faith! There are things which by their very nature do not allow for any kind of previous knowledge. Any kind of prior reflection on a certain type of acts kills its authenticity. We may want to be spontaneous, but a spontaneous act is prior to reflection upon the act (Mt 10:19).

I am not saying that there are no chosen people; I do say that any justification of our actions because of such chosenness destroys that same chosenness. We cannot have it both ways. Is there not an Arab saying that tells us you cannot have both the cabbage and the lamb?

We can put it differently. The moment that we claim a privilege because we are chosen we rely on power and not on authority to fulfil our mission. Authority is bestowed upon us. Power we assume. We are invested with authority. We possess power. The relation is a delicate one, and the difference subtle. We can never sever the two. The moment that we cling to the authority given us and do not put it at stake on every occasion, we rely on our power and no longer on the conferred authority. Democracy confers authority on the chosen ones, they are representatives. The moment they seize power by themselves it becomes the tyranny of sheer power. *Gott mit uns* can become a blasphemy, *In God we trust* a cowardice, *Dieu le veult* an aberration.

I am not being destructive. We can understand Germany, the United States and the Crusades represented in the three slogans. I do not contest that the sense of being chosen is a powerful experience. I do not deny that vocation, which is another way of saying that one is chosen, is a reality. What I am trying to say is that when, in a reflective way, we manipulate these vocations, attempting to justify the very thing which is inherently a risk, for which we cannot offer any defense, we invalidate ourselves; a man caught in a traffic infraction offers no excuse if he is in good faith. The essence of being chosen entails not using one's chosenness to justify the thing for which one has been chosen.

The experience of being chosen, I said, is a powerful experience. It is so powerful that without it, in a very fundamental way, we would not rise to the consciousness of being what we are. Our individual personality is the fruit of a series of relationships of which the most important are those in which we are on the receiving end. Without nurture the child dies. We discover ourselves when somebody calls us, when we experience that we are a thou for somebody. Our I emerges in relationship with a thou. We feel we are somebody when we have responsibility for someone; we learn to love when we are loved.

All this is well known. But it applies also to our individual and collective relationships with the transcendent reality, in whatever sense we may interpret it. Prayer is more listening than talking. We could put it more theologically the other way round: human relations are a reflection of our constitutive relationship with transcendence. We are, because we are known and loved by the God, the Earth, the Nation, Party, Tribe, Family, Friend.

When chosen, in whatever sense, either merely sociologically or anthropologically, one experiences the rise of one's own personality, acquires self-confidence, feels responsibility, takes courage, senses oneself to be somebody endowed with a mission, to

perform which gives meaning to one's life. One is no longer
forlorn, a nonentity, lost in the anonymous mass of a faceless
crowd.

History shows us that the very feeling of peoplehood usually
emerges out of a myth narrating how a particular people has been
chosen by a transcendent power in order that that people may
fulfill a certain role among the other peoples of the world. Transcendence here, obviously, is a philosophical notion and not a
monotheistic concept.

We insert these considerations, sketchy as they are, in order to
show that our critique does not refer to chosenness *per se,* but to
its connection with universality.

3

To be chosen entails being picked out, special, separated, set
apart, sacred, holy, different. This whole group of words betrays
a certain mentality. The "woman of distinction" is, so it seems, a
great woman precisely because she is distinct from others; and
thus, obviously, the more different the better. *Sanctus,* separated, chosen.

All the Abrahamic religions have the central idea of being
chosen, of being set apart, of being different. They accord to this
specialness a high positive value; chosen because special, rare.
Not everyone is chosen; otherwise what is the point?

There is here a dialectical mentality which is based ultimately
on the principle of non-contradiction. This means that something
is all the more *it-self,* the more it is *it,* and not something *else.* We
apply the primacy of the principle of non-contradiction in order
to understand what a thing is. We do this by differentiating this
thing from what this thing *is-not.* This leads to the kind of
mentality that affirms the sacred to be distinct, the holy to be set
apart, the chosen ones to be unlike others. Difference connotes
the highest value.

I am not saying that this is right or wrong. It is one particular
way in which the human mind works: to oversimplify a little, it is
a deeply engraved feature of the three Abrahamic religions.

Perhaps the classic example is the very concept of God in these three so-called monotheistic religions. In order to know what this God is or is not, these traditions put Him outside all possible categories. Because God is the highest Being, He has to be the most different, the most special, the most set-apart, transcendent—outside all things, totally Other, absolutely Holy. The concept of God in these three Abrahamic religions is of God the Different, the Other, the Holy, the set-apart. Any other idea of the Divine is deemed pantheism, wishy-washy thinking in which everything is just the same.

However, there are other traditions. Another type of thinking is observable in the Indic mentality, a kind of thinking characterized by the primacy of the principle of identity over against the primacy of the principle of non-contradiction. We say the primacy because we are well aware that in India, as in Greece or anywhere else, both principles are known and applied. Primacy indicates that the upper hand is here given to the principle of identity, so that in order to know that a thing is, these traditions do not look at what a thing is-not, but at what it *is*; and the more a thing is it-self the more it has selfhood. So, when classical India is struggling to say what "ultimate reality" is, she is not saying it is something which is apart, different. She does the opposite: she tries to discover that which is most common, most present everywhere, most immanent, most identical to itself and identical to everything to which any identity can be applied and affirmed: *brahman*. What the three monotheisms call holy, classical India calls basic; 'ultimate reality' is not so much transcendent as it is immanent.

In order to deal with this type of issue across cultural and religious boundaries I have elsewhere introduced the notion of *homeomorphic equivalents,* lest we should fall victim to grave misunderstandings. Cross-cultural criteria of comparison are different from criteria within a single culture. A culture is full-fledged when it segregates its own criteria of discernment. To be chosen may be thus meaningfully positive within a certain world-view, but may be interpreted as irritatingly negative if interpreted from the outside.

Let me give one example to illustrate this double type of

mentality. It has been written in Hindu, Buddhist, and Chinese scriptures, all much before the Christian era: "Love your neighbor as yourself." For me this is an ontological and not just a moral principle, and my understanding of it is almost the reverse of what some readers may think when they quote the same text from the Hebrew and Christian scriptures. These latter understand: Love your neighbor as *another* self which has the same rights as you and which, because it is an equal self to you, you must treat as you would like to be treated yourself. Thus, love your neighbor as *another* self and consider that this other self, which is different from you, has the same rights you do. Equality here does not mean identity but non-contradiction. The other is not incompatible, not an enemy, but is equal to you as a second self. Love your neighbor as (another) yourself.

In Hindu, Buddhist and Chinese scriptures, however, "Love your neighbor as yourself" is understood as "love your neighbor as *your* self," and unless you reach that kind of identity, all your love for the other person is make-believe, artificial—for the sake of possessing or for the sake of something else. *Love* your neighbor as your self amounts to saying *know*, discover, realize your neighbor as your self, because as long as this saving knowledge of the *self* has not dawned upon you, you cannot truly love the neighbor as your self. True love always entails knowledge and this knowledge will lead me to love and know both my neighbor and myself as the *self*, or at least sharing in selfhood. I cannot love my neighbor as my self as long as I have not exploded the *ego*. In fact, the other person is myself in as much as the *self* does not belong to "me," I don't want you to feel you should thank me if I love you: I don't love you as another self who has to thank me because I am going out of myself in order to reach you. I do not welcome your thanks as if you were paying a bill by giving me thanks. I love the neighbor as *my*-self because I love the "other" individual as self—and doing it, I love the neighbor for what really the neighbor is. This is, incidentally, the reason why the word "thanks" in most languages of the Indian subcontinent does not have the same connotations as in western languages.

In sum: the experience of chosenness is valid and lofty, but it is also partial and not a universally human way of entering into

contact with some of the greatest mysteries of life. The common
feature of the three great Abrahamic traditions is precisely their
sense of chosenness. Yet this feature is counterbalanced by another type of mentality in which this sense of chosenness either
does not appear or is interpreted in a way which defeats the
purpose of the other tradition. You are "chosen" when you are
not chosen; you are "chosen" when no exception is made with
you. You are loved by me when I do not love your *differences,*
but precisely that substratum which makes you exist; when I
love your self rather than just your different little nose and face
(*Brahadaranyaka Upanishad* II, 4, 5). A familiar metaphor illustrates the difference between the two mentalities.

The metaphor, common to both East and West, is that of the
drop of water falling into the ocean, symbolizing the destiny of
the human being, which is to be united with the Divine or the
Infinite. What is the drop of water? The *drop* of the water, or the
water of the drop? If the drop of water is the (differentiating) *drop*
of the water, then when the drop falls into the ocean, it certainly
disappears. We are then full of anguish since we feel that we are
bound to disappear. If the drop of water is the drop of the *water,*
i.e. the surface tension which maintains the drop of water, then
the drop is annihilated when the drop drops into the ocean.

But if the drop of water is not a drop of the water but the
(common, plain) *water* of the drop, the water of the drop certainly does not disappear when it enters into the ocean. Just the
opposite, the water is not gone. The water is there more than
ever. The water of the drop of water is totally there in the ocean.
So much so that this water of the drop, if it has been too small (it
all depends on the temperature), wouldn't be visible, let alone
important; in the ocean, however, it overcomes all separateness
and merges with the entire ocean. And all the *water* of the
particular drop remains in the ocean.

Is it not possible that many a misunderstanding comes from
the fact that some believe themselves to be the *drop* of the water
while others believe they are the *water* of the drop? Do we need
to be chosen to be *water* or do we need to be chosen only to be
drop? Which are we: water or drop?

In point of fact the drop of water is both drop and water.

Without the drop we would not be aware of the water; without the water there would be no drop. Perhaps some drops are chosen precisely to consciously disappear as drops in order to reveal the water. Is not the salt asked to lose its separate identity as salt in order to enhance the taste of everything?

We could formulate the same idea in a more philosophical way. Every human being is an individual, has individuality, is a definite particle of water. But our singularity is only apparent for a certain period of time and is just superficial; it is the surface tension that makes the drop of the water by which we also differentiate the waters. Divine calling confers on us individuality, not singularity. Individuality is uniqueness. Singularity separatedness. A whole christology stems from this insight. The identity of Christ is not our identification of him.

Nor is the concept of universality universal. It goes without saying that the universality I speak about is not a factual consensus of opinion at any given time and place, like the present-day universal conviction that, under normal circumstances, cannibalism is to be repudiated, or that the institution of slavery, ethically acceptable for centuries, is detestable.

It should further be pointed out that our universality refers to value statements and not to *a posteriori* statements of fact. "All terrestrial bodies are somewhat heavy" would be a statement of this latter type. On the contrary, "All weight is due to the 'law' of gravitation" would be an instance of a statement which needs to be proven universally valid. We do not refer, either, to merely *formal* statements, like $2 + 5 = 7$, which could be said to be universally true, although the moment they are given a material meaning, they lose their universal validity. Two of my rocks and five of my stones are not equal to your seven pebbles for obvious reasons of nonhomogeneity.

But what of the claim of Christianity not only to have a universal validity but to be *to Katholikon*, i.e., to contain a message valid, and suitable, for any human being of whatever time and place? Here I argue that the original notion of the catholicity of the Church was not that of its being universal in the above-mentioned and geographical sense, but of being complete, perfect in the sense of offering her followers all they needed for attaining salvation. I would like to refer here to the profound discussion of catholicity and the church in Yves Congar's *The Mystery of Faith*. He shows the double sense in which the church understands itself as catholic: it is open and directed to the whole world, on the one hand; it is authentic and true, on the other. Both meanings, he says, must be kept in balance.

I take Congar's interpretation as a valid starting point. I start from the deep insights of classical theology, especially in its cosmic understanding of the universality of Christ and of the trinitarian process through which the entire universe goes in order to reach its goal, so that "God may be all in all." It is a fascinating and coherent view, authentically expressed in the Christian language of the last twenty centuries, as it tries to convey the mystery of the sum-total of reality.

But I pointed out at the beginning the widely accepted idea that we are now at a turning point in history and that the encounter of present-day Christian consciousness with other cultures and religions can no longer follow the homogeneous and evolutionary pattern of what is sometimes termed fulfillment-theology. Reflection on universality today can no longer follow the injunction of Benedict XV who, in his Encyclical on Catholic Missions (*Maximum illud*) presented the goal of the missionary activity of the Church as "rescuing that mass of souls from the savage tyranny of the devils" (AAS, XI [1919] 453).

We are discussing here the contemporary problem of a universal doctrine (of truth and salvation) enshrined in the Christian church. In this context I submit that this claim to universality cannot be convincingly maintained, for two main reasons. First, because any claim of universality is bound to be identified with our understanding of it; otherwise the sentence has no meaning. If we claim that "A is C" has universal value, it means that we claim "A is C" in the sense that we understand each of the three terms—"A" and "C" and "is," as well as their meaning in conjunction. No claim to universality can be separated from our understanding of this claim, i.e., from our concept of this universality. This implies that our understanding of universality is also raised to the status of being universal.

Let me elaborate. If I were to affirm that the universality of the church implies that her sacraments are the means of salvation for everybody, this might be regarded as a possible, because non-contradictory, statement. But the language used implies, to begin with, that the notions of sacrament and of salvation are universal, which is not the case. Furthermore, these two notions are imbued with assumptions and presuppositions which entail a very definite cosmology. This means that in order simply to understand what the sentence says, one has to adopt one particular form of thinking. We arrive thus at an alternative conclusion: *either* any other form of thinking is insufficient, even false, and the Christian terminology is alone universal, *or* the Christian affirmation is one particular way of formulating a more general problematic which may not even have a univocal articulation.

Could we not, however, translate, accommodate, proceed towards a profound "inculturation"? Certainly we could, but one must then inquire—leaving all other problems aside—to what extent the translation is a Christian one. Would it be correct to affirm by dint of "translation" that *samskaras* are the means to *moksha*? But would Christians admit the notion of *samskaras* without Christ, and *moksha* without God? Further, does *moksha* postulate *samskaras?* Formal concepts like "means of liberation" and "final stage" could be *a posteriori* universal, but we would then have formal and not Christian universality.[2]

We may revert to the defense of one particular language with a universal meaning, saying that it is the language used by "God." However, even accepting God's claim as universal, the fact remains that the meaning for us of these "revelations of God" depends on our notion of "God" and our understanding of what he is saying. Any revelation is meaningful only if we fill these words with some meaning. This means that God's alleged universal language cannot be totally disengaged from our understanding of it. Faith is a prerequisite for theology, Christian scholasticism stoutly affirmed. Thus, unless we say that our understanding of things is a universal understanding, the claim of universality cannot be meaningfully raised.

Secondly, no claim of universality can be meaningfully raised because no human group or mind can claim to exhaust the totality of human experience. No human group can claim to have

access to the whole of Man. Even if we had the totality of human
experience today, we could not know in this temporal world
whether it would not alter tomorrow. This temporal fragmentation of the real makes it impossibe for us, in any kind of critical
way, to put forward a claim to universality. "How can we know
the knower?" as the Upanishad puts it (BU II, 4, 14).

Yet the human mind can work only if it assumes that what we
consider to be the case is in fact, at least to some extent, the case
for others as well as for ourselves. If it were not so, if we did not
postulate that what we are saying is also valid for others in
equivalent conditions, no sentence could be meaningful. We
require an intentional universality within a certain myth—a certain cosmology, one could also say, as a universe of discourse.

Today, theologians and philosophers have become more and
more critical of any claim to unrestricted universality, and universal theological doctrines are on the wane. A certain religious
pluralism is making inroads into theology. Ironically enough,
scientific and political thinkers seem to have inherited the colo-
nialistic features of "one God, one Pope, one Religion" and
defend with the same zeal "one Science, one Technology, one
Democracy." Let me adduce as just one concrete example, the
"Universal Declaration of Human Rights." There has been serious debate and much talk on this problem, which proves that
the said human rights are not universal. The universal validity of
the Human Rights Declaration is in fact only relative; it uses
non-universal language, concepts and assumptions. Yet, there are
homeomorphic equivalents, so that the negation of universality
does not mean condoning abuses against human dignity. But
there is no universal notion of human rights. The theoretical sum-
total of such equivalents would yield only a purely formal universality.

5

Christians nowadays, Roman Catholics in particular, like to
use an Old Testament expression and call themselves "people of
God." Even if some, with Karl Rahner, "envisage the possibility

of calling humanity itself the people of God," the phrase is a continuation of Jewish consciousness of being a chosen people.

How are we to understand this idea of being a chosen people, whether it be Israel or the church or Christianity in general? How are we to understand the impulse which incites these groups to such a universal proclamation?

The concept of being chosen is vital and important for the three great Abrahamic religions. It would not be desirable for them to dispense altogether with this belief, which both gives them a sense of self-identity and enables them to fulfill in the world at large the important task that they feel they are commissioned to perform. I think the world needs this push and enthusiasm. I would, however, make two points.

First, I would ask for a certain ingredient of collective humility which recognizes that this "chosenness" is neither a right, nor a justification, but simply a certain way of understanding one's own identity, and of risking one's own life to pursue an ideal and adhere to a certain belief.

Second, I would warn against extrapolating the conclusion that, if we are chosen, others by implication are not. If Israel is chosen, if Christian people are chosen, and if Islam constitutes monumental historical proof of the belief that God does choose people, this in no way means that other people may not also be chosen for other tasks, although this is neither the language nor the self-understanding of those other traditions. Nevertheless, our problem remains.

Here is one of the greatest challenges to Christian self-understanding today. Israel offers the paradigm for chosenness, but she does not aspire to the type of universality Christians claim. Islam lays a special emphasis on universality: everyone is born a Muslim inasmuch as all are creatures of Allah, but Islam has a qualified notion of chosenness: all are called to share in the most perfect of monotheistic faiths, but Islam will not thematically consider adaptation or inculturation into other cultures. It will preach conversion but not concede validity to other cultures. They are to be tolerated, but eventually need to be converted. The Quran is indivisible, the literal word of God which as such does not allow translation—though the interpretation of this is not necessarily fundamentalist. Islam has validity in itself. Love it or leave it, one could say. In this way, by and large, it has been more "tolerant" than Christianity.

The primitive Christian church has a sort of transcendental relation to cultures and religions. She inspired and transformed them by a kind of continuation of the Incarnation dynamic. But at that point she did not claim to be a religion. In point of fact, the church crystallized as a full-fledged religion by adapting and adopting the religiousness of the peoples who "converted" to Christianity. It then took a definite shape and became a religion.

Christians since at least the last millennium have wanted to have it both ways: to be chosen and yet universal. This creates a tension which needs fundamental rethinking. I would like to expand on one concrete aspect of this complex and delicate situation. If the Christian church represents one single chosen people, it is understandable that she should keep her way of worship, her doctrine and life-style—even her culture—as closely linked as possible with the concreteness of the chosen people and the likeness of the Founder. Anybody wanting to join the flock is welcome, provided the candidate adjures all the "errors" or imperfections of the former way of life. The Christian church is the concrete way provided by God to save people. All are called to join her, accepting her particular ways as sanctioned by God . . .

However, if the Christian church puts forward at the same time a claim to universality, different from the Jewish one which implies identity by differentiation and the Muslim one which entails a specific Muslim culture—that is to say, if the Christian church claims to be ready to accept every culture, language and way of life because her message is allegedly not tied to any particular human phylum, and aspires to be at home in Africa, Asia and the whole world—then such a chosenness demands her renunciation of any claim to be a particular religion.

There has been, of course, a standard answer to this. The church can accept any culture and adopt any way of life because she belongs to a supernatural order higher than any created structure. Yet this is hardly compatible with the oft-asserted historical claim of Christianity, unless we accept Hegel's divinization of the particular history of those western people who accepted Christianity. In that case, conversion means entering into the mainstream of this particular world history. This implies a linear and evolutionary conception of history. The *mysterium salutis* is *Heilsgeschichte*. In spite of marxism and liberal Christianity Hegel is still the towering figure of modern times. History is still seen as the place of the unfolding of the spirit. But that is another subject.

Is it possible to have it both ways: *chosen* with a particular, though unique mission, and *universal* with an equally unique but exclusive mission?

Both options are open, but not the two simultaneously—unless Christianity claims to be the exclusive and perfect way of realizing the *humanum*, or to use Christian vocabulary, the divinization of mankind, relegating all other religions to mere approximations of Christian fullness.

The church may understand herself to be the remnant of Israel, the *pusillus grex*, the selected—and elected—few who reach the goal, the only *fully* true religion; or she may understand herself as a symbol of the invisible mystery transcendentally present in any religion, people and ideology. Two ecclesiologies are here at work: the church as a visible human society and thus a sociological construct, although with a divine mission; and, alternatively, the church as a mystic reality, a cosmos within the cosmos, as some of the Fathers expressed it, as the inner light latent in everyone coming into this world. Both options are legitimate, both have a long Christian pedigree, both could offer an orthodox understanding of the Christian "fact." But the two options cannot be held simultaneously—without subscribing to a Christian totalitarian imperialism.

In the first case the church is either the *societas perfecta*, visible, although perhaps with invisible boundaries—it is the most perfect religion—or it is a particular religion contributing in her own unique way to the ultimate welfare of Man along with many other institutions striving towards the respective homeomorphic equivalents of Christian salvation. In the second case, the church is either the leaven which disappears into the fermenting mass, or it is a kenotic principle indistinguishable as a separate entity. Two main ecclesiologies are here discernible with a respective subdivision: church as the only true religion; church as one religion; church as a distinguishable community performing a unique service to the most diverse religions; church as an invisible bond uniting all those who, to use gospel language, seek the Kingdom and its Justice.

During twenty centuries this tension has been present in Christian history. The great challenge of the religions and traditions of Asia today is the awareness that this tension may now become destructive. Innocence is lost. Perhaps a momentous decision has to be taken. This is the ecclesial translation of the 'turning-point' of which many are speaking. What is Christian identity today?

This decision has to be taken ecclesially. It should be possible to say that "it appears to the Holy Spirit and us" that circumcision or baptism is no longer needed. It is for this reason that I am asking for a Council of Jerusalem II in order that humankind as a whole may discern the signs of the times.

To conclude, I shall pose concretely the question of the *communicatio in sacris.*

When Christians celebrate the Eucharist or when they pray *to* the Father *through* the Son *in* the Spirit, they are performing the ritual not only for themselves but also, vicariously, *for* everybody. But are they ready to perform it *with* everybody in so far as there is good intention, respect and desire to share in that trustful thrust? Vice-versa, provided neither scandal nor apostasy is involved, is the Christian ready to share in the rituals of other religious traditions?

If Christianity is one religion among the others, we should keep distinctions, jurisdictions and boundaries as clear as possible. If Christians believe in their commitment to a universal mystery—revealed to them in Christ—they will also share in the manifestation of the Sacred found in other religions, without imagining that they are betraying their own beliefs or despising those of the others.

Let me offer one example of the above-mentioned ambiguity. It accounts for the acute divergences at the very heart of Christian theology. It is the issue of "inculturation," or whatever word one may prefer. For most civilizations, the obstacles to the separation of religion from culture loom as insurmountable. Both are knit together. Some modern Christians may have a different opinion, but by all accounts, seen from the other side, inculturation amounts to *communicatio in sacris*. To accept cultural forms of Hinduism, for instance, amounts to appropriating religious symbols of and even participating in the religious world of Hinduism. One cannot have it both ways: either this is a nonlegitimate intrusion or the third Christian millennium has to undergo a radical *metanoia*.

Here we have again at a very concrete level the play of two mentalities. The Abrahamic mentality will prefer distinction and separation; the Indic mentality will prefer to show respect for sharing. There are two anthropologies at work. Should there also be two existential ecclesiologies?

Most probably, for the time being, we shall have the more or less peaceful coexistence of Christianity reforming its self-understanding and christianness striving towards one. But the Spirit (Wis 1:7) "has knowledge of every voice."

Notes

1. Man, with capital M, means *Mensch, homo, purusha*, the human being and not the male. On the same principle, I speak of Mankind.
2. *Samskaras* (often translated as "sacraments") "represent, as it were, the various landmarks in man's progress through the course of life, which aim at building up a full-fledged physical and spiritual personality" (*Gantana pharma Sutra*, 8). *Moksha* consists in liberation from the phenomenal world. [Editors]